HANDS that built NEW HAMPSHIRE

The Story of Granite State Craftsmen
Past & Present

COMPILED BY WORKERS OF THE WRITERS' PROGRAM OF THE WORK PROJECTS ADMINISTRATION IN THE STATE OF NEW HAMPSHIRE ᪰ SPONSORED BY HIS EXCELLENCY, FRANCIS P. MURPHY, GOVERNOR OF NEW HAMPSHIRE, AND THE HONORABLE COUNCIL, SPONSORS OF THE NEW HAMPSHIRE WRITERS' PROJECT ᪰

STEPHEN DAYE PRESS · BRATTLEBORO, VERMONT
1940

Library of Congress Cataloging in Publication Data

Writers' Program. New Hampshire.
   Hands that built New Hampshire.

   At head of half title: Federal Writers' Project.
   "Sponsored by His Excellency, Francis P. Murphy,
Governor of New Hampshire, and the honorable Council,
sponsors of the New Hampshire Writers' Project."
   Bibliography: p.
   1. Art industries and trade—New Hampshire.   2. Arts and
crafts movement.   3. Handicraft—New Hampshire.
4. Artisans—New Hampshire.   I. Federal Writers' Project.
II. Title.
NK835.N4W7   1975   709'.742   73-3635
ISBN 0-404-57935-3

Reprinted from the edition of 1940, Brattleboro
First AMS edition published in 1975
Manufactured in the United States of America

AMS PRESS INC.
NEW YORK, N. Y. 10003

FEDERAL WRITERS' PROJECT

HANDS that built NEW HAMPSHIRE

AMS PRESS
NEW YORK

TABLE OF CONTENTS

CHAPTER		PAGE
I	BASKETMAKING: A LEGACY	1
II	OUT OF SEAFARING DAYS	12
III	MEN WHO MADE NEW HAMPSHIRE BUILDINGS	25
IV	CABINETMAKERS, PAST AND PRESENT	39
V	TIME AND MUSIC	54
VI	THE CRAFT OF THE WOODWORKER	67
VII	MODERN ORNAMENTAL WOOD CARVING	79
VIII	CLAY KILN AND POTTER'S WHEEL	90
IX	STONECUTTERS	105
X	NEW HAMPSHIRE GLASS	118
XI	WORKERS IN METAL	131
XII	SPINNING WHEEL AND HAND LOOM	148
XIII	WITH THREAD AND NEEDLE	162
XIV	SAMPLERS AND QUILTS	176

XV	Home Rugmaking	192
XVI	Art and Near Art	206
XVII	Shaker Crafts	220
XVIII	The Country Fair	236
XIX	Trends in Organized Handicrafts	250

LIST OF ILLUSTRATIONS

TITLE	PHOTOGRAPHIC SOURCE	OPP. PAGE
ARTHUR CORLISS	*League of N. H. Arts and Crafts*	4
INDIAN BASKETMAKER	*C. T. Bodwell*	5
FIGUREHEAD, LADY OF THE LAKE	*WPA N. H. Art Project, Herman V. Wibel*	20
SHIP'S EAGLE AND FIGUREHEAD	*WPA N. H. Art Project, Herman V. Wibel*	21
FRANKLIN PIERCE HOMESTEAD	*The Manahan Studio, courtesy of the State Planning Board*	36
MEETINGHOUSE, HANCOCK	*League of N. H. Arts and Crafts*	36
WOOD CARVING, WEBSTER BIRTHPLACE	*WPA New Hampshire Art Project*	37
PARLOR, PIERCE HOMESTEAD	*The Manahan Studio, courtesy of the State Planning Board*	37
DOLL'S CRADLE, WINDSOR CHAIR, HIGHBOY	*WPA N. H. Art Project, Herman V. Wibel*	52
TABLE, DESK, BUREAU, CHEST	*WPA N. H. Art Project, Herman V. Wibel*	53
CLOCKS	*WPA N. H. Art Project, Herman V. Wibel*	56
GREAT HISTORICAL CLOCK	*Clarence Collins*	57
EARLY MIRROR, BANDBOX	*WPA N. H. Art Project, Herman V. Wibel*	64
INTERIOR OF A HOME WORKSHOP	*League of N. H. Arts and Crafts*	65
WOODEN OX AND CART	*League of N. H. Arts and Crafts, Dunlop Photo Service*	88
GRANDPA AND GRANDMA DOLLS	*League of N. H. Arts and Crafts, L. M. A. Roy*	88
MARY WHITTIER	*League of N. H. Arts and Crafts*	89
LEO MALM	*League of N. H. Arts and Crafts, L. M. A. Roy*	89
HAND-CARVED CORNER CUPBOARD	*WPA N. H. Art Project, Herman V. Wibel*	96
WOOD CARVING OF COVERED BRIDGE	*WPA N. H. Art Project, Herman V. Wibel*	97
CHARLES CLOUGH	*League of N. H. Arts and Crafts, L. M. A. Roy*	97

TITLE	PHOTOGRAPHIC SOURCE	OPP. PAGE
Glazed Osborn Pottery	WPA N. H. Art Project, Herman V. Wibel	100
Keene Pottery	WPA N. H. Art Project, Werner Kohlenberg	100
Lloyd Burt	League of N. H. Arts and Crafts, Russell E. Clark	101
A Jewel Craftsman	WPA N. H. Art Project, Werner Kohlenburg	116
Bottle and Inkwells	WPA N. H. Art Project Werner Kohlenberg	117
Roscoe Grant	League of N. H. Arts and Crafts, Russell E. Clark	132
Walter Rogers	League of N. H. Arts and Crafts, L. M. A. Roy	133
Loom and Clock Reel	League of N. H. Arts and Crafts, L. M. A. Roy; WPA N. H. Art Project, Herman V. Wibel	148
The Weaver	League of N. H. Arts and Crafts, Russell E. Clark	149
Doll Dressed in 1852 Clothing	WPA N. H. Art Project, Herman V. Wibel	164
Embroidered Panel	WPA N. H. Art Project, Werner E. Kohlenberg	165
Sampler	Mrs. William Bready	180
Log Cabin Quilt	WPA N. H. Art Project	181
Concord Wreath Hooked Rug	WPA N. H. Art Project, Herman V. Wibel	196
Wheat Pattern Hooked Rug	WPA N. H. Art Project, Herman V. Wibel	197
Mrs. Elvin Prescott	Martha Sackett	197
Rocking Chair, Tin Ware, Window Shade	WPA N. H. Art Project, Herman V. Wibel	212
Hand Painted Wall	WPA N. H. Art Project, Herman V. Wibel	213
Shaker Colony Building	WPA N. H. Art Project, Herman V. Wibel	228
Shaker Latch and Lock	WPA N. H. Art Project, Herman V. Wibel	228
Weaving at the Shaker Colony	WPA N. H. Art Project, Herman V. Wibel	229
Shaker Sister	WPA N. H. Art Project, Herman V. Wibel	244
Wooden Buckets	WPA N. H. Art Project, Herman V. Wibel	244
Shaker Rockers and Cupboards	WPA N. H. Art Project, Herman V. Wibel	245

ACKNOWLEDGEMENTS

The Workers of the Writers' Program of the Work Projects Administration of the State of New Hampshire wish to express their appreciation to the craftworkers and other interested persons of the State who have co-operated with them in compiling the material used in this book, and to all authors whose published works have been studied in gathering information on the subjects covered in it. They are especially grateful to Brigadier-General Charles F. Bowen, the Adjutant General of New Hampshire, acting agent for the Sponsors, the Governor and Council of New Hampshire, and to the consultants, Dr. Carroll S. Towle of the Department of English of the University of New Hampshire and Director of the New Hampshire Writers' Conference, Miss Margaret V. Cobb, Director of the Community Guidance Center, and Mr. Fred W. Lamb, Secretary and Director of the Manchester Historic Association, all of whom read and criticized the complete manuscript. They wish also to thank the staff of the State Library, Concord, the Librarian of the New Hampshire Historical Society, Concord, the staff of the Baker Memorial Library, Hanover, the staff of the Nashua Public Library, Nashua, the staff of the Keene Public Library, the Librarian of the Athenaeum, Portsmouth, the staff of the Manchester Institute of Arts and Sciences, Manchester, members of the Council and the Director of the League of New Hampshire Arts and Crafts, and the Director of the Currier Gallery of Art, Manchester, for their unfailing courtesy and patience in aiding in the gathering of material. They are profoundly grateful to all the members of the staff of the Carpenter Memorial Library, Manchester, especially to Miss Caroline Clement, Librarian, and to Mrs. Olie M. Kibbee, Miss Charlotte R. Garvin, and Miss Mildred J. Peaslee whose concrete suggestions and able assistance have been invaluable in preparing the manuscript of this book.

Many of the photographs used in this book were selected from the files of the WPA New Hampshire Art Project, Omer T. Lassonde, State Supervisor. Others were furnished through the courtesy of the League of New Hampshire Arts and Crafts, the State Planning and Development Commission, and private individuals.

Manchester, New Hampshire. July 5, 1940.

FOREWORD

Some years ago, the idea of writing a book about the arts and crafts of New Hampshire first occurred to the present supervisor of the WPA New Hampshire Writers' Project. Without any attempt at systematic research or formal organization, she began to gather material about the subject. Even a casual survey of the matter soon convinced her that such an undertaking was too ambitious to be attempted by any individual. The research alone would have been impossible for one person to handle in a satisfactory manner. Therefore, she reluctantly abandoned the plan, until, through the Work Projects Administration, a group of competent New Hampshire people became available for the enormous task of unearthing and assembling information, checking and rechecking facts, and finally organizing the vast amount of material they had accumulated.

From the very first, a book dealing with certain aspects of handicrafts in the State seemed desirable for a number of reasons. During the Colonial and post-Revolutionary periods, New Hampshire's development was typical of that of the other New England States. During the nineteenth century, it was similar to that of other northern industrial regions. Thus the subject would by no means be restricted to a small area. Even more important, however, New Hampshire, the first State to have subsidized the handicraft movement and to have set up a commission as part of the State Government, occupies an important position in that field. Since its inception and subsequent successful functioning, the League of New Hampshire Arts and Crafts and its work has been studied and followed by other States. It is especially appropriate, therefore, that the story of New Hampshire handicrafts be told.

In writing this book, we have kept certain definite objectives in mind. We have placed the emphasis on the craftsmen, letting the crafts themselves occupy a secondary position. As far as was possible we have tried to confine our discussion to arts and crafts; art, in the sense of original creative work, has been mentioned only incidentally and in its relation to craftwork. Many New Hampshire craftsmen are also artists; this phase of their work is, however, outside the province of this book.

With one or two exceptions, the general plan of each chapter has been to follow a chronological sequence from Colonial days to the present time. Each chapter begins with the craftwork of the early settlers, when the men and women of the Piscataqua region were trying to create for themselves conditions of a life similar to those which they had known in England. It continues through the eighteenth century, when great advancement had been made in the comforts of living, into the more sophisticated years of the early nineteenth century, when craftwork flourished during the period of maritime prosperity that followed the Revolutionary War. It is the story of two centuries of artisans and of their work, as it developed until the industrial expansion of the mid-nineteenth century pushed aside the product of the individual craftsman.

We have told this story briefly, because our space was limited, and because we wished to bring in also the work accomplished in the handicrafts movement as it has been revived in the twentieth century. In telling of craftsmen of the past, we have mentioned only a few typical examples. The descriptions of modern craftsmen are more detailed. Those we have mentioned were selected because they are especially well known or because they have been available for interviews. Others, equally expert, are at work in every section of the State.

The modern revival of handicrafts in New Hampshire owes much to two outstanding influences, the Manchester Institute of Arts and Sciences and the League of New Hampshire Arts and Crafts. Both organizations are mentioned in many chapters and are discussed at length in the last.

Two chapters are devoted to subjects which, at first thought, may seem out of place in a book of this type. That on the Shakers has been included because their crafts are distinctly folk arts, still practiced in the colony at Canterbury. The story of the country fair is included because of its importance in keeping alive rural arts and handicrafts during the industrial era.

As first planned, the book was to have contained a chapter on the handicrafts of the different nationality groups which are a part of the social and cultural picture of the State. However, it later seemed that a better portrayal of their contributions could be made by describing the work of individuals.

The members of the staff of the WPA Writers' Project who assembled and wrote up the material are either experienced writers, research workers, or recent college graduates. The names of the staff who did special work in preparing the book are as follows: Herbert Blais, Irene Bourdon, Mary C. Burpee, Susan Caldon, Lillian Campbell, Florence Crosby, Milton Crowell, Barbara Dickey, Gladys Duhaime, Harry Flanders, William T. Gardner, Lucille Hodge, Lucien C. Jutras, Victoria Langlois, Paul Martineau, Luna Osburn, Henry Pratt, Julia Sample, Francis Sheridan, George Smith, Eugene Stuckman, Dorothy Van Houten, Ola G. Veazie, and Eunice Weed.

In gathering their information, they have consulted sources, such as State and Provincial Papers, probate and town records, State, county, and town histories, newspaper files, and authoritative books on the various subjects. Invaluable assistance has been given by administrators of handicraft organizations and craftsmen themselves, who gave generously of their time and information in interviews. After each chapter was written, all data were checked carefully and were edited under the supervision of Clare A. Cheetham, editor.

The manuscripts were sent to three consultants: Dr. Carroll S. Towle of the English Department of the University of New Hampshire, who read for literary form; Miss Margaret V. Cobb, former Research Assistant of the New Hampshire Foundation, who read for New Hampshire content; and Fred W. Lamb, one of the State's outstanding historians, who read for historical authenticity. The manuscripts were read also by various members of the organizations interested in handicrafts. They were finally criticized by Brigadier-General Charles F. Bowen, Adjutant General of the State of New Hampshire, who acts in the matter as the agent for the Sponsors, the Governor and Council.

The book makes no pretense to being an exhaustive survey of the subject of handicrafts. Such a study would be impossible in a work of this size. It is submitted to the public in the belief that they will gain from it a clearer impression of the craftwork done in the State both at present and in years gone by, and with the hope that it may prove a key to unlock an even more productive future in finding material for use in writing other books on various phases of New Hampshire arts and crafts.

ELLA SHANNON BOWLES, *State Supervisor*

I

BASKETMAKING — A LEGACY

The picture of a man engaged peacefully in what is probably the oldest form of handicraft in the world, impresses even the casual observer with a feeling of the stability of a way of life which continues from one generation to another. Wars come and end, but work with the hands goes on. For man's existence depends upon his ability to appropriate the materials supplied by nature and adapt them to his daily needs.

The late Arthur Corliss, a rural craftsman who was perhaps the finest in his line that New England has produced in recent years, was a man who felt that basketry was more than a means of livelihood, that it was an expression of a personal philosophy of life, a philosophy which exemplified contentment in carrying on a craft he loved and in producing wares as beautiful and perfect as his skill and creative ability could make them.

Someone who saw Mr. Corliss at work in his South Tamworth home said it was a joy to watch him expertly bending the handles over his knee to form the curve he wanted, or swiftly weaving the fillers around the uprights as he created a basket. He learned the craft from his father and, in turn, passed on his inheritance to his stepson.

In his own work he followed the methods of old-time craftsmen like Benich Whitefield of Brookfield and Daniel Hall Sanborn of Wakefield, and made the bushel baskets, melon-shaped baskets, wood baskets, and waste paper baskets for which he was famous from native materials, especially brown ash, without the aid of nails. He refused to use machine-made materials and prepared his own stock, cutting down the ash trees himself and removing the bark carefully so that it came free in long strips. In this procedure Mr. Corliss followed an ancient tradition; experts say that no machine has ever been invented which can imitate the specialized hand-technique used in the various steps of basketry as practiced by the primitives.

Every pioneering period in the world's history has encouraged all types of handicraft. This is especially true in basketry where the wares produced have been designed, for the most part, to store food and to transport supplies.

Usually, woman was the leader in primitive handicrafts. But she was not overburdened with them, for she had all of her known world for a storehouse and plenty of time to carry out her ideas. Roots, flexible grasses, barks, skins of animals, birds' feathers, and clay were her media. Coarse textiles made of straw, leaves, the bark of trees, grass, or feathers were fashioned only after hour upon hour of splitting, twisting, weaving, netting, and dyeing. Pottery was made from coils of clay, patted and moulded with the hands. Fine roots of spruce, twigs, rushes, and strips of bark furnished the materials for baskets.

The American Indian's outstanding craft was basketmaking; as Allen H. Eaton says in *Handicrafts of the Southern Highlands,* he created the finest baskets in history. It is his greatest legacy to New England handicraft workers. The art of basketry, however, was not restricted to the Indian, for the white man brought a knowledge of basketmaking from rural England, but he added to it many tricks of the trade shown him by the Indians before he taught the craft to his children.

The colonists, like the Indians, made their first baskets for utilitarian purposes: to store maize, nuts, and other surplus commodities; to carry produce when harvesting or traveling; and to measure and sift grain and coarse meal.

By the opening of the nineteenth century, some kind of a basket was used in almost all of the ordinary household and family tasks. When the early New Hampshire farmer went to town, to Portsmouth, to Rumford (Concord), or to Boston, he carried his week's supply of home-cooked food in the "mitchin-box", or food hamper. Square baskets with closely woven sides and loosely woven bottoms were used to separate the curds from the whey in cheese making; and even the unpleasant task of goose picking called for a basket to cover the fowl's head while a crop of feathers for plump mattresses and downy pillows was harvested.

In rural communities, the men made baskets while winter storms were raging, or in the slack season after the end of sledding and before planting time. In some cases, moreover, they became so proficient in the art that those of their neighbors who did not have the gift of basketry at their finger tips were glad to buy their wares.

Basketweavers like many early craftsmen were so important in their communities that the names of those especially skilled in the art have been recorded in certain town histories, along with the names of the town officers and other local celebrities. Nathan Hunt of Boscawen, who earned his living making baskets and bottoming chairs, was one such craftsman. Others having more diversified talents to their credit were Stephen Messer of Gorham, "the only praying man in town", a maker of baskets and snowshoes, and "the homespun genius", David Welch of Plymouth, listed as poet, paper-hanger and preacher, as well as neighborhood basketmaker.

During the nineteenth century, itinerant basketmakers, like those of Gilsum and Sullivan, traveled from town to town peddling their wares; and in certain sections of the State, vans piled high with farm baskets are seen today on country roads.

Families of basketmakers lived for years in Swiftwater, on the Ammonoosuc River, and as late as 1905 journeyed to Bradford, Vermont, to the country fair to sell their products. There was great excitement in the hamlet when they set out on these vending expeditions. At daybreak, twelve or fourteen teams assembled and started in a procession for a three days' trip in which business and pleasure were combined, with pleasure predominating. Men, women, and children had their provisions and baskets hung from every corner of the great wagons; barking dogs dashed about madly; there was a cracking of whip lashes, a sound of creaking wheels; and the caravan disappeared in enveloping clouds of dust. At the fair, they swapped their baskets for horses and then went home full of pride in their bargains.

The "Leatherses", as their neighbors called them, were other well-known traveling New Hampshire basketmakers who lived in a section of Barrington known as "Leathers' City". During the winter, they made various kinds of baskets in preparation for their long trips over the countryside and to the villages and cities of southern New Hampshire and Massachusetts. These basket-selling expeditions, when the Leatherses piled huge hayracks with their wares, tucked in their wives and children and a number of old women to tell fortunes, usually began soon after mudtime and continued off and on until the snow flew.

Amzie Childs of Peterborough was another New Hampshire man whose name went on record as a fine basketmaker of the nineteenth century. He was not an itinerant basketmaker, for he bought some simple machinery and opened a shop where he carried on a profitable business with the farmers in the vicinity. Nor are the names of women basketweavers omitted from local annals when the excellence of their work warranted their inclusion. Betsy Colby of Weare earned a reputation in her community as one outstanding basketmaker, and around 1840 a certain Mrs. Glover of Pike, in the town of Haverhill, was making and selling baskets in the upper Connecticut Valley towns. Mrs. Anabel Glines of Haverhill, New Hampshire, owns one of this weaver's baskets, which holds a peck and is made of white ash with a sturdy handhewn handle. Mrs. Glines has a fine collection of early New Hampshire baskets, among them a square cheese basket, a small egg basket, a bonnet basket, and several work baskets which her family has owned for three generations.

Basketry is still carried on in Haverhill where one man, at least,

THE LATE ARTHUR CORLISS of *Tamworth*, *making baskets of split ash.*

INDIAN BASKETMAKER at the Flume.

has acquired a considerable reputation for his work. Using brown or black ash Manley Coffrin weaves baskets of both bushel and peck sizes and also reseats chairs with native materials which he gathers and carefully seasons. For rush bottoms he uses the ordinary cattails, bringing them home in August and spreading them to dry, until they are pliable enough to weave seats into the framework of the chairs. Charles A. Sprague, a well-known basketmaker of Center Effingham, also employs native materials in his work, using brown ash which he turns into baskets of all sizes, varying from containers which hold five bushels to little baskets the size of teacups.

Like Mr. Coffrin and Mr. Sprague, Mrs. Charlotte Cooper, who has made and sold baskets in Rye for over sixty years, uses split ash wood gathered in New Hampshire for many of the wares she displays at her stand on the Ocean Boulevard. Others are woven of striped sweet grass picked in the salt marshes. The method of fashioning the sweet grass baskets is somewhat different from that employed in weaving baskets of ash and similar materials. In braiding grass for these baskets an experienced weaver working at one of the Rye stands throws the long blades over an antique iron pothook to hold them firmly. Asked where he found the grass, he replied, "Oh, near by, way back in." This vaguely indicated locality proved to be in Seabrook. He says that the grass is gathered "when it seeds itself," in July and August.

"We handle the grass six times," he explains. "First, we pull it up by the roots, never mowing it down, as that spoils the sweetness, and then dry it with the roots on. Next, we lug it a quarter of a mile to the truck, and load it, then we bring it home and unload it to be stacked up and cleaned."

This man never glances at the grass while he is cleaning it, for his fingers tell him at once what portion to throw away. As his hand moves, out come the flat soft flag, the wiry witch grass, and the thin marsh grass, leaving bunches of cleaned, scented grass, which are hung up by the roots until they are needed for the baskets. Any surplus which cannot be used locally is sold to Indian basketmakers at Oldtown, Maine.

For many years Indian basketmakers have come from Maine and Quebec during the summer months to carry on their trade in a number of New Hampshire resorts. In some places, the grandchildren and great-grandchildren of the men and women who first undertook these business ventures are making baskets at the original stands occupied by their families season after season. A typical example is Mrs. Joseph Laurent of Odanak, Quebec, a careful and conscientious craftworker with great creative ability who spends from four to five months of each year in Intervale on the Saco River. Her wares are made by the same methods that her people have followed for generations.

"Our baskets are made of ash wood and sweet grass which grows wild near water or can be cultivated. The ash is always used as a foundation and dyed different colors and the sweet grass either left in strands or braided and then woven in," she says.

Miss Stella Collins of Manchester owns an interesting collection of forty raffia baskets woven by her mother, Mrs. Eliza Lane Collins, who was born in Sanbornton in 1834. Each large covered basket, woven vase, candlestick, hanging vase, or tray was constructed with exquisite precision. Mrs. Collins, who took up basketmaking as a hobby a few years before her death in 1922, colored the raffia herself and planned her own designs.

Raffia basketry was taught in the art classes of the Manchester Institute of Arts and Sciences as early as 1906, and very shortly afterwards instruction in reed basketry was added to the curriculum. From then on, for about twenty-eight years, the basketry classes for children and adults were among the Institute's most popular courses. One of the outstanding instructors was Miss Mary Slason, an active member of the Boston Arts and Crafts Society, nationally known for her skill. Her theory of basketmaking as an art involved the fresh and imaginative use of old combinations of weaving designs, colors, and shapes. She was expert at reviving odd types of baskets that had been made in other days: the dainty cap basket that ladies of a hundred years ago used to carry when they attended tea parties, or the capacious darning basket that was an essential part of old-time housekeeping. Miss Slason had studied, collected, and reproduced the designs made by the North American Indian basketmakers. One of them was the "Peterborough basket", a sturdy affair with a square base, round top, and reeds that had been dyed in many different shades of brown. Originally this type was made by a lone Indian who worked in the Monadnock region of New Hampshire long after his kinsmen died. In her work with settlement house children, Miss Slason taught them to design heart-shaped baskets, first made by the Choctaw Indians, Navajo ceremonial baskets interwoven with strange symbols, and imitations of the tiny baskets that were made in Mexico from colored horsehair.*

The baskets produced in rural New Hampshire today are, for the most part, just the old-time, handy utensils that Yankee farmers use for this and that around the barn, and that their wives find handy for a hundred and one things around the house. The men who make them do not pretend to be professional basketmakers, but they turn out honest, sturdy wares which they sell whenever there is the opportunity.

One who watches a basketmaker at work and asks a judicious question now and then can acquire a fairly good idea of the general methods followed in the production of baskets. Practically all of them are made of native woods, which are felled in winter or in early spring and then are quartered in the required lengths. All of the first steps in basketmaking seem to be involved with variations of the word, "rive", meaning to split or tear apart. The lengths of wood are placed on a *rivinghorse* and the worker splits each of them into pieces about two inches wide and three inches thick by means of a *riving* chisel and a wooden hammer. Then he pounds the *rivings* until they split with the grain of the wood into strips approximately a half-inch thick, called splits. Usually, the splits are soaked in water to make them pliable.

The basketmaker seats himself astride the shavinghorse which extends in front of him and supports the split lengths of wood

* *Boston Evening Transcript. Boston. Tuesday, February 19, 1907.*

while he smooths them with a drawknife. The next step is weaving or cross-hatching splits together to form the base of the basket, which is held together by means of a narrow split run completely around it. When the craftsman is constructing a number of baskets at the same time, he carries the work on each one to this preliminary stage before he begins weaving the sides. Then he weaves the first fillers around the uprights and continues until he has made the basket as deep as he wishes it to be. Finally he tapers the ends of the splits, which have been left about four inches long, and turns them under around the upper edge of the basket. When the baskets are dry he binds on the rims and handles with finish splints, and the baskets are ready to be used or sold.

Basketmaking, as carried on by Mr. and Mrs. Joseph Taylor of West Rindge, has developed beyond the simple processes used by farm workers into a real industry with an output estimated at about three thousand baskets a year. Many of the baskets are shipped all over New England, and to New York, Ohio, and Pennsylvania.

Ash, oak, and birch are the materials most commonly used by the Taylors. Some baskets are made entirely of one material; others are a composition of two or more. Shopping baskets and novelties are made of birch, while heavier baskets, such as those used for firesides or for clothes hampers, are made of ash. Sometimes the uprights are of ash and the fillers of birch. The selection of stock is an art in itself. Mr. Taylor says that the wood is sliced so thin that it splits when the craftsman's knife strikes a knot. The stock for the hoops or rims is cut about a quarter of an inch thick, the uprights one-sixteenth of an inch, and the fillers to a paper-like texture. Each filler is from twelve to forty-eight inches long, according to the type of basket being made. A power knife, guided by hand, cuts the bolts into the needed widths of one-half or three-eighths of an inch at the same time that it splits them into the required thickness.

Mr. Taylor follows the usual steps in basketweaving, but he has substituted a hot water bath for the steaming process done in a large shop. He places the woven frame over a tub and pours water that is almost boiling over the wood to make it pliable. Next, the frame is shaped while wet between two blocks, one pushed down inside the other. Hoops or rims and handles are made flexible by an ingenious steaming method which Mr. Taylor invented himself. Such heavier material is placed in a pine box, with an opening in the bottom, resting on a small laundry boiler over a low stove.

After the frame is dried (a half-hour process), the fillers are wet and woven in and out around the uprights to form the sides. The fancy striped pattern around the sides of many of the baskets is obtained by dipping some of the fillers into dyes of various hues.

The pie basket, having a capacity of one to three pies and equipped with a cover, two handles, and little trays with feet to hold the pies in place, is perhaps the most popular type. The picnic hamper is another favorite and is made in several variations: the tall, narrow type with compartments for food and thermos bottle; a deep and narrow basket with a lid and two handles. Other utilitarian baskets include market and knitting baskets, all sizes of dog baskets, fireside baskets, waste baskets, egg baskets, and baskets in which school children carry their lunches.

Only a step or two away from the art of basketry is an unusual craft that probably no one in New Hampshire pursues today. But for over thirty years following 1800, when the craft was promoted by some girls in Massachusetts and Rhode Island who made hats to sell locally, the braiding of straw hats supplemented spinning and weaving as a major industry for women. Soon the popularity of commercial straw hatmaking spread northward to New Hampshire, where farmers' wives and daughters who needed extra money began plaiting, sewing, starching, and pressing the pretty and extremely fashionable straw bonnets. Nor did they overlook the opportunity to supplement their income by making headgear for the men folks. Some brides earned their wedding finery by weaving wide-brimmed sun hats for men to wear in the hay fields. In

Salem, New Hampshire, one woman paid for the material to build her homestead by selling such hats to a local trader, who distributed them to different markets all over the United States.

Since most New Hampshire farmers grew rye, rye straw at first was used exclusively to make hat and bonnet braids, though it had to undergo a complete curing process to make it suitable for weaving. The steps involved were long and laborious. Before the rye crop was thoroughly ripened, women gathered it into bundles, soaked it in soapy water, and left it to cure. Then the dried straw was cut at the joints into ten-inch sections and bound into bundles, which were again soaked in hot suds. This double soaking made the wisps tough and pliable, and suspension over a pan of hot coals, upon which sulphur had been sprinkled, bleached them. At first the straw was used whole, but the workers soon learned how to split it and then weave the finer strands into braid that brought two to two-and-a-half cents a yard in market.

Palm leaf was another popular material for hatweaving. It was introduced into New England by two traders, William Hazelton of Chester and John Ordway of Hampstead. In March, 1827 while disposing of a stock of hats in Boston, they became curious about bales of recently imported palm leaf they saw on the docks. They made some judicious inquiries and were told that a man in Newport, Rhode Island, used the leaf to weave hats of a superior quality. The traders at once set out to find the hatter. He had a strange story to tell them. He said that he had been a sailor and on one of his voyages had been captured and thrown into a Spanish prison. There the inmates were taught how to make palm leaf hats and he, too, learned the craft. When he was set free he returned to New England, where he was hired immediately by Jabez Boyden of Dedham, Massachusetts, to teach a staff of factory girls the trade.

Within a few days the ex-sailor was on his way to Hampstead with Hazelton and Ordway to interest local women in the work. He received two dollars for each pupil, and the girls themselves were paid one dollar for every hat they produced. The leaf was split by hand, and the hats, after they were woven, were pressed by hand.

The business of palm-leaf braiding spread swiftly to other New Hampshire towns. In Boscawen, women and children quickly acquired the knack of plaiting the strands. Traders imported the leaf from Cuba, circulated it among the housewives, and then came back later to buy the hats that had been made since their last visit.

Gradually, small factories, staffed by women and girls, were set up in Salem, Rindge, and Candia, and in 1830 a firm began the manufacture of palm leaf hats in Fitzwilliam, selling them in their local store until 1868, when the company reorganized in New York City. This was practically the end of straw hatmaking in New Hampshire country towns. Unlike basketry, which has largely remained a craft, weaving hats and bonnets advanced to a point where certain local situations, under the operating conditions of the times, made the continuing of their manufacture impossible. At last the straw hatmaking business entirely disappeared from the State, and soon after the Civil War even the "Bonnet Saloons" of Concord and Manchester, which had advertised straw braiding made to order for their fashionable patrons, knew it no more.

II

OUT OF SEAFARING DAYS

New Hampshire has but a fringe of seacoast extending fewer than eighteen miles from the wide estuary of the Piscataqua to the sands of Salisbury in Massachusetts. Yet the sea has made a definite imprint on the work of the artisans and craftsmen living in the vicinity. This maritime influence is not restricted to the coastal area. You can trace it west to the Connecticut River and into northern mountain valleys, miles away from the tidewater arms of the Atlantic.

Some of the men who served apprenticeships in the shipyards of old Portsmouth, Dover, Exeter, and Hampton, or who sailed as carpenters on the square-rigged ships sent out to foreign ports by the Piscataqua merchants, settled inland after they gave up the sea. They might have farmed a little or even engaged in trade, but usually every one of them could be called upon to ply his craft of woodworking whenever his neighbor needed his help. The names of these men with "a drop of salt sea-water in their veins" come to light again and again in the records of towns where their reputations as meticulous workmen have survived the years. A bit of fine carving above the mantel in a Merrimack Valley house, the precise joining in the woodwork of a low-eaved cottage near the Ossipee Mountains, a neighborhood folk tale of a daring workman at a barn-raising in a town north of Mt. Washington survive to prove that the men who learned their craft within sound of the Atlantic worked in every section of the State.

Many of the finest shipwrights of old Piscataqua came from a line of farmer-fishermen who took up boatbuilding through the sheer necessity of getting food and a living for their families. In the golden days of Portsmouth's great maritime glory, their descendants were employed by master shipbuilders like George Raynes, who, according to John Mead Howells, will probably go down in history as the town's most famous man in the business.*

Raynes launched many proud ships, but in the eyes of the newspaper men of his times, his greatest achievement was the *Sea Serpent* of which one enthusiastic reporter said, "Her model fills the eye like a full moon." But beautiful as the *Sea Serpent* was, she was outrivaled by the magnificent *Nightingale,* a clipper ship without peer in point of construction and workmanship, and, at the time of her launching, the fastest vessel afloat. No expense was spared by her owners to make her a thing of exquisite loveliness.

Designed to make her first voyage with passengers for the International Exhibition of 1851, held in London, builders and carvers joined forces to put on ornamentation that would give a light and delicate appearance to the outside of the ship, and to make the interior finish elegant with carvings of carefully selected woods elaborated with sumptuous gilding. In her cabins, instead of the ordinary ships' bunks, were built-in bedsteads, a great innovation at the time.

A man who had passage on the clipper when she made one of her trips on the famous "tea and silk" course in 1853 has left us a vivid description of the *Nightingale* as she appeared when the whole country was stirred by her beauty, her speed, and her triumphs. Writing in 1904, he says, "In the construction of the Nightingale only the best materials were used,—live oak and locust and hard pine. In port she wore mahogany belaying pins in her rails, which were replaced at sea by stouter oak. Her rigging was capped with brass, highly polished; her rail was finely carved and gilded; her cabin was finished in mahogany and satinwood; her rigging was a-taunto, and her decks were holystoned, as on a man-of-war. At

---

* *The Architectural Heritage of the Piscataqua. John Mead Howells. New York. Architectural Book Publishing Co., Inc., 1937. p. 140.*

sea she was equipped with all canvas possible to be carried; including skysails, staysails, outer jibs, and stun'sails in successive suits. In all waters, as she lay in port, she was the object of frequent inspection and admiration. She sat the water like a duck."*

The *Nightingale* was built in the Hanscom shipyards up the Piscataqua on the Maine side of the estuary. Beginning with the year 1683 when the first Hanscom settled in Eliot, then Old Kittery, the family line was known to the Piscataqua people as "the family of shipwrights". From it came some of the most noted builders and ship architects in New England. William Hanscom, born in 1783, was famous for both his workmanship and his integrity. "I will never drown any man by using poor stock," was his invariable reply when asked to cut corners on the expense of building a ship. His son, William L., became one of America's greatest naval architects. Another son, Isaiah, born in 1815, designed the *Nightingale,* which was constructed under the supervision of the architect's uncle, Samuel Hanscom, Jr., who was in charge of the yards while the ship was on the stocks.

In 1851 Yankee clippers and Jenny Lind, the talented singer, were, without doubt, the two subjects of most interest to the American public. So it was natural that the beautiful ship which came from the ways of the Hanscom yard that year should be given the nickname of the lovely "Swedish Songbird".

The clipper bore on her bow a finely carved figurehead of the prima donna, and on her transom, a reclining full-length figure of a woman, with a bird poised on her finger. Some authorities believe that a certain figurehead now in the Mariners' Museum in Newport News, Virginia, is that of the *Nightingale.*

These exquisitely modeled wooden figures which for centuries adorned the bows of sailing vessels were outstanding examples of the art of carving. By 1830, when American shipmasters were competing with each other in elaborate decorations for their vessels, the most skilled and expert craftsmen in their line were hired to carve

---

* *The Atlantic Monthly. Volume XCIV (November, 1904). "A Clipper Ship and Her Commander." Frank J. Mather. p. 649.*

and to paint them. In their simplest form, the figureheads of New England ships were carved, ornamental billetheads; a large per cent of the Piscataqua schooners and merchant ships had no other decoration. Occasionally billetheads were replaced with more ornate carvings, as in the case of the merchantman *Grandee,* first registered with a billethead and afterwards with a genuine figurehead, the latter a magnificent carving of a Spanish "grandee" wearing an elaborate costume of the eighteenth century.

Figureheads were carved in various forms, but they usually were designed to personify in some way the names of the vessels for which they were made. On the stern of the *Sea Serpent* were two huge, carved representations of the "Great American Sea Serpent".

Models of human beings, such as the male busts on the brig *John Decatur,* the ship *John Hale,* the *Isaac Newton,* the *John Taylor,* or the full-length figureheads of the *Governor Gilman,* the *Cato,* and the *James Brown* were often portraits of historical characters or important political men of the early nineteenth century. These large and valiant figures were supported on carved and gilded scrolls, which were themselves splendid examples of the wood carver's skill.

Female figures might be effigies of the masters' wives or sweethearts, and many a New Hampshire Eliza, Felicity, Ann, Mary Jane, Arabella, and Caroline were true guiding stars on the sturdy, well-built vessels which sped through tempestuous waves and furious winds, when Yankee skippers carried the American flag to distant ports.

The figureheads were very lifelike, but were of the proportions of goddesses rather than of human beings. A typical example was one formerly owned by a Portsmouth woman and familiar about fifty years ago to many residents of that city. It came from the ship *Brussette* of Boston, which went ashore on the rocks of Odiorne's Point in Rye and never came off except in pieces. This fine carving represented a woman with hair dressed in huge puffs on each side of her face, and her back hair kept in place by a gilded comb. Gold earrings as big as silver dollars hung in her ears and a gold belt encircled her waist.

Some of the able wood sculptors who fashioned the figureheads on New England ships were very famous in their day. According to Nathaniel Hawthorne, the earliest of these was Shem Drowne of Salem, Massachusetts, the first American to attain a degree of success in the art of wood carving. He carved ornamental pumpheads, urns, gateposts, mantelpieces, and apothecaries' mortars but achieved his greatest fame for his figureheads. Copley, the great portrait painter, often visited his shop to watch him at his carving.

Simeon Skillings, who worked with his brother, John, in Boston, was probably the ablest wood carver of his time. He was one of the few early craftsmen who were true creative artists rather than skilled artisans. He made the first real figurehead and carved other ornaments for the famous *Constitution*. Isaac Towle and Joseph Doherty of Boston and Joseph True of Salem were other Massachusetts figurehead carvers of note. James Sampson of Bath and W. L. Seavey of Bangor, Maine, made figureheads which were romantic in conception and distinguished for their fine carving. Woodbury Gerrish and John Bellamy of Portsmouth are New Hampshire's outstanding contributions to the list of famous wood sculptors whose names are still remembered.

Only a few specimens of these carvers' work remain in existence. Many New Hampshire figureheads have been sold for large prices and carried out of the State. As far as can be ascertained only two of the female figures are in local collections, and a third, which was purchased by a Portsmouth collector of maritime items, is now displayed in the Museum of Fine Arts in Boston.

One well-known figurehead, owned by the New Hampshire Historical Society, never was greeted by flying seagulls as she came to port; for forty-five years she stood as if poised for flight on the prow of the *Lady of the Lake,* and was saved when the old steamboat, after long years of service, was honorably buried beneath the waters of Glendale Bay in Lake Winnipesaukee. The figure was then taken to Spindle Point on Meredith Neck and placed on the roof of a boathouse; later it was given to the Historical Society and can be seen in the Old Building on North Main Street, Concord.

Woodbury Gerrish sculptured the only figurehead extant in Portsmouth at the present time. The heroic figure is lightly poised as if it were leading the way to unknown lands. It is attired in flowing draperies of bright colors, rich blues arranged against shades of deep cardinal. It is known that Gerrish made the figurehead in 1865, but there are no data about the ship it was to have adorned. The traditional story is that it was a Boston-built vessel which was burned before its "guide" was set in place. The figurehead is owned by the Portsmouth Yacht Club and is considered one of the finest of its type in America.

The identity of the sculptor of the third figurehead—that of the *Creole,* now in the Marine Room of the Musem of Fine Arts, in Boston—has not been settled. Some antiquarians believe it was carved by the late Lieutenant W. T. Spicer of Kittery, Maine; others say it has strong characteristics of the work of John Bellamy. The *Creole* belonged to John Howard March, a wine merchant, who in the early nineteenth century was engaged in trade between Portsmouth and the Madeira Islands. After the ship went out of commission, its figurehead stood for years on the lawn of the old March farm in Greenland, a few miles out of Portsmouth. Though minus an arm, it was an object of great beauty; and in spite of wind and rain, it kept its lovely colors without repainting. In 1900, the family that bought the farm sold this piece of lovely wood sculpture to the collector who presented it to the museum.

John Bellamy is best known as the designer of the wooden eagles which began to appear as ships' figureheads about the middle of the nineteenth century. Although he turned out eagles by the hundred, few of them are found today. His largest eagle, preserved in the Mariners' Museum, was designed for the bowsprit decoration of the Philadelphia-built *Lancaster* and was placed on the frigate when it was reconditioned at the Portsmouth Navy Yard in 1880. The eagle weighed thirty-two hundred pounds, and four cords of wood were used to build it.

In this type of work Bellamy had no peer, and under his skillful handling the "Bellamy eagles" became pieces of real sculpture.

They are noted for the grace and the simplicity of their execution and for the individual character of their fierce beaks, symbolic of vigor and strength.

John Haley Bellamy, poet and thinker as well as master craftsman, was a native of the Piscataqua region; he was born in the old Pepperell home at Kittery, Maine, in 1836. He attended the public high schools, received private tutoring, and completed his general education at New Hampton Literary Institution in central New Hampshire. Then he studied art in Boston and New York. He began his career in Boston, where he was employed by the United States Government. However, his work took him frequently to Portsmouth and he finally went back to live in the vicinity of his early home. During slack periods in the Navy Yard, he executed carvings for private individuals and for public concerns.

Many stories have been related about Bellamy's individuality in thought and speech. It is said that one day while at work on the *Lancaster's* head at the Charlestown Navy Yard, he suddenly decided that he was tired of working. He climbed onto one of the wings of the Bird of Freedom and proceeded to take a nap, only to be discovered by an officer and scolded roundly. But the artist was not in the least disconcerted; he knew that the eagle was not completed and that he alone could finish it, so he chased the indignant officer out of his shop with a carving tool, and finished the famous eagle in his own good time.

His shop was located at Kittery Point, and he had an establishment at 17 Daniel Street in Portsmouth, where he carved house and ship furniture, signs and frames, and garden figures. The sign of the Daniel Street shop read: "John H. Bellamy, Figure and Ornamental Carver."

At his Kittery shop, which was formerly his father's storehouse, Bellamy's room was located on the second floor with windows opening on the seaward side. Visitors entered the room by climbing a ship's ladder. Above the work bench on the south side, hung examples of his finished work, patterns, designs, and tools. The walls were covered with pictures and cartoons; curios and old papers were everywhere. A pot-bellied stove standing in a sand box supplied heat during the cold weather. Comfortable chairs were on hand for his friends, among whom were George Wilson, Tom Burns, Mark Twain, William Dean Howells, and other distinguished men of the day.

He has had many imitators. One of them was John Williams of Kittery Foreside, a skilled workman who is credited with carving the eagle on Bellamy's home, and John R. Pridham of New Castle, who carved about forty figures while he was cook at the Wallis Sands Coast Guard Station in Rye.

Miss Mary H. Pierce of Concord owns a ship's eagle, carved in the Bellamy tradition, which probably once decorated the prow of a schooner wrecked off Great Boar's Head in Hampton. The eagle was brought ashore by a sailor who survived the catastrophe. He gave it to Colonel Stebbins H. Dumas, proprietor of Boar's Head Hotel, and the eagle hung there until the building burned down. Colonel Dumas then gave the carving to Miss Pierce, whose father had been his partner in the management of the Phenix Hotel in Concord. The piece is marked with the name of "G. W. Harvey, Jr., Carver, Bath, Me.," and the present owner thinks he was one of the schooner's crew. The beautiful carving is colored. The eagle is bronzed over and the shield and the American flag which it surmounts are painted in the national colors.

Frank C. Pinkham of Kittery, a local designer of fine ships' models, is an authority on Bellamy's work. He says: "I never saw John Bellamy, but he was a friend of my family, especially of my father who was a foreman ship rigger at the Navy Yard for over fifty years." Mr. Pinkham has made many models of historic ships, but his outstanding accomplishment is a model of the *Pennsylvania*, fully rigged.

Making ships' models is a craft in which many old seamen have engaged for years. Among them is Bernard Linchey, of Portsmouth, a bland and gentle old sailor who served his sea apprenticeship on the *Kearsarge*. He gives his children models of ships for wedding presents and rigs a miniature ship for each new grandchild. Besides models of the *Flying Cloud* and other vessels out of Massachusetts yards, "Barney", as all his friends call him, has built and rigged four intricate models of New Hampshire ships: the beautiful *Nightingale*; the *Clotilde,* made for the guano trade between the Chincha Islands and England; the stately *Grandee,* and the *Annie F. Conlon,* a coastwise schooner. He was an officer on the "Annie" when he gave up the sea to be married, and this model is his most prized possession.

Another model-maker who followed the sea in his youth but gave it up to become an inland carpenter and mill sawyer, was the late William W. Scott of Derry. His best known models are the three miniature replicas of the clipper *Alice,* the sailing vessel *City of Rome,* and the steamship *Titanic,* the last portraying the famous liner just as she started to sink after she struck an iceberg in 1912. The models and the woodwork of the cases which hold his masterpieces were fashioned with no tool except a jackknife.

Mr. Scott always refused to call himself a wood carver. "I am just a Yankee whittler," he said. "I guess whittling runs in the family. My grandmother said her father was always quite a whittler and my youngest son is quite a whittler, too."

Ship model collecting as a modern hobby was coincident with the disappearance of square-rigged sailing vessels. Models interest two types of people. The first are those who have a natural aptitude for constructing mechanical objects, and who, like the Piscataqua craftsmen just described, enjoy "puttering around" making miniature ships for a hobby. The other is the collector, who is interested in poking around old warehouses, ancient dwellings, and antique shops along the waterfront in search of models made by long forgotten craftsmen. Today, many of these tiny vessels are preserved in museums or in the collections owned by the Government, where they serve not only as permanent records of the days when "wind-driven ships sailed the seven seas", but also as real models for present-day craftsmen to study and copy.

There are two full-rigged models and a number of mounted half-hulls in the Portsmouth Navy Yard and a small collection at the

FIGUREHEAD *from the prow of the "Lady of the Lake."*

SHIP'S EAGLE *owned by Miss Mary H. Pierce of Concord and* FIGUREHEAD *owned by Portsmouth Yacht Club.*

Portsmouth Yacht Club. But it is the old Athenaeum on Market Street which antiquarians and craftsmen visit when they are studying ships' models, for it houses one of the most famous collections in the country outside of the Smithsonian Institution in Washington. The present exhibit consists of forty half-models, and the three full models of the frigate *America,* the *Montgomery,* bearing a figurehead of General Montgomery, and the French ship *Clovis,* carved out of white whalebone with ivory ornamentations by French fan carvers confined as prisoners of war in England's grim Dartmoor Prison.

The Marine Room in the John Paul Jones House (Portsmouth Historical Society) contains a number of good models. Some of them, however, like the old *Dover Packet* and two gundalows with lateen sails, are copies of river boats used on the Piscataqua.

Gundalows, defined in the dictionary as heavy flat-bottomed barges or boats, used especially in New England, disappeared from the Piscataqua region at the end of the nineteenth century. According to an investigation made in 1937 under the direction of the Historic American Merchant Marine Survey, the hull of the wreck of the last known New Hampshire gundalow was demolished in 1925.

The gundalow probably received its name from the light, dainty boats of Venice and Greece, but in appearance it was quite unlike them. It was at its best pictorially, when lying on some tide-deserted beach, its yard on a line with the deck, and the sail loosely brailed up.

In 1884 when John Albee wrote the history of New Castle, he described the appearance of the gundalow as it was nearing the end of its existence. The historian says, "Nothing in our day is seen upon its waters so picturesque and foreign-looking as the gundalows, which creep along the shores and in and out among the islands. They have one short, stumpy mast, and a very long yard, rigged with a lateen sail. The yard is held to the mast by a chain hooked into an iron band around the yard and rove through a sheave-hole in the mast-head; thus enabling it to swing horizontally, when passing under bridges, or when at anchor. . . . The yard is weighted at the forward end, in order, when lowering, to balance the weight of the sail, which is mainly aft of the mast."*

The boat described by Albee was the third type of its kind to sail up the waters of the Piscataqua, the Oyster, the Lamprey, and the Exeter Rivers, for the gundalow passed through three definite stages of construction.

No one knows when the gundalow first began to circulate around the arteries of the Great Bay. Albee claims to have found allusions to such a craft existing in 1696. But whatever date is set, it is safe to say that for over two hundred years they were in constant use in the coastal region for transporting lumber, bricks, coal, and passengers to such towns as Newmarket, Dover, Durham, and Exeter. In addition, they took the place of hayracks for carrying the marsh hay, the black grass cut along the creek borders in June, and the fox-thatch in September—bringing them back on high-running tides to the town and farm landings.

Unlike other types of shipbuilding, the making of New Hampshire gundalows never reached commercial proportions, but remained a craft carried on by local farmers and river captains who made the boats in limited quantities. No fine work was put into them, but their construction required a certain knowledge of local conditions which had to be "born and bred in the bone".

Today only one known gundalow is extant: at Adams' Point on Great Bay, a partially completed hull, started by Captain Edward H. Adams in 1933, lies on the ways. In design and craftsmanship, Captain Adams' partially completed gundalow resembles those of his father's time. In 1882 he modeled a gundalow, built it during the following three years, and named it the *Fanny M.,* after his wife. The half-inch scale model is now in the Watercraft Collection of the Smithsonian Institution. The captain, now in his eightieth year, still carves and fits out models of boats, and at present is engaged in carving from wood and assembling a collection of water birds, native to

---

* *New Castle, Historic and Picturesque.* John Albee. Boston. Cupples, Upham & Co., 1884. pp. 55-56.

the region, which have been painted in their natural colors by his son.

Captain Adams selected and cut the principal timbers for his gundalow during the winter, searching many acres of woodland to find natural ships' knees and bow legs. Oak was chosen for the heavy timbers of the frame, and pine was used for the hull planking and corner pieces. It was often difficult to find pine trees with the natural curvature needed to make bow logs of one piece. Thus the bow planking usually was constructed of short pieces well-braced inside by extra curved logs, "trunneled" transversely over them.

Usually gundalows were built with one foot more beam forward than aft. Captain Adams increased the difference to two feet. His boat had no keel and was flat-bottomed. The bow timbers averaged six inches in thickness and ten inches in width. Every piece of lumber was personally selected for size and shape, and cut on his own or the adjoining property. Crooked pieces were shaped with an adz, and other logs were carried up the river to a saw mill and cut on two sides, to specific dimensions.

Drilling holes for the large hardwood pegs, or treenails—colloquially called "trunnels"—was a task in itself; but the hardest part of gundalow construction was carving the spoon-shaped bow and the sharply-curved corner pieces which helped to hold the flat bottom and perpendicular sides together. These, like the knees and the frames, were placed in position and fastened together with oak trunnels.

Neither the roughhewn nature of the gundalow's construction nor the character of the business for which it was designed, warranted much concentration on beauty of exterior design and finish. Gundalows were painted whatever color was available when they were ready to slide off the ways. It was a pure waste of time to paint the bottoms, since frequent groundings and scrapings on mudbanks and sandbars would soon remove every vestige of color. The most common pigment used was a mixture of white lead and lampblack, which resulted in a battleship grey resembling unpainted, weather-beaten boarding. The farmer gundalow-owner often covered his boat with the same red paint that he slapped on his barn.

The half-completed gundalow which Captain Adams is building lies on the shore of a little cove, a hundred yards from the family homestead on the Point. The "skipper" started it in 1933, but sickness, depression, and death in the family have delayed the work. The boat lies a few feet from the water, with its top and sides covered by grey boards, some of which were picked up adrift. The hull has been completed and the deck is on. Now only the cabins and the interior work are needed to finish it. Recent delay in the construction of the gundalow may possibly be caused by the progress being made on a new modern river gundalow which the skipper started building in 1938. He is making it for family use, but, as has occurred many times before in the history of Adams' boatbuilding, some interested buyer may pop up at its launching and offer a bid. In dimension, the gundalow is little more than half as large as the *Fanny M*. It differs also in that it is to be schooner-rigged with two masts, where the original had only a lateen sail. It will have a bow-sprit nine feet long, where the original had none. Like all gundalows it has a flat bottom, with a lee board taking the place of a keel.

The two gundalows show the wide range of Captain Edward H. Adams' versatility as a craftsman. All around Adams Point, scattered high up on the beach, hidden among the reeds, and moored offshore, are at least two dozen boats of all types and sizes, built by the skipper and his son, Cass Adams, in the last three decades.

Out of seafaring days have come boats and vessels with personalities all their own. The figureheads of some have pointed out of Portsmouth Harbor towards strange shores; the flat bottoms of others have helped to develop the industry of home waters. They are remembered as men are remembered for the part they had in building New Hampshire.

III

MEN WHO MADE NEW HAMPSHIRE BUILDINGS

> "Here is a fine house! It stands high on dry land.
> The owner is rich, and a very fine man.
> At home he is honored, and abroad it's the same;
> May he still keep increasing in honor and fame.
> This house it stands square, and in a fair view
> Of a river, fine meadows and neighbors a few.
> The timber is square, and is well put together;
> May God bless the owner, forever and ever!"

This was the toast proposed by Kimball Fletcher in 1835, when Parker Tabor's frame house was raised near the river in old Indian Stream Republic, now the town of Pittsburg, which lies just under the Canadian border.

In New Hampshire, as elsewhere in pioneer America, a "raising" brought out all the neighbors for miles around. Every available able-bodied man came to lift the heavy timbers when the masterbuilder gave the signal and cried, "Heave O heave!" The women gathered to serve the mammoth noon meal and early supper; the boys, accompanied by their dogs, scampered around everywhere, carrying tools and water to the workmen and running errands for the women.

Unless there was a bad accident like the one which happened in 1773 when the Wilton meetinghouse was raised and one of the center beams supporting the frame broke and pitched timber, axes, board saws, and fifty men to the ground, raisings were gala occasions for the whole countryside. During the day there were intervals of relaxation from the hard work of lifting the great sills, plates, posts, and beams, when the young men held races and wrestled while their elders smoked and gossiped and watched the fun. Everybody had access to the hard cider and to the West India rum, which was furnished by the town if a public building was raised or by the host when a house was put up.

Liquid refreshments usually helped out even in the raisings of meetinghouses. In Mont Vernon, when the church was framed in the late eighteenth century, the building committee was instructed to provide one barrel of rum, two barrels of cider, and "one quarter of sugar" for the workmen. Tradition also tells us that the lack of rum at the raising of the Sandown meetinghouse, completed in 1774, was responsible for the first labor strike in New Hampshire. The supply ran out just as the workmen were about to put on the roof; so the men refused to work for half a day while a messenger was sent down to Newburyport for another half-barrel.

But in some communities there was opposition to so much drinking at raisings. The master builder, William Abbot of Boscawen, framer of churches at Somersworth, Cornish, Wentworth, Unity, Thornton, Henniker, and West Concord, took an active part in temperance reform. When the question of buying liquor for the raising of the West Concord meetinghouse came up in 1820, Mr. Abbot opposed it vigorously. He was told that there was always drinking at raisings and that it would be impossible to get workmen without rum.

"If there are not enough temperance men in Concord, I'll try and get them elsewhere," he answered. "Send me down twelve good men," he told Thomas Coffin of Boscawen. There were so many volunteers that nearly one hundred men arrived to raise the meetinghouse, without rum.

The high point of a raising came after the body of the frame was actually up, the beams put in place, and the rafters placed in position, a pair at a time. Then the final task of pinning the ribs, to which the shingles were to be fastened, was divided between two crews, both ready for a merry contest to see which team would get its allotment of ribs placed first. The honor of setting the ridgepole and naming the building went to the victors, so the rivalry between the teams was great. When the last nail had been pounded down, two men from the winning team, each one with a bottle in his hand, clambered out on the ridgepole. Reaching the center of their high perch, up they stood, one of them facing the south, and the other, the north.

"This is a fine frame and deserves a good name!" one man cried, following a recognized custom of the North Country.

"Oh, yes! Oh, yes!" chanted the crowd below him. "What shall we call it?"

The man facing the north answered by giving a very humorous or elaborate name; and when his companion sang out "Oh, yes!", each of them took a long drink from his bottle.

An eye-witness of a barn-raising held in Coös County in the mid-nineteenth century says that, in this particular instance, one of the pseudo godparents was a sailor who added an original note to the customary procedure by reciting at the top of his lungs,

"The owner is a cooper, a jolly old soul,
We'll drink all his rum, but leave the ridgepole."

Sailors were particularly popular at raisings, for they dared to climb to any height and to perform all kinds of daring feats. They stood on the ridgepole or hung down by their heels as they drank the toast and christened the building, according to their own doggerel:

"Some oak and some pine,
Some coarse and some fine,
Some old and some new,
Hand on the bottle and that will do."

Raisings were hard work as well as fun. A Lancaster man who attended many similar celebrations in his youth has left us a vivid description to prove it. He says: "First the two sides of the structure were put together on the sills and underpinnings and securely pinned in the joints. Long poles called, in the vernacular of the trade, 'follerin poles', were chained to the upper and outside corners. The next step, generally, was to stop and take another drink preparatory to the tug of war that was coming. This feature of the business being attended to, and all being in perfect readiness, the master workman distributes the men at such places in which he thinks they can best serve. The oldest and most trusty men were assigned to the task of tending the foot posts, to guide the tennon into the mortice as the framed side rises serenely in the air. The master workman now took a position from which he could see all his men, and from which all could see him as he gave orders. He called out in lusty and commanding tones, 'Are you all ready?' When all had responded affirmatively to the question, he commanded, 'Pick 'er up', in response to which every man laid out his strength to comply with the command. The frame was lifted as high as men could lift by hand, when handspikes and pikepoles were brought into use. The master workman next called out, 'Heave at the follerin-poles.' The 'follerin poles' having been duly 'heaved on', the frame was raised until the tennons sank home in the mortices, and the whole side reached a perpendicular position. It was then securely fastened by temporary braces and stays. The second side went up after the same manner as the first, after which 'all hands took another drink', and had a short breathing spell. They next proceeded with ends, and middle timbers of the frame, in the same manner as with the sides. At this point a situation of affairs was reached in which the courage and agility of the more venturesome and level-headed young men could show off their skill to great advantage. Someone was needed to mount to the corners and guide the tennons into the mortices and pin them together. This task generally fell to the lot of apprentices at the carpenter's trade, or the carpenter's assistants, called joiners and finishers, or in the absence of such, to some young man possessed of the requisite courage and skill for a task so far above the ground."*

* *History of Lancaster. Rev. A. N. Somers. Concord, N. H. Rumford Press, 1899. pp. 205-206.*

MEN WHO MADE NEW HAMPSHIRE BUILDINGS

Framing buildings was a specific trade which required great judgment and knowledge. Any farmer or minor artisan could nail boards in place, but it took a man of extensive experience to know how to cut each piece so that it would fit when the whole frame was made, and to raise the frame without mishap. William Durgin was one such master builder of the late eighteenth century. He framed a number of buildings in Portsmouth, and, after he went to live in central New Hampshire, still carried on his trade. He framed the Sanbornton meetinghouse on the southern crest of the hill, at the Square. It had few architectural attractions and no steeple.

"What is that great building on the hill?" Squire Stephen Perley asked his traveling companion when they arrived in town in 1789.

"It is the Lord's House," was the answer.

The Squire looked at the building again and said dryly, "I should think it looked more like the Lord's barn."

Early New Hampshire meetinghouses were built simply and plainly for use. When the Northwood meeting house was built about 1784, the work was divided so that one man could board the west half of the front; another, the east half of the front and the south end of the east side; and so on, until the entire frame was covered.

When the vogue for putting steeples on churches swept over the countryside, Ephraim Potter, the only framer of buildings in Concord at the beginning of the nineteenth century, was called upon to construct the four-square steeple of the historic North Church. Potter had been a sailor; when not at sea, he had worked on one mechanical device after another. With remarkable ingenuity, he framed and finished the steeple inside the porch of the church, and raised it by means of a tackle contrived by himself.

The versatile carpenter and joiner, Joel O. Patrick of Jaffrey, was as famous a steeple builder as the Concord man. The tower which he added to the old meetinghouse, now the Jaffrey Town House, when it was remodeled in 1822, is proof that he was not only an expert artisan but also an architect who could have been successful in a larger field than the one he chose.

Patrick's steeple shows the influence of Sir Christopher Wren, the noted English architect. Wren raised the standard of taste in England and his ideas, in turn, affected American architecture. A number of steeples based on his designs were added to New Hampshire churches, among them the beautiful meetinghouse in Hancock.

The most stupendous piece of framing accomplished in early New Hampshire was done in the wilderness of the Connecticut Valley when Old Dartmouth Hall, at Reverend Eleazar Wheelock's Indian School, was built at Hanover. The building was three stories high and had a frame made of massive pines, cut on the site. The principal timbers were fifteen inches square; the cords of the roof, fifty feet long; and the longitudinal sills and plates, seventy-five feet. A large number of men, working ten days under the direction of the master carpenter, John Sprague, were required to raise the frame.

The master builders often took their work under contract for sums which seem very small to modern eyes. In 1777, Samuel Jackman—called "Joiner" Jackman to distinguish him from Samuel Jackman, the blacksmith—agreed to furnish the frame of the Boscawen-Webster meetinghouse for ninety-four dollars, but he fulfilled the contract so well that the town voted him the additional sum of sixteen dollars and sixty-eight cents. Some years earlier, John Thompson, Sr., contracted for the frame of the Durham meetinghouse at around two hundred and fifty dollars for the job. One-half was to be paid when the lumber was hauled and laid in place; the other half, when the frame was ready for raising.

The early town proprietors urged carpenters and joiners to settle in the new communities. Nathaniel Burley, a carpenter and joiner by trade, brought his family to fifty acres of land in Sanbornton, which had been awarded him because he was the first house carpenter to settle in that community. Sarah, his wife, and her two youngest children rode horseback along with the barnyard poultry, which were caged in a straw tick with breathing holes from which the hens' heads protruded. The two oldest boys, six and seven years old, walked with their father and drove the cows. When they came

MEN WHO MADE NEW HAMPSHIRE BUILDINGS

to the claim, Burley helped his wife to dismount in front of the log cabin he had built for her. Then he swung open the bark door and said politely, "Walk in, Ma'am". We are told that Sarah both laughed and cried as she entered her wilderness home.

In places where an artisan did not immediately "make a pitch", workmen from neighboring settlements came to help out with house building. In 1775, Wells Chase and Moses Haskell, fellow apprentices, put their tools on their backs in Newbury, Massachusetts, and tramped through the wilderness to Chester to build a house for Stephen Morse. Hopestill March, a mulatto of Dover, was another of these traveling master carpenters. Before the Revolutionary War, he was called from one Piscataqua town to another to ply his trade. He built many houses in Portsmouth, all of them on the same general plan—two-storied houses with gambrel roofs.

These early carpenter-architects seem to have been not merely jacks-of-all-trades, but masters of many. Looking over a list of New Hampshire artisans of the eighteenth and early nineteenth centuries, we find that a number of carpenters and master builders also followed other trades and even learned professions. They worked under difficulties of which our modern craftsmen are ignorant, for every step of building from start to finish was done by hand with simple tools.

The joiners who worked on the inside finish of churches and houses were men of as much local importance as the framers and master builders. Caleb Woodman, described as "a man of influence, decision, and energy" was a prominent joiner of Canterbury. He was often called upon to do the finish work on meetinghouse interiors. A well-known joiner in the western side of the State, Ebenezer Crehore, came to Walpole before 1780. He built a footlathe on which he turned all the pieces for the pews of the meetinghouse, put up in 1789. In Gilford, the Hunts, skilled journeymen workers, did expert finish work on panels and banisters and were noted for their skill in ornamentation.

For the most part, master builders had little to do with the raising of the first New Hampshire houses, which usually were started and completed by their owners. As in all pioneer communities framed houses were preceded by temporary shelters put up in a crude fashion without any plan for permanency. Pioneer building methods were very crude and were similar to those used by John Fawcett, who made his first home in Fitzwilliam in 1769. He set split logs in the ground to form a palisade and covered the sides with hemlock bark, which had been dried on the ground, beneath stones to prevent curling. Then he passed green withes around the posts and through holes in the bark before cutting the rafters and lashing ribs across them. The shingles of this primitive wilderness dwelling were double thicknesses of bark, and the bark door had withe hinges.

The log cabin era was of comparatively short duration in New Hampshire. This was as true of the western and northern sections as it was along the seacoast and in the lower Merrimack River Valley. In Lancaster, far up to Coös County, there were eight frame houses, only nineteen years after the town's settlement in 1763. The first two-storied house to be framed in the town was the large, flat-roofed Holton House which still stands at the north end of the village. In 1780, the first owner, Major Jonas Wilder, brought his wife and ten children to Lancaster, and with them came carpenters, masons, and glaziers to build and finish the house.

The Jackson House at Christian Shore, owned by the Society for the Preservation of New England Antiquities, is an example of the permanent early houses built in Portsmouth. It was erected in 1664 by Richard Jackson, a shipbuilder, and six generations of his family have lived in it. It has many features of the Elizabethan houses which, in England, had been familiar to the Piscataqua settlers.

Although built over a hundred years later than the Jackson House, the first frame house in Wentworth was much more simple in form and more typical of early frame houses. It was the home of Phillips White, and was designed and built in 1772 by Reuben Whitcher. The frame was hewn from small pines; and the joists, studding, and braces were of red oak, split from the log. The building was never clapboarded, but the cracks were bat-

MEN WHO MADE NEW HAMPSHIRE BUILDINGS

tened by means of a narrow board nailed over each one. There never was any lathing or plaster; the floor boards were fastened down with wooden pins; the doors were hung on wooden hinges and had wooden latches. The house was only 20 x 23 feet square, but was two stories high, so that an old dame characterized it as "all tall and no big". These little "half-houses" with one room on each floor were built at an early date. If more space was needed, the half-house plan was repeated on the other side of a great chimney, making a four-room house. If it was necessary to enlarge it again, a lean-to was added at the rear, producing the famous "saltbox" house style.

By the mid-eighteenth century, the wealth of the Province of New Hampshire had increased greatly through its lucrative trade with the West Indies and its shipbuilding and lumbering industries. New demands for more luxurious and comfortable ways of living gave a decided impetus to the building trade.

Elaboration in house architecture began with gambrel-roofed houses of much larger size than those previously erected, and was followed by the imposing "three-decker" mansions characteristic of Portsmouth and other New England coastal towns.

The names of some of Portsmouth's master builders of this period of a maturer culture have been preserved because they were members of important families of social standing. In 1750 Mr. and Mrs. Charles Treadway, who gave fine houses to all their children, built the Cutter-Langdon House for their son, Jacob. It is known that the master carpenter was George Gaines, a famous cabinetmaker, whose father, John Gaines, constructed the Treadway's own home. The younger Gaines, who became very prominent in local civic affairs, was born in 1736 and lived until 1808. He developed a large business as a cabinetmaker and housebuilder. It is conceded generally that George Gaines was the builder of a number of Portsmouth's stately mansions and that he and his father are responsible for some distinctive features in the architecture of the period in which they worked.

Like Gaines, Langley Boardman was a cabinetmaker. It is

thought that he was his own architect and master-craftsman when he built his residence, the beautiful Langley Boardman-Marvin House, which modern architects say is a perfect example of the town type of house at the turn of the nineteenth century. The Boardman family was very well-to-do, and the young cabinet-maker had money enough to set himself up in business as soon as he finished his apprenticeship. He had considerable social standing in Portsmouth, and he designed his house to meet the needs of a man of culture and wealth.

The general education of all well-to-do young men of the times was along cultural lines, which included instruction in all art forms. When they came to build houses, they often acted as their own architects. In some instances they designed buildings other than their residences. In 1773 John Wentworth, last Royal Governor of the Province of New Hampshire, furnished the plans from which the master carpenter, Ebenezer Rice, built the Union Church at Claremont. Governor John probably made the plans for his magnificent manor house, which he built in old King's Woods, now the town of Wolfeboro.

The influence of Charles Bulfinch, the famous Boston architect, is found in a number of buildings, like the Public Library, the Larkin-Rice House, and the Peirce Mansion in Portsmouth, and the Wheeler House in Orford on the Connecticut River; but there are no records to prove that he made the plans from which they were erected.

The hand of Asher Benjamin, the first agent of the Nashua Manufacturing Company, who is noted as the author of the earliest American books on architecture, is distinctly evident in certain buildings in Nashua. Benjamin's influence on architecture, however, extended much farther than the lower Merrimack Valley; in the first half of the last century there was scarcely a region in New England where moulding profiles, cornice details, church spires, or houses did not reflect his ideas.

Samuel Shepard, a Nashua architect, seems to have been associated with Asher Benjamin in a number of ways and is spoken

MEN WHO MADE NEW HAMPSHIRE BUILDINGS 35

of as his pupil. Apparently, he was better known as a manufacturer and inventor than as an architect. With David Baldwin, he set up the first shop in the country for building doors, sash and blinds, and is credited with having invented machines for making these fittings.

Ralph Adams Cram, sponsor of the Gothic revival for church architecture, is the only great architect having more than casual connection with the State. He was born in Hampton Falls in 1863. The Phillips Church at Exeter, built in 1897, and All Saints Church at Peterborough are outstanding examples of Dr. Cram's work in the State.

In comparison with other sections of New Hampshire, the seacoast region had a headway of almost one hundred years in which to form a culture sufficiently leisured to produce ornamental carving of high artistic skill. While the newly chartered towns in the western counties were notching timbers for their first houses and barns, the sawmills of the Piscataqua were preparing pine boards for paneling rooms in the houses of the mill owners. The decorative woodwork, used so lavishly in the mansions along the coast, shows faithful imitation of certain English schools of architecture, with designs based on some characteristics of a Renaissance style originated by Andrea Palladino, the Italian architect.

Wood carving in New England reached its most refined stage during the middle of the eighteenth century. Wood needed broad surfaces to display the beauty of its grain, and craftsmen treated it with very different methods from those used in working with stone. The emphasis in wood carving was on ornamentation rather than on symbolism, and such structural features as pilasters and capitals were held in high regard.

Portsmouth has been called a city of architectural layers. Examples of wood carving characteristic of the changing moods of its history are found in all sections of the town, for succeeding generations of carvers tried out their skill on fireplace decorations, stairways, and doorways.

The local carvers who decorated the homes of Piscataqua merchants were looked upon as artisans rather than as artists. However, the system of apprenticeship which trained boys for woodworking in the shipbuilding trade, provided for a high standard of workmanship. Some of these boys, who were talented beyond an ordinary degree of skill, eventually devoted their time to the better-paid business of architectural carving.

The Wentworth-Gardner House in Portsmouth, built in 1760 for Thomas Wentworth, is an outstanding example of the methods used by local craftsmen. Three ships' carpenters spent fourteen months on the beautiful interior carvings, which are typical examples of the finest craftsmanship of the times. The pine paneling of many of the walls forms a chaste background for the delicately molded cornices and medallions, for the fluted Ionic pilasters and Corinthian capitals, which run the full height of the walls, and for the graceful curve of the front staircase. The effect of this handiwork is one of sensitive culture as well as of wealth and leisure. Even the pineapple motif, within the scrolled pediment over the door, seems a hand-carved symbol of the gracious hospitality dispensed by the leading figures of Portsmouth's aristocratic society.

At least one architectural phenomenon, the so-called Portsmouth baluster, found in a number of houses in the Piscataqua region, is attributed to John and George Gaines. The staircases of the eighteenth and early nineteenth century houses afforded wood carvers ample opportunity to display their dexterity. The newel post of the staircase in the Wentworth-Gardner House is carved from a single block of wood, probably fashioned by a ships' carpenter. The spindles in the railing are carved of old black cherry. The handrail itself is painted pine, for mahogany and maple veneer did not become popular until the height of good taste had passed, and the glorification of humble woods was characteristic of eighteenth century craftsmanship.

The doorways on the old Piscataqua mansions have great interest for both the artist and the craftsman. In their entirety they are distinguished for their pediments and their columns, which in design and in execution show the exquisite skill of master carvers.

FRANKLIN PIERCE HOMESTEAD, *Hillsboro.*

OLD MEETINGHOUSE, *Hancock.*

WOOD CARVING *of Daniel Webster's birthplace, Franklin, N. H.*

PARLOR *of the Franklin Pierce Homestead.*

Harry M. S. Harlow, an artist who lives in Portsmouth, has made a detailed study of these doorways with their triangular and curved pediments, heavily carved cornices, fluted Corinthian columns, and Ionic porticoes; he has interpreted their beauty in a series of paintings which faithfully portray the chronological sequence of their development as American art forms. Fifty doorways, no two of them alike, have been portrayed. Much of the research for the paintings has been done by the artist's wife and by her father, Charles H. Magraw, a retired carpenter, who has worked on many of the old houses, and who remembers the details of construction on those he has repaired.

One outstanding example of the way a genuine architectural feature of the seacoast section was taken inland and transplanted by craftsmen and artisans is found in the "widow's" or "captain's walk" which surmounts the "Dr. Hamilton House" in Lyme. Its hanging stairway winds around a perfectly circular inner well to the level of the roof top, which is surmounted by a large square cupola with windows on all sides. The external balustrade has been removed, but a door still opens onto the roof.

This house stands on the "Plains", west of the common, and evidently was designed to accommodate a large household with servants. It is an almost perfect example of the methods of construction used by the old master builders, who put up a house to last for centuries. The framework is so massive and the double walls of the brick foundation so thick that when the house was modernized the electricians had great difficulty with their work. The fact that the external architecture has certain similarities to the village church, leads architects to believe that the two buildings were both erected about 1813 by the same builders. The present owner of the house, Dr. Mary Conant, has no family connection with the mansion, but she knows that her grandfather, born in 1793, worked on it.

The carpenter-builder is still an important figure in New Hampshire, especially in rural towns where he is called upon to do all kinds of jobs from building and repairing his neighbors' homes, as the goodwives want them done, to building and remodeling houses for the "summer folks", according to trained architects' specifications. Unlike the woodworker of metropolitan centers who works from blueprints and is skilled in one particular branch of the trade, the modern carpenter-builder is as versatile as his grandfather. He can turn a corncrib into a studio, change a woodshed into a summer cottage, shingle a barn quickly and efficiently, or build an entire house from garret to cellar. To be sure, he works by square rule instead of the old scribe rule, where every part of the building was fitted and scribed (marked for a certain place) before framing. His tools are up-to-date and would make his ancestors green with envy; the material and stock he uses are prepared in modern woodworking plants. But he is still the typical New Hampshire carpenter of three hundred years, an ingenious Yankee craftsman who knows how to use his head as well as his hands.

IV

CABINETMAKERS PAST AND PRESENT

New Hampshire people who wish to refresh their memories of the social life and customs of Portsmouth in its prosperous days, when sailing vessels from Norway, from "red Ceylon", and from the "blue Azores" anchored in the Piscataqua, usually take the pleasant and easy way of consulting records set down by the chatty "Rambler", Charles W. Brewster. This versatile newspaper editor, a member of a substantial Portsmouth family, died virtually with a pen in his hand in August, 1868.

From the "Rambles", we get our first inkling of the fine work of a noted cabinetmaker who lived in the "Old Town by the Sea" during the first third of the eighteenth century. Brewster says: "We have in daily use, and as good as new, four chairs made by our great-grandfather, John Gains* in 1728. He built the house in the rear of Mechanics Reading Room in that year, and these chairs were made for his parlor."†

For years no one took more than a passing interest in the history of the chairs, which, according to the Rambler, were "handsomely and faithfully made". Some years ago it was learned that Charles Brewster, through one of Gaines' daughters, was a descendant of the cabinetmaker, and the history of these chairs was traced directly to the present time. They are made of native hardwoods and,

---

* As spelled by Brewster. Modern spelling used in text.
† *Rambles About Portsmouth. Second Series. Charles W. Brewster. Portsmouth, N. H. Brewster, 1869-1873. p. 355.*

except for their rush seats, retain their original finish of brown paint, grained to imitate walnut. They are still owned and used by descendants of John Gaines.*

Gaines' dexterity in woodworking was handed down to his son, George. But the younger Gaines was a mere lad when his father died, and he served his apprenticeship under other cabinetmakers. He was very young when he took over the family shop and started making fine furniture for his Portsmouth neighbors.

There are no means by which George Gaines' products can be absolutely identified, but reliable data attribute two lots of chairs to him. One set consists of ladder-back side chairs in the Chippendale style. They were owned originally by the shipbuilder, Captain Tobias Lear, father of the second Tobias, who was President George Washington's private secretary. The Rambler mentions these chairs in his annals and says that they were made from cherry wood cut in the Lear garden. The other set consists of a pair of large, beautifully constructed Chippendale sidechairs, fashioned from dark, rich mahogany. They are branded with the name of their owner, Captain William Rice, sea captain and privateersman of the War of 1812, famous for his "Calico Party", where the women were invited to cut dress patterns from bales of calico captured from the British by one of the good captain's ships. George Gaines was on intimate terms with the Lear and Rice families, so it is reasonable to assume that they ordered their chairs from their personal friend, who, around 1760, was the finest cabinetmaker in town.

The latter part of the eighteenth century brought the flowering of the cabinetmaking designs established in England by the great Thomas Chippendale and copied with certain adaptations by American craftsmen. Examples of Portsmouth furniture made during this period are very rare. Between 1802 and 1813 the town suffered from three great fires, which laid waste an area of over fifteen acres. Much of Portsmouth as it was in the Royal Provincial

---

* *American Collector. Vol. VII (November 1938) "John and George Gaines of Portsmouth, N. H." Stephen Decatur. (Used by permission of the author.)*

Period was destroyed. The furniture was burned with the houses, so that practically the only types of finer furniture forms in the city today are representative of the styles of the Early Republican or Federal era.

A series of advertisements in the *Portsmouth Gazette* indicate the increasing business of the cabinetmakers. Josiah Folsom displayed a cut of a Windsor chair and advertised that he had chairs of every description for sale; and on August 4, 1798, Langley Boardman announced that he was making furniture.

Boardman was a fine designer and a superb craftsman, and amassed a fortune from the cabinetmaking business, which he carried on from about 1795 until his death in 1829. Stephen Decatur, an authority on early furniture and silver, has made a study of Boardman's life and work, and has reached the conclusion that certain furniture forms—including an early American Empire sideboard, a mahogany sofa, and three sets of Sheraton chairs—were made by this distinguished craftsman.

Mr. Decatur, himself, owns two chairs, which, he says, have a distinctive design, making them easily recognizable as having been made by Boardman. Their structural details are examples of the transition from the Hepplewhite to the Sheraton designs, but the shape of the seat and legs and the employment of the stretchers are definitely in the Hepplewhite tradition. The front legs of each chair are moulded and slightly tapered; the uprights and cross members of the rectangular back are reeded and have a carved conventionalized flower in a small square at their intersection.

During the first decade of the nineteenth century, cabinetmakers' advertisements continued to appear in the *Gazette*. In 1808 Judkins and Senter announced that they had taken a shop and would engage in the cabinetmaking business. They kept together very well as a firm, for in 1814 they again were advertising their business, stating that they had on hand all kinds of cabinet furniture of the newest fashion.

Paul Burroughs of Pembroke has compiled a list of early New Hampshire cabinetmakers. In it he names the men who produced pieces of furniture that he has seen and examined, including items made by the Portsmouth firm mentioned above, and by such craftsmen as Stephen Adams of Haverhill; Moses Bohonon of Salisbury; Eliphalet B. Briggs, Jr., of Keene; John Gould, Jr., of New Ipswich; Moses Hazen of Weare; David Young of Hopkinton; Henry Wiggin, Jr., of Newfields; John Peters of West Henniker; Josiah Hosmer of Littleton; and the famous Dunlaps of the Merrimack Valley. Today, only a few meagre facts are known about the men in Mr. Burroughs' list and other early craftsmen working in the same line. News items concerning them are to be found in town histories and genealogical records, but none of these items gives us any idea of the way they worked or how they made their designs. A survey of the information available shows us that they plied their trade in all sections of the State and were not restricted to the Piscataqua region. Wherever a settlement was established, one or more cabinetmakers eventually set up business.

Very early in the nineteenth century, Stephen Adams came from Lexington, Massachusetts, to the lower Cohass meadows, where he carried on his trade of cabinetmaking and kept a general store. Michael Carleton, another fine craftsman of the Connecticut Valley, worked at the "Corner" in Haverhill. His furniture is still found in homes of this vicinity.

The Salisbury cabinetmaker, Moses Bohonon, born in 1774, was the son of Ensign Bohonon who fought under General John Stark at the Battle of Bennington. The Ensign married Susannah Webster, aunt of New Hampshire's famous "Black Dan'l". Salisbury people long remembered their wedding because the guests danced on a floor sprinkled with sugar, ground from a large conical sugar loaf, instead of stepping out the measures on sand-sprinkled boards. The elder Bohonon, a builder and joiner, taught the trade to his son, Moses, who produced a great amount of furniture and who employed a number of journeymen and joiners in his shop.

Eliphalet Briggs, Jr., of Keene, born in 1788, was one of six brothers, all cabinetmakers. They learned their trade from their father, a carpenter and joiner and a master of the "scratch and scribe rule", the old-method of framing buildings without the use of plans. For years Eliphalet, Jr., made furniture for the people living along the Ashuelot River.

The outstanding cabinetmakers of central New Hampshire were the Dunlaps. Major John of Bedford, John, Jr., of Antrim, and Samuel of Salisbury are the best known. Major John was the son of Archibald, a Scotch-Irish cabinetmaker from Ireland who settled in Chester in 1741. John, Jr., who learned his trade from his father, was very inventive and made an ingenious handloom for weaving "gentlemen's underclothing", a great innovation for the times. In 1844 he got the Western fever and moved to Zanesville, Ohio, where he lived for twenty years. Then he returned to New Hampshire and died in Nashua.

Major John's brother, Samuel, resided in Chester but worked at his trade in Concord and Henniker. He moved to Salisbury in 1797. His son, Samuel, Jr., followed the family trade "probably inheriting the feel of the tools from his father". Many Salisbury people own pieces of his furniture, which a local historian described in 1890 as being "sound as the day it left his shop".

The Dunlaps were noted for the excellence of their work, which is recognized by certain distinctive characteristics. These craftsmen worked out details that set them apart from the ordinary cabinetmakers. Some of their pieces carry basket work of Greek grille tops, and the skirts are distinguished for the Flemish scrolls with intaglio shells. Paul Burroughs believes that the finest forms were made by Samuel Dunlap, and that John, Jr., produced the inlaid cherry items prized by New Hampshire collectors.*

Robert Parker, born in 1797, was another Bedford cabinetmaker of repute. His products were noted for their expert workmanship and beauty of line. Bedford is located south of Manchester on the west bank of the Merrimack River, which, after the building of the Middlesex Canal (opened in 1803), became a commercial waterway between Concord, New Hampshire, and Boston, Massa-

* *American Collector, Volume VI (June 1937) "Furniture Widely Made in New Hampshire."* Paul Burroughs. pp. 6-7.

chusetts. Rand and Abbott had this in mind when, advertising their cabinet shop for sale in 1825, they made note of the fact that it was located "where furniture may be easily and very cheaply transported to Boston by water".*

Designing fine furniture for out-of-State trade is still carried on in the Merrimack Valley. A query often heard at the showrooms of a famous furniture firm is, "Where was this piece made?" and the answer is, since 1936, at least, "Up in New Hampshire, at our factory at Nashua." One of the outstanding designers and decorators is Frank G. Ranney of Hudson whose work indicates that the art of making fine furniture did not die with our ancestors.

Luther Alden, born in 1797, was a well-known cabinetmaker of Lebanon, in the Connecticut Valley. He worked for many years at Center Village, and was noted especially for his sideboards. In Newport on the Sugar River, about twenty-five miles southeast of Lebanon, cabinetmaking was an extensive industry from 1820 to 1837.

Chairmaking was a specialized business in New Ipswich, with the name of Isaac Appleton standing foremost in the trade. Many of the pine-seated, curved-back, painted, and ornamental chairs used in New Hampshire houses in the early nineteenth century came from the shop of Peter Wilder, located in a section of Keene known as "Tophet Swamp". Later, Wilder made rocking chairs, which Yankee women considered a great luxury. They became increasingly popular and sold in quantities.

New Ipswich was famous for its furniture, for many of the town's early settlers came from Ipswich, Massachusetts, a cabinet-making center, and continued to work at their trade in their new home. The early Ipswich cabinetmakers probably obtained some of their ideas from Thomas Dennis, who lived in Portsmouth in the period when good, substantial, oaken chests were the outstanding furniture forms. His identified pieces embrace a wide range of designs, and prove him to be the unrivaled master craftsman in his

* *New Hampshire Patriot and State Gazette. Concord, N. H. Monday, October 24, 1825.*

line in all New England. In 1664 he purchased land in Portsmouth, but four years later he married the widow of William Searle of Ipswich and moved to the Massachusetts Bay Colony.

The first New Hampshire settlers seem to have brought very little furniture with them. The inventories of the Laconia Company make no reference to any form except linen chests. Probably the women who followed their husbands to Pascataway transported their possessions in chests; and after they arrived, had other similar pieces made for storage purposes and for settles. A few of these early chests are still in existence. One, made in 1891 of oak with an original pine lid in one piece was found in the vicinity of Portsmouth. Another old chest, showing traces of coloring, was discovered in a kitchen in Fitzwilliam, and a pine chest of the late seventeenth century came to light in a Hampton barn.

The pioneers in the new settlements added to their meagre supply of furniture by making things they needed out of materials at hand. However, it is probable that few New Hampshire men were asked by their wives to bring in a hollowed log sap-trough and make a cradle for their first born, as was Shubeal Dearborn of Northfield in 1779; nor did every housewife demand that her husband build their hut around the stump of a large maple tree she could use for a table, as did Mrs. Josiah Ward of Henniker in 1763. Nevertheless, the first furniture forms were very crudely constructed: single loose boards supported on a three-legged trestle became a table; a piece of scantling set on a three-splayed standard served as a stool. From such humble origins came trestle tables, joint stools, and Windsor chairs.

The shop of the late Harvey Large, Haverhill cabinetmaker, still stands but a stone's throw from the kitchen window in the yard of his home, now occupied by his sister, Mrs. Anabel Glines. The house contains many examples of the work from which he earned a livelihood for over seventy years. Pieces still in use include a chamber set of light grain pine, a sofa with a butternut wood frame, a kneehole desk, and several chairs.

In this house there is a child's chair which is about eighty-two years old. Mrs. Glines says that when her mother was a young woman, she was very anxious to have a "little chair" for her child. She did not have money enough to hire a cabinetmaker to put it together, so she went out into the fields, picked a pound of wild strawberries, and carried them with a pound of rags to the general store. She received twenty-five cents for her wares, and this sum paid for making the tiny straight-backed red chair which has been cherished by four generations of children. In Concord the young mother might have taken the strawberries and rags straight to the cabinetmaker himself, for in October, 1810, no less a person than the well-known furniture-maker, George W. Rogers, was advertising all kinds of cabinet furniture to be sold for cash, country produce, or approved credit.

Cabinetmaking began early in Concord. Ebenezer Virgin, one of the original proprietors of old "Pennycook", was engaged in the trade in Salisbury, Massachusetts, before he settled in New Hampshire, in 1726. By the early nineteenth century Concord had become an important cabinetmaking center. Rogers was advertising for apprentices and journeymen to work at "the best stand in town, opposite the Walker Bank", and was assuring his customers that nothing would be lacking on his part to have his cabinet furniture made "in the newest and most elegant fashions".* He had among his competitors Levi Bartlett, who, besides his Concord stand, had a shop in Salisbury. Bartlett carried everything a housewife would need for outfitting a home, even to "Fresh Bedfeathers" to fill the plump mattresses used on all "four-posters". Porter Blanchard, born in Milford in 1788, bought out both of Bartlett's shops and advertised the fact in the *New Hampshire Patriot,* saying he would "spare no reasonable pains in ornamenting furniture to have it please".

Today Concord still has its cabinetmakers, all of them able to produce diversified types of work. Some of them concentrate on meeting the popular demand for smaller articles, such as trays, boxes, mirror frames, and a variety of other novelties.

* *New Hampshire Patriot. Concord, N. H. Tuesday, November 14, 1809.*

CABINETMAKERS, PAST AND PRESENT

George A. Chandler, now in his early seventies, has carried on the craft of woodworking for fifty years. For the past twenty years, he has been reproducing early American furniture and repairing antique pieces, such as four-poster beds, highboys, bureaus, cupboards, chairs, tables, and clocks. He does much of his work by hand, though he uses a band, bench, and circular saw, driven by electricity, and a turning lathe. He has a large shop, separated from his house, which contains his machinery, his treasured tools, and all kinds of cabinet woods.

In 1919 John A. Batchelder came from Claremont and started a cabinetmaking business in Concord. He has been a woodcraftsman ever since he was seventeen years old. His specialty as a cabinetmaker is restoring antique furniture, which he says covers several branches of craftsmanship: the actual cabinet work, refinishing, decorating, clock repairing, upholstering, wood carving, marquetry, and wood turning. He makes drawings and sketches of fine antique furniture, and he refers to these sketches when he is called upon to repair or reproduce rare pieces. He uses mahogany, maple, pine, and cherry for most of his work, though he also makes use of walnut, rosewood, beech, oak, ash, birch, chestnut, linden, whitewood, butternut, and elm. He is very particular about his stock; from the very beginning of his career as a cabinetmaker, he has made it a point to buy up cabinet woods and have them seasoned for future use.

Another expert cabinetmaker and master craftsman located in Concord is J. Albert Johnson, who was born in Sweden and who learned his trade there. He came to Concord to work for a piano company. Later he was employed in the cabinet shop of the silverware company, where he and Alfred Rydholm made mahogany inlaid serving trays with silver trimmings. Eventually he became foreman of the company's carpenter shop and had charge of making wood patterns for the machines. He is noted for the beauty of his custom-made furniture. His pieces include chests of drawers, highboys, dressers, buffets, tables of all kinds, chairs, beds, cedar chests, hand-carved and inlaid sewing cabinets, and mirror frames.

Mr. Johnson's son, Walter Leonard, has made model airplanes ever since he was a small boy. For Christmas, 1939, he made twenty-six models, all different.

Harry P. Hammond of Concord did not take any special course in cabinetmaking. But he was interested in American antiques at an earlier age than most young people are, and, he says, he bought his first collector's item when he was only eleven years old. It was this interest which led him to take up fine cabinet work. He has made chairs, lowboys, mirror frames, carved chests, and has restored many valuable pieces of old furniture.

Woodworking in its various branches was an outstanding business in Sanbornton in the early nineteenth century. At that time Sanbornton was the third largest town in New Hampshire with a population of 3800 people. There were thirty-eight thriving businesses in operation, with trade extending as far as Philadelphia and to points north of the State. Now the town has about 650 inhabitants and one tiny store run by the postmaster. In the early days, William Durgin, the framer of the "Lord's Barn", supplemented his work as a master builder by making furniture. His talents in producing articles from wood were so diversified that it was said he could make anything in the world but rennet bags.

Today George Lauder, a retired Concord business man, makes his home above the Square in Sanbornton, and does cabinetwork as a hobby, producing many fine pieces. In speaking of his work, Mr. Lauder says: "It is amazing how much knowledge one acquires in an art such as I have had for a hobby for nearly forty years."

In the region north of Mt. Washington, stories about the skilled cabinetmakers, "Uncle Sammy" Blake and "Uncle Jimmy" Lewis, are told to this day. Uncle Sammy lived just over the line in Northumberland, but his fine pieces of furniture adorned the "best" rooms in many of Stratford's houses. Uncle Jimmy was an Englishman who lived in the family of a Stratford innkeeper. He usually made his wares of cherry-wood, and they were so beautiful that people paid large prices for them. It is said that Elisha Baldwin, a leading citizen of the town, gave the cabinetmaker his best cow in payment for the cherry case of a tall clock, which stands today in the lovely Baldwin homestead.

Of the many cabinetmakers who worked in the Ammonoosuc River Valley after 1830, Deacon John Merrill is perhaps the best known. He learned his trade in Pembroke and came to Littleton when he was only twenty-four years old. Certain pieces of furniture, made of native woods, sometimes veneered with mahogany, which have been identified positively as his work, are still in use in North Country homes. The family of Woodman L. Wallace, on the Cherry Valley Road in Bethlehem, owns a black cherry table having two drawers with mahogany fronts, made from wood turned out at an old up-and-down sawmill on the next farm. One piece was of such fine grain that the owner saved it. It was carefully dried and taken to Deacon Merrill's shop to be made into this table which probably is the finest existing specimen of the Littleton cabinetmaker's work.

Charles Keyes of Littleton has restored a Deacon Merrill bureau which is a typical example of the methods of construction used by nineteenth-century cabinetmakers. The ends of the bureau are each made of one solid maple board. The drawers are of pine, with their backs hand-planed and bevelled and their fronts veneered with mahogany. The bureau is put together without nails, the pieces of wood being carefully dovetailed together. It also has the original brass escutcheons which Deacon Merrill put on many years ago.

Besides Mr. Keyes, three Littleton men are producing excellent handmade furniture "just for the fun of the thing". Frank Jesseman specializes in making furniture from bird's-eye maple, a difficult wood to handle. He has made a number of fine maple chairs, the maple case of a grandfather clock, a library table of maple and walnut, and other pieces constructed of native curly birch and black cherry. His greatest achievement is a nine-piece bedroom set, fashioned from solid bird's-eye maple which was cut just over the town line in Bethlehem.

Bird's-eye is a popular cabinet wood in that neighborhood and was used extensively by local craftsmen. Mrs. Elwyn Nelson of Franconia still owns a fine bird's-eye maple secretary which was made by a Littleton cabinetmaker just prior to 1852. The trees from which it was constructed were cut on the home farm of her grandfather, Luke Brooks, who in 1793 bought a tract of land in the Franconia eastern reaches.

A retired antique dealer, Charles Patenaude, a native of Canada who has lived in Littleton for many years, has turned out excellent copies of old pieces. His most famous items are two corner cupboards of basswood, fashioned from a log which he discovered as it was being drawn on a sled in the Littleton Winter Carnival Parade of 1930.

On the third floor of his home, Justus H. Beal has fitted up a workshop where, in his spare time, he produces exquisite furniture. He has made two tall clock cases of mahogany with boxwood inlays, a mahogany desk with inlays on each serpentine drawer, a gate-leg table of mahogany, mirror frames of varied designs, several four-poster beds, and various types of chests of drawers. One of the latter is a beautiful swell-front bureau of solid mahogany with mottled mahogany veneer on the front of the drawers.

Wooded acres of beech, maple, and birch, and swift, tumbling streams furnished the materials and the water power which made the section between the Ossipee and Sandwich Mountains an ideal location for small wood-turning shops. They were often owned and operated by succeeding generations of the same family.

The story of the Tappan family is typical of the old New Hampshire way of life. At the opening of the nineteenth century Abraham Tappan, an English cabinetmaker, settled in Sandwich in that part of Whiteface known as Bennett's Loop. There he began the Tappan tradition of making sturdy chairs; a tradition that was well established by his son, Daniel, after 1851. Daniel and his wife had fifteen children, each of whom had a particular task in the chairmaking industry carried on in their home. The youngest of the children was Walter S. Tappan, who died in December, 1939.

One of his memories was of the day his father discovered him turning out chair rounds on the old foot lathe for amusement, and gave him this chore as his part in the business.

Tappan chairs were designed for everyday use and were sold as fast as the family could make them, especially in the immediate vicinity of Sandwich. Many a newly married couple furnished every room in their house from the fourteen patterns of Tappan chairs. Their special virtue was substantiality. The materials used were standard: maple and birch for the posts, ash or maple for the slats, and brown ash for the splint bottoms. Handwork predominated in their construction; the posts and rounds were turned on the lathe, the back slats bent in sets, and the ash splint pounded and stripped from the logs.

The only method of retail distribution ever employed in disposing of the chairs was through the general store in Ashland, which agreed to take all the chairs the family could bring to them, provided that pay be taken out in trade. It was often a difficult matter to transport chairs to Ashland through winter drifts and spring mud ruts. For this reason the Tappans sold most of the chairs in the local market of Sandwich, a town which, at that time, was larger than Manchester.

The fifteen Tappan children grew up and the homestead was finally abandoned. The chairs continued to be made at a small mill until it was flooded during the spring freshet in 1882. Fortunately, not all the patterns for the chairs were destroyed, and the Tappan tradition has not died out. It is carried on today by Albert B. Hoag, a Sandwich cabinetmaker and teacher, who took up woodworking as a hobby. After several years of teaching, he invested in a woodworking shop. He soon saw that if the enterprise was to be a success he must concentrate on a single staple item which would support the rest of his products. Walter Tappan had been encouraged by the League of New Hampshire Arts and Crafts to make some specimens of the Tappan chairs. It was with his advice and assistance that Mr. Hoag started making chairs from the century-old patterns, nine of which are still in existence. Mr. Hoag says: "Over one hundred years of history in one town, in one family, and with the original designs and materials still being used is, I believe, as severe a test as could be given any product. It is therefore with a feeling very close to veneration that I am continuing the work of a man who could design and make a line of chairs so sound that, a century later, they meet a ready sale."

Not only does Mr. Hoag use the identical patterns of the Tappans, but he also follows much the same methods of handwork. He takes special care in the selection of wood. Only native wood has ever gone into Tappan chairs, and in order that it will respond properly to his tools, he checks its quality himself, saws it himself, and controls the seasoning. He can continue making and selling his chairs under the Tappan trade name only as long as the quality and design remain the same as the originals.

Harry Clark is another modern Sandwich cabinetmaker. Besides producing a wide range of miscellaneous articles, he specializes in fireside seats and serving trays. Also he makes such hard-to-find things as odd-sized trestle tables and corner cupboards.

About three years ago Earle R. Griffin, who lives in the neighboring town of Holderness, began working in wood for recreation. Now he is making settles, chests of drawers, and dressers, based on colonial designs. Examples of his furniture were shown in the League of New Hampshire Arts and Crafts Exhibit at the New York World's Fair in 1939-40.

It was noticeable that many of the pieces of furniture shown in the exhibit were constructed of native woods. The reason for this is apparent when the trends for workmanship are examined. Under League guidance, local craftsmen are experimenting with woods, and are making plans to conserve and build up the supply of native material. To quote Mrs. Foster Stearns, editor of the *Bulletin,* issued by the League, "Our woodworkers who are educated in their subject and are willing to add continually to their knowledge, can do much toward the rediscovery of past materials and their adaptations to new uses. How else than by the trial and error

DOLL'S CRADLE, *made in 1867, owned by Miss Ruth Whittier.*
WINDSOR CHAIR *originally owned by Moses Bayley, probably made in 1870.* HIGHBOY *owned by Fred E. Beane of Manchester.*

CARD TABLE, DESK, BIRD'S-EYE MAPLE BUREAU *and* CHEST, *probably all made by the famous Samuel Dunlap of Salisbury.*

system over an untold period of time, have we amassed the great volume of knowledge of wood lore, the secret grains, hidden in the hearts of trees, which can be cut in different slants to expose beautiful patterns, and all their endless variety and uses?"*

* *Bulletin, No. 55 (January 1940). League of New Hampshire Arts and Crafts. Mrs. Foster Stearns, Editor.*

V

TIME AND MUSIC

In 1762 Isaac Blasdell brought the clockmaking trade up to New Hampshire from Amesbury, Massachusetts. He brought it in a wagon, piled in with his wife and children, with his tools and dishes and clothes. He brought it over a blazed trail, wet and boggy from spring mud. A four-year-old sat by his side; on a chest, swaying with the pitch of the wagon, his wife sat holding the baby; and Isaac stood in the cart to shout and snap his willow whip at the straining beasts.

Grey skies must have brought out the deep reds of the soft maple buds, the deep greens of the spruce and the pine, in the country which was to be the Blasdell's new home. Perhaps Isaac thought, "They need me in this place. A place that's any size at all needs a clockmaker these days. Man's got to know what time it is, so that he can plan things and can do more with himself and his beasts and his seeds."

In 1762, then, the first known clockmaker came to New Hampshire. Although another such artisan was reported to have worked in Portsmouth in 1719, there are no actual records about him.

Blasdell found a house for himself and his family in Chester, and started right in to make clocks—good solid clocks with brass works. He made the teeth of their wheels sharp so that the linen line wouldn't slip, and he built his clocks so that one line and one weight carried both the time and the striking. A man had to pay him twenty good hard dollars for a clock movement, or the equivalent in cord wood or some other product.

Isaac learned his trade from his father, David, and taught it to his own son, Richard. It looked as if the Blasdell family would continue to be a clockmaking family for generations to come. But the boy died in 1790; Isaac himself, the next year; and there was no more clockmaking by the Blasdells.

Chester people who wanted a new clock had to pay some stranger for it, or had to fetch it from outside the village—from Concord or Portsmouth, or from Boston or Newburyport, Massachusetts.

But up the Merrimack River in Concord, Ephraim Potter, who framed the steeple on the Old North Meetinghouse, worked at clockmaking when he was not putting up buildings. Ingenious Ephraim was a fine craftsman, who lived hard and died poor. In 1775 he started whittling out wooden clocks that have ticked to the song of many a teakettle in homes along the plains of Penacook. Before this time, there had been only two clocks in Concord, and these had been imported from England by the Reverend Timothy Walker and Deacon Joseph Hall. People used to watch for the deacon on the Sabbath, and when they saw him coming through "Eleven Lots", they knew it was time for them to go to church.

Over in Weare, there were several clock shops. As early as 1780 Abner Jones was building large eight-day brass timepieces. They sold high—fifty dollars! Jones' clocks had a beautiful finish and gave the correct time of day, the day of the week, the day of the month, the name of the month, and the changes of the moon.

Jones had been working for years when Jesse Emery set up a clock shop in this same town. James Corliss became his chief competitor, and there's a story about the two that the good wives of Weare may have whispered under each other's bonnets after Sunday service. Corliss worked for a farmer as a miller and had never been apprenticed to a clockmaker. But one day he announced he'd made some clocks to sell. The town gossips said that the only possible way Corliss could have learned this trade was to have followed the meadow brook from his own millsite to Jesse Emery's place in the dark of night. They said that he probably went right up to the window of the room where Jesse worked at his clocks, and watched the craftsman saw at the tiny wheels, fit them together, and thread a line over them. The mere thought that Corliss might have taken such trouble to appropriate the craft, as gossip half-humorously, half-seriously, had it, was high praise in a way. The New Hampshire trader, William Fitz, valued clocks in terms of fish and nails, stating that a clock was worth so many pounds of the other commodities. In 1797 he advertised that he had clocks and watches and "experienced workmen to execute my commands expeditiously". One day, it was tar and molasses Fitz listed as acceptable for trade or barter; again it was rum, gunpowder, and tanned calfskin.

Around 1790 Robinson Perkins, a blacksmith of Jaffrey, became interested in clockmaking and studied the trade. His work was very good and several of Perkins' grandfather clocks still keep time accurately after a century and a quarter or more. Perkins' clocks had wooden works. He took great pride in them and marked on the dial of each one "R. Perkins, Jaffrey, N. H." He also identified each clock by a number on its dial. He must have found the business a profitable one, for he became the owner of the first two-wheeled shay in the town.

In Keene, the townspeople wanted a clock they could see from the street, since many of the people could not afford an individual timepiece. So in February, 1794, a committee of citizens entered Luther Smith's shop on Federal Row. Rather cautiously one of them asked how much Luther would take to build a clock for the town. He said that he might be able to do it for sixty pounds, that he would not be making anything on the deal, but that he was willing to do it for his own community. The spokesman for the committee said ten pounds was as much as the town could afford to pay; all the money would have to be raised by subscription, anyway. Finally, they came to an agreement. Luther was to make the clock and keep it in order for ten years for the sum of thirty-six pounds.

In the spring, a couple of ladders were set against the meetinghouse tower and two men climbed up with the clock between them.

TIMOTHY CHANDLER CLOCK *in the collection of the Manchester Historic Association.* BANJO CLOCK *made by Abel and Levi Hutchins.* SHORT CASE CLOCK *made by Daniel Pratt.* SERAPHINE *made in 1832 by Abraham Prescott & Son.*

GREAT HISTORICAL CLOCK OF AMERICA, *which took eight years to make. From the Old Clock Museum, George's Mills.*

TIME AND MUSIC

It was set in place, and the inhabitants of Keene began to plan their days from it. This was the beginning of New Hampshire town clocks, set high so all the people could see them.

At the annual town meeting of 1812, the people of Amherst decided to have such a clock. To raise the necessary funds, they pulled some of the benches out of the meetinghouse, built pews, nailed them in, and then charged rent for them. When they found that this income was not sufficient to pay Thomas Woolson, Jr., the clockmaker, they got the rest of the money by dunning their more prosperous townsmen, and the clock was installed.

An old New Hampshire clock usually had much beauty and dignity of line. It rested a man's body to sit back in his chair after a day's plowing and watch it standing there, shining and solemn in the fading evening light, and to know that the pendulum was swinging back and forth, regularly and unceasingly, inside the wooden case. A good clockmaker built a clock strong, so that it would run more than just a year or two. And even today, many men set right their mass production clocks by the works of these early craftsmen.

Some people in Haverhill, New Hampshire, are still sending their children to school and setting their tables for supper by John Osgood's clocks. Folks liked to come into Osgood's shop just to pass the time of day and watch him at work. He limped badly, and was very quiet; but they say he could break into a smile easily. People pushed past the open Dutch doors, walked through the front room where his new clocks, spoons, and shoe buckles were displayed, and stood beside him while he worked. They watched him cast his wheels blank, squint as he rounded up the teeth with a file, and lean over pivots in the lathe which was made up of a spring pole overhead with a line passing from it around the piece he was turning to the treadle he pumped with his foot.

People in every town felt grateful toward the craftsmen who served them well. When Timothy Chandler, who made clocks in Concord over a period of fifty-five years (from 1785 to 1840), suffered financially through the burning of his shop, his neighbors did their best to help him. As recorded by a local historian,

"Major Chandler's loss was estimated at $5000; for his relief $1200 were generously subscribed by inhabitants of the town and of the vicinity."* Chandler was a clockmaker who gave himself wholeheartedly to the affairs of the town. He helped name the streets, aided in the founding of a singing society, and took part in temperance work. A member of the family of Mrs. C. F. M. Stark of Concord, New Hampshire, has a beautiful Chandler clock which has great historic interest. Formerly it belonged to Benjamin Pierce, the father of President Franklin Pierce, and is still a good timekeeper. Its face records the movements of the sun and moon, and the days of the month. The works are brass; the case, maple with mahogany trimmings and inlay of satinwood; and there are brass ornaments on its top. Among Chandler's apprentices was Cyrus Eastman of Amherst. He worked seven years for the Major and then went back to his home town to carry on his trade until the mid-nineteenth century.

Levi Hutchins and his brother, Abel, built clocks in Concord for a total of sixty-four years. When Levi was ninety, he could still put in a good day's work. Towards the end of his life, his hand was a bit shaky, but there was a sharp nod to his head and a gleam in his eye as, tapping a neighbor's chest, he told him, "Our names may be seen on the faces of many time-keepers, standing in the corners of sitting rooms in houses situated in all the New England States."†

The Hutchins brothers were very highly trained, they learned the trade from the great Simon Willard of Roxbury, Massachusetts. Levi never tired of telling folks that he got most of what he knew from watching Willard's skilled fingers as the clockmaker worked.

Levi Hutchins had enlisted as a fife player in the Colonial army when he was only fourteen years old. He was seventeen when he started his apprenticeship with Simon Willard. Abel Hutchins is remembered in Concord as a famous innkeeper, as well as a clock-

* *The History of Concord.* Nathaniel P. Bouton. Concord, N. H. Benning W. Sanborn, 1856. p. 349.
† *Autobiography.* Levi Hutchins. Cambridge, Mass. Riverside Press, 1865. p. 121.

maker. He built the Phenix Hotel, and when it burned in 1819, put up another inn on the same site. His daughter, Martha Currier Hutchins, was the mother of Miss Mary H. Pierce, who still lives in the house in which her grandfather lived after he gave up the Phenix Hotel in 1832 and where he died. Miss Pierce owns one of the very few banjo clocks made by the Hutchins brothers. She says the timepiece, which was made sometime between 1786 and 1819, is not marked, but adds that it hung in her father's kitchen for years, before a clock repairer cleaned the case and brought out its original beauty. She also has a tall Hutchins clock made in 1790.

In 1807 Edward Moulton started a clockmaking business in Rochester. Later James Cole, who had been his apprentice, took it over. Cole hired several youths as apprentices to help him make the movements, and a cabinetmaker to make the cases. His journeymen traveled from farmhouse to farmhouse far into the country. Once a journeyman was sitting in a kitchen, he might persuade the good wife to let him set the clock up for a while "just on trial". He'd promise that he would come back for it in a few days if she didn't want it. But when he returned, he generally found that the lady of the house had developed such a liking for the clock that she couldn't bear the thought of losing it.

Contemporaneously with Cole, Samuel Wright made clocks in Lancaster, and Joseph Chadwick worked in Boscawen. Both of them had their businesses ruined by new, machine-made clocks. Benjamin Morrill, however, opened a shop in Boscawen in 1816 and became one of the few artisans who adapted themselves to the new order. He got machinery and helpers, and made cheap clocks, too. He was also a scalemaker and at one period of his life manufactured melodeons and seraphines.

When clockmakers first came up into New Hampshire's backcountry, folks were building their houses straight on a north-and-south line, so the women could tell by the shadow when to prepare a meal and when to sound the horn to call men home from the fields. First, handmade clocks were brought to the rural people. Next came cheaper wooden clocks that sold for twenty dollars. But when the woolen and cotton mills began to sprawl along New Hampshire rivers, people needed still cheaper clocks and watches to get them to work on time. As a necessary and inevitable part of America's industrialization, machine-made clocks and watches were introduced and accepted.

Clarence Collins of George's Mills on Lake Sunapee has a collection of over two hundred clocks, which is visited annually by guests from every State in the Union and from Europe. Mr. Collins owns a number of items of great interest to antiquarians. One is a kidney shelfclock of mahogany, made in the eighteenth century by Simon Willard. Mr. Collins owns also several shelfclocks designed by Eli Terry of Connecticut. They are of a delicately carved Chippendale pattern. His best example of the work of a New Hampshire craftsman is a Timothy Chandler shelfclock, made in 1785. It was purchased during that year by a young man who wanted a gift for his bride, and who carried it forty-five miles on horseback and gave it to her on their wedding day. Another very interesting example of the clockmaker's craft is the "Great Historical Clock of America" on which little figures in action portray scenes in America's history. Eight years were spent in building it.

Another collection of clocks is owned by Arthur J. Morrison of Enfield, a watch and clock repairer. He owns the old Dartmouth Hall clock which was in a Hanover repair shop during the fire of 1904 and so escaped destruction. Mr. Morrison uses it as a "regulator" in his own work. His finest clock by a New Hampshire maker is the work of David Dutton, an obscure Mont Vernon craftsman.

* * *

In its delicate precision, the craft of constructing musical instruments is closely akin to that of clockmaking. It is a craft that has often attracted the artisan who works in wood. According to contemporary reports, Massachusetts' distinguished wood carver, Samuel McIntire of Salem, was considered "the best person to correct defects in musical instruments that could be found in that vicinity". Jonas Chickering, a New Ipswich cabinetmaker, achieved a world-wide reputation with his pianos. Abraham Prescott, famous New Hampshire designer of stringed and reed instruments, informed the Concord people in the 1830's that at his shop "umbrelloes and walking-canes could be made and repaired, box-wood, ebony and ivory turnings done to order in the best manner". Haverhill's present-day recordermaker, William Koch, is an expert cabinetmaker and also a repairer of fine antique furniture, a specialized craft in which he is an authority.

Mr. Koch makes his recorders of Cocobola wood which comes from South America. The wood is first "roughed out" into tubes and allowed to season for about two months before actual work on the instrument begins. Care is taken to keep together the pieces of the same stick to make a single recorder since the grain of wood must match the length of the instrument. These pieces are turned and polished and put together with cork joints. The way the holes are bored regulates the pitch. There are sixty-five operations in the construction of one flute; and all require painstaking craftsmanship.

In 1921 William Koch came to Haverhill to live in the beautiful General Montgomery House, built in 1790. The original owner of the mansion, General John Montgomery, purchased the first piano used in the town. It was made in London by Christopher Gaverand for Princess Amelia, daughter of King George III. The princess gave it to a chaplain of the royal family; and later his daughter, who married an American, brought it to Boston with her. But the most important thing about the old piano was the effect it had on the life of Jonas Chickering, a great lover of music, and at the time a young apprentice in the shop of the New Ipswich cabinetmaker where the piano was overhauled. The work Chickering did on the piano made such a deep impression on him that he set out for Boston to learn the piano business. Eventually he became one of the greatest pianomakers in the world.

Interesting also is the story of the founder of a well-known Concord piano company. Abraham Prescott was a farmer and not a cabinetmaker, but like Chickering he loved music. Early in the nineteenth century he began his long career as a maker of musical instruments. To quote a biographer, "As early as 1810 or 1812, Abraham Prescott . . . conceived the idea of making an instrument similar in shape to the violin, but of larger size. He had never seen but one violin. . . . There were no Bass Viols made in this country, to his knowledge. . . . He succeeded, however, unaided, in producing a remarkably fine instrument of the violoncella class."*

Reverend James MacGregor, the first pastor of the Londonderry church, shocked his people by playing the violin which he had brought to America with him and was reprimanded severely by the church officers when an elder passing the good parson's cabin at night heard a "linked sweetness long drawn out" issuing from it.

When Samuel Graham carried his bass viol into the Chester Congregational Church on Thanksgiving Day, 1806, up got Deacon William Clarke, "took his hat and left in hot haste". He was followed immediately by Moody Chase, "nearly ready to burst and give vent to bile". The Henniker people were more broadminded: at a meeting of the parish, they voted to allow the use of a "bass-viol and a tenor one".

A bass viol was used in the Jaffrey church, but some of the parishioners could not make up their minds as to the right or wrong of singing to its accompaniment. So they called the instrument "Dagon"—after the old god of the Philistines—and this name clung to it as long as the bass viol was played in church.

Despite such stringent opposition, by 1820 Abraham Prescott had found a good market for his wares. Ten years later, his business had grown so rapidly that he decided to open a shop and a music store in Concord. In 1833 he left Pittsfield and concentrated on building up his Concord business. With him went the Dearborn brothers, David M. and Andrew P., master craftsmen who knew how to make "Bass and Double Bass Viols, Violins, Bugles, Trombones, French Horns, Orpheclydes, Trumpets, Clarinets, Flutes, Fifes of all kinds, and Accordians".

An elbow melodeon designed by a Massachusetts man furnished Abraham Prescott with the idea of extending his business. This fore-

* *Concord Daily Monitor. Concord, N. H. Monday, January 6, 1868. p. 2.*

runner of the reed organ had only three octaves and stopple keys. Prescott bought a melodeon to study, made improvements on the idea, and began to put out accordians which were really the grandfathers of hundreds of parlor organs, later sold by him all over the State.

Abraham Prescott and his eldest son had entered into partnership. Deacon Prescott retired in 1850, and a new firm, known first as Prescott and Brothers and later as Prescott Brothers, was formed by three of his sons. They concentrated on developing the popular pianoforte. With variations in personnel, the firm continued into the twentieth century until the talking machine and the radio seriously affected the piano business.

At the present time in New Hampshire the production of musical instruments is, for the most part, a hobby. A number of local musicians and craftsmen, however, have achieved some degree of distinction in the art. Forty-four years ago, a future citizen of New Hampshire, newly arrived from Quebec, sat on a doorstep in Manchester and listened to the strains of a violin coming from a house across the street. The lad was so delighted with the gay music that he scampered over and asked the fiddler, who was nearly blind, to teach him to play. The boy had no money to buy a violin, but the would-be musician's new friend told him that he could make his own fiddle, and sent him to a man who had learned the craft in Canada. In this way, Charles Perreault of West Manchester started on a craft at which he has worked during most of his spare time.

Since he carved his first violin, Mr. Perreault estimates he has made at least one hundred instruments, using native spruce and hemlock, and finishing them with a characteristic uniformity of color which he has worked out through years of experimenting.

Many lively medleys of Canadian jigs and reels and accompaniments to old French folk songs have been played on Perreault fiddles. The maker says that the kind of violin a person uses is a matter of individual opinion, for no two players are alike in their taste and judgment. "Choosing a violin is like choosing a wife; men have different tastes, yet each one believes the woman he has selected is the best of them all."

In Candia, a typical northern New England village with houses, general store, and garage strung out along the highway, lives Lewis L. Litchfield, ticket seller, baggageman, switchman, telegrapher, and general caretaker at the "Depot". But the Candia station-agent has another interest besides his railroad work—music. During the half century that he has worked for the Boston and Maine railroad, Mr. Litchfield has kept up the study of music, which he began in his boyhood. His craftwork did not start with musical instruments, but with fishpoles, which he learned to make from Charles Mitchell, a Penobscot Indian.

The Candia man began making violins by accident when he sent his violin away to be repaired and did not like the work done on it. After fixing the instrument himself, he became convinced that he could put one together. So he bought materials and an instruction book and he started to make his first violin of one hundred and five different pieces. It took him five weeks to complete the work.

Mr. Litchfield is interested in the history of violinmaking and, through his research, has made many friends among distinguished musical people. He was allowed to examine thoroughly a valuable Stradivarius, which has served as a model for most of the violins he has made himself. "Violinmaking is sort of an accident. We make them good and bad," he says. Then he adds that he has produced more than fifty instruments and intends to make others when he retires from business. Two of these instruments journeyed to the far north with Donald MacMillan, the explorer, who was his schoolmate in Freeport, Maine. Mr. MacMillan had planned to give the violins to the Eskimos, but he grew so attached to the instruments that he brought them back home to Provincetown.

The New Hampshire violinmaker is frequently called upon to appraise violins. He believes that many of the really good instruments in New England have been brought in by sailors from foreign ports. Franklin Fenderson of Barrington, who collects violins, has a few which he picked up in Gloucester, Massachusetts; Mr. Litchfield rates these highly. Mr. Fenderson, a keen-eyed man who has seen eighty-eight winters come and go, has made about eighty violins,

EARLY AMERICAN MIRROR, *made in late 1700's, owned by Mrs. Scott Sandborn of Boscawen, and* HANNAH DAVIS BANDBOX, *in the collections of the Manchester Historic Association.*

INTERIOR OF A HOME WORKSHOP.

all of which have brought good prices. He made his first instrument fifty-two years ago while he was living in the home of a Maine fiddler. He used native maple for the back and the sides, and White Mountain spruce, which has a fine grain, for the tops.

Some twenty-five years ago, Rudolph Schiller, a distinguished Manchester musician, passed an afternoon with Walter Ewing Colton of Exeter who, prior to his death in 1913, was probably New Hampshire's finest maker of stringed instruments. Mr. Schiller remembers him as a man of great learning, steeped in the history and tradition of music. Mr. Colton personally knew many of the famous violinists of his day, and so had an opportunity to examine their instruments. He showed Mr. Schiller his patterns, tools, selected woods, and violins in various stages of construction, and discussed his craft with great enthusiasm.

Concord has its violinmaker, Edgar Quint, who has turned out some very good instruments; and Manchester has Martin Schoepf, who has built up a spendid reputation as a musician and is now a member of the WPA New Hampshire Symphony Orchestra. Mr. Schoepf has produced many beautiful instruments, all of which have great volume and fine tone. He served an apprenticeship with three well-known violinmakers, among them the famous Albert Lind of Boston.

Mr. Schoepf says that the building of a violin is an engineering problem first and last.* He considers that the wood which goes into the making of a first-class instrument is of vital importance. In the line of craftsmanship he believes that violinmaking, from the first steps of carving the plates from solid blocks of wood to the last operation of applying the varnish, requires all the skill and dexterity which the workman can bring to the task.

But the making of a violin requires something more than manual dexterity. The craftsman must also have the sensibilities of an artist. Like Irmi Whitney of Henniker, an early nineteenth-century music

* *The Sunday Union-Leader. Manchester, N. H. July 29, 1923. Manchester Resident, Martin Schoepf Makes Violins. Quoted by permission of the author, Rudolph Schiller.*

teacher and composer, the modern violinmaker may make a half-dozen instruments which do not please him; again, he may produce one that fully rewards him for the hours he has spent in the delicate work of carving the plates and fitting the neck of the violin, and in pitching the interval to obtain rich, sonorous tones, resembling those of the instruments made by the Italian master craftsmen.

VI

THE CRAFT OF THE WOODWORKER

Wood furnished the foundation of the early pioneers' economic existence. The first two centuries of New Hampshire's history might well be called the "Wooden Era", for a good proportion of the articles used by the people at that time were made by them from wood. Except for the higher summits of the mountains, almost the entire area within the present State boundaries was heavily timbered with virgin spruce, pine, hemlock, and hardwoods. Year by year many acres of the primeval forest disappeared. However, in the early nineteenth century much of the first-growth timber was still standing. Articles made from this timber had lasting qualities which have never been equalled by those made from trees that had a later and quicker growth.

Wooden utensils were manufactured for nearly every household need. Hop-yeast for the family supply of bread was left to rise beside the banked fireplace in a deep bread bowl, hewn from the heart of a log. Square and oblong trenchers held the bean porridge of the English settlers and their descendants, and the barley broth of the Scotch-Irish.

Treen—as the common wooden tableware of the seventeenth and eighteenth centuries was called—was made at home by a family craftsman who needed only a sharp knife to produce bowls, trenchers, and wooden containers for dry foodstuffs. He found his "dish timber" in the forest or selected it from a pile of logs intended for fuel. He liked the close-grained woods such as walnut, pine, oak, birch, ash, and wild cherry, but maple held the leading place as desirable material.

Wooden utensils were used as commonly in barn and field as in the house. The early agricultural implements were very crude. The first sledges used in Hampton were simple ones, fitted on runners and drawn by hand, and the first harrow used in Keene was merely a number of wooden pegs driven into holes bored in the forked branches of a tree. Ploughs had heavy, hand-turned wooden shafts, with short iron points; and even as they continued to improve in design, they were still of home manufacture. A carpenter might make the frame and a blacksmith the iron parts, but the implement was usually put together by the farmer who planned to use it. Wooden shovels and axe helves likewise were made at home, from seasoned hardwood.

Sawmills were very important in the early communities, and mill rights were given out by vote of the town. Provision for a sawmill often was inserted in the charter of a newly founded town. One of these old-time sawmills played a leading part in the history of New Hampshire industrial life. It was established in 1743 in old Rowley-Canada, later called Jaffrey, and developed into a mill system known as the Squantum Mills, a business undertaking maintained for many years by a long succession of owners. Shortly before the Revolutionary War, John Eaton, "a man fit to rank with the minister in solid worth to the community", came from Bedford, Massachusetts, and succeeded Ephraim Hunt as owner of the mills. He was a man of many trades; and his journal, a homemade book with covers of shaven oak held together with leather thongs, shows the usefulness and variety of his life. He made "tuggs", "collers", sleds, "corfens", leach tubs, "ches-preses", saddles, and plows; and in addition he plastered chimneys and fashioned casements. Eaton was the first man to use the equipment of the mills for wood turning. He produced flax wheels, thousands of spindles, and the balustrades for the pew walls in the Jaffrey meetinghouse. He also repaired the big wooden wool wheels, used for spinning, and made

THE CRAFT OF THE WOODWORKER

wooden clocks. He is remembered particularly as the grandfather of Aunt Hannah Davis, famous maker of wooden bandboxes.

Another owner of these mills was Captain David Sherwin, a veteran of the Revolutionary War, who conducted a singing school, a tavern, a store, and owned potash works in Rindge. In 1825 John Prescott, a representative business man of the time, was manufacturing household woodenware as well as lumber and chairs in the mills. Several years later Ephraim Murdock, one of New England's leading industrialists, was doing very well making lumber, pail staves, clothespins, and miscellaneous woodenware. It was he who made the neighboring town of Winchendon, Massachusetts, the woodenware center of the world. He expanded his interests by means of a co-operative system of partnerships with small mill owners. Murdock looked with a jealous eye on the boxmaking industry, which was almost a monopoly in the next-door town of Rindge.

Gaily painted nests of boxes, known as pantry sets, were popular products in this period, when domestic supplies were bought in large quantities and had to be stored away safely from mice and dampness. Like veneer spice boxes, these containers were specialties of the Rindge woodworkers. One of the bright young men in this business was Thomas Annett, whom Ephraim Murdock hired to take charge of the boxmaking enterprise of the Squantum Mills. Eventually Annett became sole owner of these mills. Boxes for all purposes were made profitably with the aid of saws and planing machinery, but a certain amount of manual skill was required to slice the wood thin enough to use for the rims.

The manufacture of wooden clothespins was an outgrowth of the New Hampshireman's innate fondness for whittling, and the fact that he had plenty of material at hand to work up a business. Richard Kimball of Rindge was one early craftsman who utilized his dexterity with the jackknife to meet the needs of New England's traditional Monday washday. He made clothespins at home from oblong blocks of white birch wood, which he sawed and tapered to the desired shape with a handsaw and knife. When he had a sufficient quantity of the "wooden sugar tongs", as the shrewd tin peddler and skilled clothespinmaker, Arad Adams of Jaffrey, called the indispensable little articles, he set out over the countryside selling his wares from house to house. Richard's son, Samuel, was a wheelwright, but two of his grandsons, Elipha S. and S. Warren Kimball, made woodenware. The Civil War was just ending when Warren began manufacturing butter prints, mauls, and rolling pins. His business was conducted on a small scale, with "two or three hands", and continued until 1902.

New Hampshire small farmers frequently took up other kinds of woodworking to put a little hard cash into the family pocketbook. Making wooden dishes was the most popular business in this line. Thomas Clark, a wholesale manufacturer of wooden dishes and spoons, came to Troy from Wrentham, Massachusetts, in 1779 and began to clear and cultivate the land. He discovered soon that he needed more money than he could earn from agriculture, so he set up a foot lathe and started turning out wooden mortars, spools, plates, bowls, and other wares, similar to those he had made in his former home. To make his products more attractive and thus add to their sales value, he colored them by holding a stick dipped in red or blue paint against each piece as he turned it. He bartered his wares for needed commodities by walking from farm to farm and peddling them himself. About thirty-five years later, Timothy Gillette and his son, Oliver, came to Henniker and set up a woodenware manufactory in an old cider mill. They used ash timber to make bowls, plates, skimmers, cups, saucers, and other useful articles. The father filled huge leather pouches with them, placed the pouches behind him on his horse, and rode out in search of customers, while the son remained at home to keep up production. In Sutton, Jacob Davis and his son turned out plates, trays, bowls, noggins, piggins, platters, skimmers, and ladles. Like Clark and the Gillettes, the Davises peddled their products on horseback.

During the first half of the nineteenth century, Joseph Kimball of Canterbury had a turning wheel where both cotton and linen wheels were made. He was as ingenious in advertising as he was in trade, and he made a point of outdoing his competitors by call-

THE CRAFT OF THE WOODWORKER

ing attention to himself and his work. One of his best publicity stunts was a verse he added to a notice he put in the weekly newspaper:

> "My timber is good,
> And seasoned complete—
> On the Shaker's construction,
> And workmanship neat.
> My axles are good
> And spindles are nice:
> Two dollars per wheel
> My usual price."*

Independent craftsmen of the jack-of-all-trades variety who could produce almost anything from wood, worked in every community and small hamlet, no matter how isolated. Uncle Joe Blodgett, who lived in Berlin around 1830, was famed for his dexterity with an axe, a draw shave, and a jackknife. By profession a cooper, he also could make three-legged stools, chamber sets, and miscellaneous woodenware. His whipstocks, axe handles, hoe handles, and rake-tails were whittled by hand as perfectly as if they had been turned by a lathe. Members of the Gove family of Wentworth were known all up and down the Baker River Valley for their skill in woodworking. Their neighbors from Moosilauke to the Pemigewasset said you could get a Gove to make you anything you wanted out of wood, from a cradle to a coffin.

A woodworking shop, which had a long and busy career, was built by Mark Marvle of Jaffrey around 1825. Marvle earned his living turning out mortars and pestles, washboards, and chopping trays. He was succeeded by several "Yankee geniuses who maintained a precarious existence by alternately making and peddling wooden articles for domestic use throughout the countryside."† Such manufacturers were their own retailers, using red peddling wagons on their trips, until the building of the railroads revolutionized freight transportation.

* *The New Hampshire Patriot and State Gazette. Concord, N. H., March 17, 1812.*
† *History of Jaffrey. Annett and Lehtinen. Town of Jaffrey, 1937, p. 367.*

The woodworking history of Weare is typical of many New Hampshire towns. The earliest settlers of the town discovered an abundance of red oak in the region, and excellent waterpower. They immediately built a mill and imported a heavy iron crank from England. Then they conveyed it over long, difficult miles through the New Hampshire wilderness to attach it to a wooden overshot wheel.

At the very period when Portsmouth was the social center of New England, the settlers of Weare were still making wooden dishes in a primitive fashion, even to spoons and forks. The Johnsons and Purringtons built mills and made an early start in furniture making after the Revolutionary War. Shingles were made in large quantities. In one instance a pine log, cut for a mast, fell into a swamp and was left there by the workmen. One hundred years later two shingle weavers dug it up and worked it into shingles, which lasted much longer than any made on machines from green wood. Two brothers, Samuel and Jonathan Osborn, who lived west of Weare Center, made wooden buttons. They were extremely ingenuous in their business dealings with the public. When Samuel returned from a trip to Boston, where he had gone to sell his wares, his friends asked what luck he had had; he was forced to admit that he had returned with the original number of buttons he had taken with him. He was very discouraged and could not understand why he had been so unsuccessful. He said that he went through every street in Boston, but not one soul asked him if he had any buttons to sell, so how could he dispose of them?

Cooperage was a very profitable way to exploit the plentiful red oak which grew around Weare. To make barrels and hogsheads, pails and keelers, the oak was "heated and bent in the cooper's great fire-place . . . the hoops driven home. . . ." Joseph Webster is reputed to have been the town's most inventive cooper, putting more artistic skill into his work than did any other craftsman in the trade. He was noted for his wooden mugs of "exquisite workmanship", some of which held a quart of liquid. Two well-known makers of woodenware were John Morgan and John Gillet. Morgan's line consisted of breadboards, mortars, and trays; Gillet's was all kinds of wooden dishes.

From the end of the Revolutionary War up until 1830, cooperage was a leading industry in the central region of the State. The New England trade with the West Indies centered around perishable goods, which could be shipped only in hogsheads and barrels. These containers were made largely by hand until as late as 1840. In Brookline, machinery for the work was not introduced until 1846. In Swanzey, the Strattons, an enterprising family, started manufacturing covered buckets by machinery, but had considerable trouble getting them sold in competition with handmade products.

Churnmaking was an outgrowth of the cooperage business. Captain Moses Gove of Andover, a noted manufacturer in this line, fashioned his churns from straight staves, larger at the bottom than at the top, and bound them with wooden hoops. About 1825 Jehiel Wilson of Keene made the first pails ever turned by machinery. He invented a block, shaped like the outside of a pail, upon which the staves could be fastened and swung in a lathe that turned them to uniform curvature. It was a revolutionary feature since, under the hand method, six pails was the capacity of a day's work. But as more progressive industrial methods became common, certain picturesque folk habits, which had grown out of the slower way of working, disappeared. Coopers had been so numerous that "Cooper" often appeared as a prefix to a craftsman's surname; and old books very often mention the peculiar "music" of the cooper's clanging instruments as he drove home his nails into a finished barrel.

The fashions of the nineteenth century played an important part in the woodworking industry in certain Monadnock towns. Bonnets of various sizes and shapes, the common headgear of women before the Civil War, were carried in bandboxes large enough to keep from crushing the daintiest fluted frills and the smartest of ribbon bows.

In 1830 Lawrence Bailey of Brookline started the first bandbox-making business in New Hampshire. He put up a mill on a stream eventually called Scabbard Mill Brook, where he got out the thin slices of wood used as foundations for his boxes. The strips of wood, or "scabbards", were taken to the old Shattuck sawmill to be steamed and bent into shape in a room fitted up for that purpose. Finally, the bottoms of the boxes were set in place, and the covers and sides were decorated with figured paper.

New Hampshire's most famous bandboxmaker was "Aunt Hannah" Davis of Jaffrey. The products manufactured by her nimble fingers during a long and busy life are now collectors' items. Aunt Hannah is said to have inherited her manual dexterity from her father, Peter Davis, a clockmaker, and from her grandfather, the capable jack-of-all-trades, John Eaton. Her powers of imagination, however, were her own. In a day when women had few opportunities to earn their livelihoods (besides housekeeping and working in the new textile mills), she was left to support an invalid mother. Finally she got the idea of making nailed wooden boxes to hold bonnets, hats, and even wardrobes for travelers. It was a tremendous task for a woman to undertake, for the stock for the boxes had to be acquired before the bandboxes could be fashioned. The first step of the new business was for the would-be bonnetboxmaker to go into neighboring wood lots and select trees of old-growth spruce to make the curved sides of her wares. When she had negotiated a deal for the trees, she hired a neighbor to fell them and haul the logs to her dooryard, where they were cut into bolts of the required length.

Proper tools for slicing up the bolts were unknown in Jaffrey, and no one had any idea where such implements could be found. Aunt Hannah gave the matter considerable thought, and one day brought out the plans for a slicing machine to be run by foot power. The machine was constructed, and for years was used by a neighbor, hired by the day, to cut the scabbards for the boxes.

After the spruce scabbards were sliced and the pine covers and bottoms cut out, the rest of the work was a one-woman, home business. The scabbards were bent and nailed and the boxes covered in the Davis home. The Jaffrey people saved remnants of wallpaper for their plucky neighbor, but this supply was not sufficient to meet the demand for bandbox coverings. Wallpapers were imported and were very expensive, so it is evident that Aunt Hannah must have found other than a local source of supply. What it was, is not known. The boxes show that the paper was used sparingly, for it never was pasted in places where it did not show. Without exception the linings are old newspapers, usually weekly religious sheets.

Aunt Hannah had her own trade sign, and every bandbox she put out had a printed label on the inside of its lid, stating,

> "Warranted Nailed
> Bandboxes
> Manufactured by
> Hannah Davis
> East Jaffrey, N. H."

The boxes were made in two sizes; the larger type sold for fifty cents, and the smaller, for twelve cents. They were popular with mill girls, who were very fashionable young ladies, and Manchester and Lowell soon became important centers for the disposal of her wares.

The bandboxmaker was her own selling agent. Having loaded her wares in a covered wagon drawn by a neighbor's horse, she set out alone over the rough roads from East Jaffrey. The journey ended at the mill gates, where she waited for her customers to emerge for dinner. When the last box was sold, Aunt Hannah began the hard trip home, and the next day started again on the long task of building up her stock-in-trade.

Bandboxes, like those produced by Aunt Hannah, no longer are made in New Hampshire; but other wooden articles equally useful and beautiful are turned out by a number of fine craftsmen. A group who have achieved considerable reputation live and work in Concord, and, like many cabinetmakers and other craftsmen, distribute their products through the League of New Hampshire Arts and Crafts. Fred E. Brown has developed a line of wooden tableware somewhat along the lines of the early treen. Pieces of "Brownie

Ware", however, are much more finely wrought than were the old-time wooden dishes. Mr. Brown makes entire dinner sets from polished bird's-eye maple, and turns out all kinds of plates, bowls, and salad dishes from maple, birch, cherry, beech, black walnut, mahogany, and gumwood.

Elba F. Horne and Ernest Kunberger devote most of their time to producing wooden novelties. Mr. Horne features wooden mirror frames and trays made of curly maple, mahogany, and black walnut. He specializes in a tray designed from the pattern of the old knife-and-fork trays, formerly used in all New Hampshire kitchens to hold the everyday cutlery. In his younger days Mr. Kunberger was a cabinetmaker. Now, in his backyard shop, he makes wooden salad and fruit bowls, boxes, sewing stands, napkin rings, candle holders, and knife and fork handles, fashioned from native applewood. One of his latest designs is a miniature wooden reproduction of the ancient New England three-legged iron kettle.

Edward Johnson is another Concord resident who carries on woodworking as a hobby. He learned the trade of cabinetmaking in Sweden and has produced some very fine pieces of furniture. His line of smaller wooden articles includes footstools, picture frames, and small clockcases.

Economic and living conditions always played an important part in determining the types of wooden objects turned out by New Hampshire craftsmen. At the present time, the recreation business has stimulated the making of wooden articles used in a number of out-of-door activities. Many of them are produced by commercial firms, but some are made by craftsmen, working by themselves or with members of their own families. Building the boats that are used on New Hampshire lakes has progressed from the construction of clumsy, flat-bottomed rowboats, used for fresh water fishing by local people, to a modern business in which high-powered motorboats are built for a luxury trade. Usually the designers of the newer models are artisans who have taken up boatbuilding as a craft. One well-known craftsman in the line is Lloyd R. Virgin of Concord, an experienced cabinetmaker. His father William E. Vir-

THE CRAFT OF THE WOODWORKER

gin, a former commodore of the Somerville Lake Yacht Club, began building sailboats as a hobby, and his wife made the sails for them. A number of the lovely oak-trimmed boats, which were constructed of native pine and mahogany, are still in use on Lake Sunapee, Webster Lake, and Somerville Lake. After his father's death, Lloyd Virgin developed the elder man's hobby into a real business, and for some years designed fine custom-built power boats of the runabout and cruiser types. Mr. Virgin believes that, with the exception of one craft which was wrecked on Squam Lake in the hurricane of 1938, all his boats are still in use on the State's larger lakes. He is still making boats, but builds most of them at home in his spare time.

Long before winter recreation became a big business, a Berlin, New Hampshire man was making his own skis and those of his friends. Back in 1883 a small *skiclubben,* which later became the Nansen Ski Club, was formed by a few Norwegians who came to the North Country to work for the pulp and paper company.

Olaf Oleson, known to Berlin people as "Spike" Oleson, was an original member of this club. For years he has profited by his experience and knowledge of skiing. A caller at Mr. Oleson's home usually finds him working on skis in his small workshop in the basement of his house. He makes them by hand, so there can be no mass production, but he claims that when he works full time he can finish a pair in a day. He has also invented and improved a binder which skiers like. He has made skis ever since 1883 when he was a lad of sixteen years.

Wood is still the foundation upon which a large per cent of the State's industrial life rests. It also remains the basis for a considerable proportion of the craftwork executed by local artisans. But there is a point where the small forest industry and craftwork in wood meet, a point so fine that it is difficult to say just where one leaves off and the other begins. It is especially noticeable in a rural community where a little woodworking plant is often run by members of one family who, with proverbial Yankee ingenuity, operate it in the fashion of the craftsman rather than that of the larger industry. As a man who has studied the local situation points out, "Where but in New Hampshire can one find at random in the course of an afternoon's excursion a miscellany like this: attached to the end of a roadside garage, a mill making shingles of hemlock and spruce; in the center of a village, a sawmill attached to an unused water wheel, apparently set up in a few hours without even a roof; and finally an interesting wood turning plant employing seven people, six of whom are members of the same family?"*

* *Forest Industries of New Hampshire and Their Trend of Development.* C. P. Cronk. Concord, N. H. State of New Hampshire Forestry and Recreation Commission, *1936. p. 82.*

VII

MODERN ORNAMENTAL WOOD CARVING

One of the few examples of decorative wood carving that has come down from colonial New Hampshire, aside from that of the Piscataqua region, is an old fiddler's throne, discovered recently in the ruins of what was formerly a busy tavern in Deerfield. This throne is gracefully curved, the platform on which it stands is slightly trefoiled, and a canopy, or lambrequin, overhangs the seat. For the old-time fiddler was the ruler of country social gatherings and such a throne was in keeping with his dignity. The pattern hewn up and down its pilasters is the familiar old-fashioned herringbone; and around the band that runs below the cornice molding, a series of tiny diamond shapes are carefully cut out. This museum piece illustrates the type of wood carving that can be done with an ordinary pocket jackknife, guided by native and untrained skill. Very few similar relics, with even incidental carvings, have been found. And specimens of ornamental wood-paneling and sculpturing, as distinguished from products of the humbler craft of the woodworker described in the last chapter, are rarer still.

Artistic work in wood became popular in this State, either as a profession or as a hobby, around 1900. At that time what was known as an "arts and crafts movement" was sweeping America. It had originated in England when William Morris formed a famous firm of designers and craftsmen who specialized in hand-wrought interior decoration. Morris was a rebel against the twin evils of the encroachment of machines on a field which he felt belonged rightfully to handicrafts, and the ornateness of Victorian taste. His ideal in design was Gothic simplicity. His motto, which became the theme of the entire movement, was this: "Have nothing in your houses except what you know to be useful or believe to be beautiful."

The spread of this movement in New Hampshire coincided with the founding of the Manchester Institute of Arts and Sciences in 1898. The arts and crafts department of the Institute started with wood carving, which was used extensively to enhance the interiors of various Manchester homes. In 1899 Mrs. Melusina Varick, a distinguished amateur carver, began woodworking classes on her own initiative in the Institute's first headquarters in the Weston Building, on Elm Street, opposite the head of Mechanic Street. So many people were immediately interested in taking lessons that she soon was supervising two classes instead of one, and had to engage two assistants. The first Institute exhibition, held in June, 1901, was a display of the articles carved in these classes, for wood carving had rapidly become fashionable in Manchester.

The search for an expert teacher of this exciting art was one of the first steps taken to promote the arts and crafts division of the Institute. In the spring of 1902 Karl von Rydingsvard of New York, noted as an artist and teacher of wood carving, came to Manchester to give a special six-weeks course. The first exhibit of the work done under his supervision was held that June. During this same visit, he helped Mrs. Varick with the decorations of her own home on Chestnut Street. Each spring and fall for the next sixteen years, he came to Manchester and instructed Institute students in wood carving. During the rest of the year, his more advanced students instructed the regular Institute classes. In this way a tradition of fine workmanship was handed down, inspired by a teacher whose ideals were very similar to those of William Morris.

Karl von Rydingsvard, who now lives in retirement in Portland, Maine, was very popular in Manchester society whenever he made his visits. A baron in his native land, Sweden, he received his early training in the art schools of Stockholm. He became a naturalized American citizen, taught at Columbia University for a number of years, and maintained studios in both New York and Boston. In Brunswick, Maine, he started a summer school which became a mecca for less experienced teachers of the wood carving craft.

Like many other professional carvers, Mr. von Rydingsvard is an individualist: hearty and genial in his manner, blunt and outspoken as a critic. The style that identifies his work is congruent with his personality; it has energy and decisivenes. He has a bold technique and uses a simple primitive design like those which have been passed down from the Norsemen of old. Most of his work is done in bas-relief.

The creative influence of von Rydingsvard was strengthened financially in 1903 through the Balch bequest, which substantially increased the funds for extending the work of the Institute. During the wood carver's fall sojourn of 1908, special evening classes for men were added to the curriculum. A separate exhibit of wood carving was held that year, and was considered far superior to those held previously.

One of the wood carver's most talented pupils, Mrs. Jessie E. Donahue, took charge of the class during Mr. von Rydingsvard's absences. She carved the first piece of woodwork to be accepted from Manchester by the Arts and Crafts Guild of Boston for its 1911 exhibition.

Wood carvers like von Rydingsvard seem to have a common characteristic: a deep love for wood itself. It was not by accident that wood came into its own again about the turn of the nineteenth century and the early twentieth century. The use of simpler, more rectilinear forms called for a material that displayed simplicity to better advantage than it did profuse detail. Wood was rediscovered as a warm, inviting substance, friendly to the touch, and extremely responsive to the application of imagination and fancy. Wood conveys the illusion of nature in isolation almost perfectly.

At an exhibition, sponsored by the Manchester Institute of Arts and Sciences in November, 1916, a display of "chests in many designs and woods" excited the interest and curiosity of the public. One of these chests was a copy of a French Renaissance design; it had been carved by a local amateur craftsman from gunstocks and black walnut planks which had been in his family for many years. Another was made of oak in a more severe Gothic design, and was equipped with a copy of a sixteenth-century Spanish lock. One of von Rydingsvard's students at the Institute, Clinton Cheney, became a master craftsman in the reproduction of similar old English carved chests. He taught courses at the Institute for several years, until 1928. Before Mr. Cheney took over this task, interest in wood carving had somewhat ebbed, but he successfully revived the craft.

Mr. Cheney, who lives in Manchester, says chests have always been his favorite work. For a few years he devoted all his time to them, and produced many extraordinary pieces. For this work he used measurements and photographs of original chests in the Metropolitan Museum of Art in New York. One of his friends, who was interested in wrought-iron work, made reproductions of hinges and locks. Only the rough hewing of the stock was done by machinery; every other operation was handwork. Native oak and pine were the materials used most often; and mahogany, occasionally, for the more ornate designs of the later Renaissance. For mahogany, essentially a "feminine" wood, can take fine detail, which oak, a "masculine" wood, cannot.

Mr. Cheney's theory of wood carving represents that of his teacher in many respects. The strictly Gothic style has always appealed to him; he believes it is the most logical type of wood carving ever conceived. The over-civilized designs of any period later than early Jacobean lose the chaste, austere beauty found in the carvings of the fourteenth and fifteenth centuries. As do most wood carvers, he likes to see wood carved so that its own intrinsic beauty is emphasized and not distorted. He feels that the early Gothic carvers were intuitively right, for they realized that wood is suitably used only when the axiom that "substance is always more important than form" is observed.

Many of Mr. Cheney's designs have definite historical derivations. The symbol of the Stuart period is the rose and thistle motif. The

"Tree of Heaven" design recalls the late sixteenth century, and the flourishing trade which the English merchant marine carried on with China. One of the very few pictorial pieces of carving in Mr. Cheney's list is a "tilting chest", copied from a fourteenth-century specimen. Across its front, knights in action at a tournament are depicted. The religious fervor which marked the Reformation period appears on the surface of another chest in carvings of the symbols of the apostles as described in *The Book of the Revelations*. Still another is of sturdy oak, decorated with a Norse design which is primitive and mystical, representing the twin spirits of good and evil intertwined with each other as inseparably as the worshipers of Thor believed they had been in real life. A chest in the style of the more refined French Renaissance is carved in a series of "lunettes", purely decorative motifs. This chest has a deep top in contrast to the shallow lids of the earlier types.

A few reproductions of early American chests were made by Mr. Cheney. Some show the influence of English tradition, but others are done in designs that are American in origin. Mr. Cheney copied the Connecticut tulip chest, one of the most famous examples of a design originated in the new world. Called the "sunflower and tulip" design, it is incised rather than done in the usual bas-relief.

Miscellaneous pieces of carving by Mr. Cheney suggest other ways in which he feels wood carving can be used legitimately. Heads carved in high relief, made from beech wood, are interesting as wall decorations. Unstained mahogany trays have very simple but graceful carved edges, with a self-stain acquired with use and the passage of time. Modern regard for natural forms, especially fruits and flowers, is carried out noticeably in frames of mirrors, pictures, and wall mottoes. The palm, the pine cone, the acanthus, and the pomegranate blend into carving that seems to belong naturally around the object it frames.

Another New Hampshire wood carver, Leo Malm of Concord, teaches the current wood carving classes at the Manchester Institute. He was born in Orebo, Sweden, in 1878, and came to this country when he was four years old. He served a thorough apprenticeship under such men as Louis Lang, Augustrofus Van Stry, and John Kirchmayer. From Lang he learned architectural carving; from Kirchmayer, the technique of working creatively in the round. For his own enjoyment he makes beautifully proportioned statuettes. He helped with the wood carvings in the Boston State House Annex and numerous churches. Twenty-one years of his career were devoted to designing and modeling silver. In this field, he developed a manual sensitivity which served him well in doing fine, delicate work when he returned to wood carving.

Bas-relief plaques are perhaps the most representative products of his fingers. A favorite piece among his own works is "The Horses", one of a series of pine plaques which was done for the Timber Salvage Administration. This series, depicting lumbering scenes, was completed under the supervision of the New Hampshire Art Project of the Work Projects Administration. Action and humor are characteristics of all of Mr. Malm's work; he proves that humor can be caught and projected in wood by such a piece as "The Musicians", a plaque which shows a negro jazz orchestra vigorously playing "hot" music. Bas-relief carving involves many of the technical problems of painting; one of these is perspective. There is a plaque of the covered bridge at the Flume, in which the water seems to flow under the bridge, and the dimly outlined mountains appear to be far across the landscape.

Mr. Malm's favorite woods are gumwood, pine, and mahogany. He says there is a persistent tradition about mahogany to the effect that it is really a sun worshipper, that even after its removal from the tropical forest, "some left-over throb of life continues to move towards the sun."

Several other wood carvers besides Leo Malm have brought a vitalizing creative influence from European countries into New Hampshire. Peter Meindl of Nashua once lived in Munich, Germany, where he underwent a four-year apprenticeship in a typical German trade school. After he came to America, he worked as one of a score of expert craftsmen who have contributed to the beauty of the Cathedral of St. John the Divine in New York. At the present time he does wood carving in his own home for a Nashua furniture company.

Edgar Keen, who lives and works in Warner, is a product of the English school of apprenticeship. He was born in the Cotswold town of Chipping Campden, which for centuries has been a center of English craft life. The village itself is a standing museum of the best in medieval architecture, reminiscent of the days when it was the market center for the Cotswold raw fleece industry. In the early 1900's it was chosen as the ideal working place for a London group, interested in the arts and crafts movement, who formed a Handicraft Guild. One of the designers in this group was Alec Miller, sculptor in both wood and stone, who became Edgar Keen's most helpful teacher. From him Mr. Keen learned the difference between the technique of carving in stone and that of carving in wood, and the limitations of each medium.

Mr. Keen began his career at the age of sixteen with an apprenticeship in architectural and ecclesiastical woodworking of the conventional style. From 1915 to 1919 he served with the British army in France; for five years after the war he worked with Alec Miller in his studio; and in 1924 he came to America. He has lived and worked in Philadelphia, Boston, and cities in the middle west; his work also appears in the great Cathedral of St. John the Divine. Of all the places he has worked, he likes New Hampshire best. From 1936 to 1938 he was the director of the League of New Hampshire Arts and Crafts, and at present he devotes part of his time to teaching woodcraft classes for the League in Concord.

He maintains that the grain of wood is the artist's greatest handicap in hewing, but it is his greatest aid in achieving final beauty. Rightly used, the grain can emphasize the modeling, yet too pronounced a grain, used for its own sake, can kill the design. In actually cutting into the wood, the artist goes across the grain as much as possible and not with it, lest the wood control him rather than it be controlled by him. In figure carving, the grain should run the longer way, because therein lies the greatest strength of the wood. To make a crucifix, Mr. Keen carves the figure of Christ from one block of wood and His outstretched arms from a second block, so that the grain will run from the fingertips of one arm to the other. In this way, there is less danger of their being broken off.

A figure carved in wood should be "all of a piece". Harmonious silhouette and well-proportioned mass are of primary importance. The material itself shows to better advantage when there are as many broad, unadorned planes as possible. The essence of a piece stands out more definitely when strong silhouette has not been sacrificed to confusing, naturalistic detail. Mr. Keen once made a caricature, in the round, of a man with a large potbelly; while it was still in roughly hewn outline, a neighbor identified it because the essential features had been caught in the simple fundamental planes, before details had been completed.

Mr. Keen often uses basswood or its English equivalent, limewood. He likes the close grain of basswood and the clean way it cuts. Occasionally, he uses pine and oak, but he likes best to carve in teak, a very oily wood. He once used teak to make a head of an African woman; to blacken it, he employed hot shoe polish which blended with the natural oils of the wood.

Mary J. Whittier, who lives on a farm near Concord, is the maker of the well-known Grandma and Grandpa dolls. The idea for the quaint little figures came from portraits of an elderly couple, a Yankee farmer and his wife, which adorned the walls of a bedroom in an old Sandwich homestead.

Omer Marcoux, a janitor at St. Paul's school in Concord, has created a wooden article which is almost as popular. He carves pairs of miniature yoked oxen, representing those which the farmers of several generations ago trained to break their land and haul their logs to pioneer sawmills. Mr. Marcoux, who is practically self-trained, gives to the rippling muscles of the oxen an appearance of hidden brute strength, and to the lines of their bodies the feeling of slowness and stolidity that is sensed in the live animals. They have been exhibited at the Rural Arts Exhibition in Washington and at the New York World's Fair.

Among the articles sent by the League to the World's Fair was a

MODERN ORNAMENTAL WOOD CARVING

carved wall panel from Bristol, which has the maple sugar industry as its theme. Articles made by New Hampshire craftsmen present regional motifs and arouse great interest. And the League shops display carved oxen, horses, and other animals, including even skunks, and representations of the covered bridges that still span many of the rivers, and of the white, tall steepled meetinghouses that face numerous town commons. Lately, the League has encouraged its carvers to try their hand at making chess sets, always a good excuse for ingenious wood carving. Lemon wood and mahogany are the materials most often used for the needed contrast of black and white.

Susan Nason Collins of Littleton, who works under the name of Suen Collins, also carves figures of New England types, such as "Aunt Sally", "The Hired Man", and "The Hired Girl", all sculptured with very simple tools in native pine. These figures are usually adorned with gayly colored costumes painted on them, and each one stands on a pedestal carved from the same block of wood as the figure itself. Mrs. Collins does another type of wood carving: symbolic religious figures similar to those that have been popular in European countries for centuries. While traveling in Italy, Mrs. Collins visited the church of St. Francis d'Assisi; her group carving of "The Crèche" is the result of this inspiration. The figures of the saints, such as St. Francis and the birds, St. Theresa and the roses, which she models, are not painted; they are either shellacked or oiled. Mrs. Collins is self-trained in this art, in which she became interested after she moved to New Hampshire from Chicago.

Marquetry or inlay work is another important division of the wood carving. A number of craftsmen do this type of work, and at least two men, Julien Lambert of Manchester and Clifford Goss of Enfield, specialize in it. Mr. Lambert is expert at combining many kinds of woods, some of them rare varieties, into unified patterns. He was a barber at one time and began practicing woodcraft to while away quiet hours in his shop. His best known accomplishment is a reproduction, on the reverse side of a large checkerboard, of the church of St. Jean-Baptiste in Manchester. Each square is made of a separate piece of wood, cemented onto a plain white pine base. The picture of the church is made up of more than 7000 very small pieces, incorporating thirty different kinds of wood, including rare imported kinds, such as white holly, olive wood, teakwood, rosewood, black ebony, snakewood, orange wood, and white boxwood, to mention only a few. The cross which tops the varicolored church is a piece of olive wood imported from Palestine. The proportions of the church are declared to be perfect by the architect who designed the original.

Mr. Goss, a former cabinetmaker, now lives on a farm and does inlay work as a hobby. He specializes in fitting tiny, irregular pieces of wood into beautiful designs for table tops, and for the lids of dainty boxes used to hold ladies' cosmetics or trinkets. These unusual boxes, made sometimes of mahogany, sometimes of cedar, are never more than a quarter inch through in thickness, and have narrow inlaid borders of ebony and white holly. Oval black walnut medallions surround the inlay design, which is usually a floral pattern. Nearly five hundred pieces of wood may be used in the making of any one of these boxes. And for color effects, the artist depends on the natural tones of the various woods, occasionally dyeing a few pieces leaf green or pink. English sycamore is used for a light tone, French walnut for a dark contrast, and cedar and mahogany for background. Four different shades of French walnut were used in an inlay representing the most familiar regional motif in New Hampshire, the "Old Man of the Mountain". The coarser grain of mahogany was employed for orientation around the "old man" to give an astonishing illusion of the mountain's rocky layers.

The inlaid pieces used in such work are not more than one-sixteenth of an inch in thickness. Great patience is required to cut these small sections, and to fit them expertly into place. The cutting is usually done on a jig saw. The design is then assembled upside down and glued together; then it is attached to a piece of paper from which it is transferred into the recess prepared for it in the box or table top. The inlay is sandpapered and finished off by rubbing in boiled linseed oil until the wood is soft and lustrous in appear-

WOODEN OX AND CART *carved by Omer Marcoux.*

GRANDPA AND GRANDMA DOLLS *made by Miss Mary Whittier of Concord.*

MARY WHITTIER *(right)* whittling the "grandpa and grandma" dolls.

LEO MALM *in his Concord studio.*

ance. The finished work is smooth to the touch, and presents an appearance of perfect blending, as though the design were painted upon the surface. Mr. Goss is able to make sliver-thin stamens for the flowers in his designs by rubbing a dark plastic wood into fine saw cuts. He gains depth and perspective in light-colored woods by a method of "shading" which is his own invention. The effect of shadows, too, can be made by the same method in satinwood on a highly polished table top.

At present, it is noticeable in the articles which the New Hampshire carvers create that individual workmanship holds its own vigorously against the products of commercial wood carving shops and wood carving machines. For the handiwork of our modern woodcraftsmen is beautiful for the same reason that an ax handle, made by a man for his own use, is beautiful: it fits its function.

VIII

CLAY KILN AND POTTER'S WHEEL

Over a century ago, a New Hampshire newspaper carried in its weekly advertising columns a series of notices announcing the public auction of a piece of real estate in the town of Barnstead. According to the advertisements, the homestead was a "celebrated farm", lying on both sides of the road leading from Barnstead to Dover. The soil was "comparatively unexcelled"; the land was well-watered, and was "suitably proportioned for hay, orcharding, tillage, wood and pasturing"; in addition there was a "valuable clay bed for the potter and the brick maker".*

A claybed added greatly to the value of any farm by supplying material for bricks to be used for various building and repairing jobs on the place, or for making small quantities of marketable brick. Only a small part of the early brickmaker's output was used in house-building. The greatest demand made upon him was furnishing material for the huge chimneys and mammoth fireplaces which for over two hundred years were important and necessary parts of all New Hampshire dwelling houses, and many farmers used their claypits for this purpose only. In 1753 Israel Mead of Hollis started burning bricks to help his neighbors solve their heating problems and found the business so profitable that he made it a lifelong work.

No place was too remote for such a craftsman to locate, and

---

* *New Hampshire Patriot and State Gazette. Concord, New Hampshire. Monday, September 10, 1827. Et seq. September and October 1827.*

within a hundred and fifty years after the Weeks House in Greenland was built in 1638 from black hand-burned bricks made on the place, practically every community where a claybed was available had at least one brickmaker on its tax list.

Comparatively speaking, however, brickmaking was not a large business, and for years the process of moulding and burning bricks took the form of a craft rather than of an industry. The craft received its first important commercial stimulation in the middle of the nineteenth century when brick factories and mills were put up in the Merrimack River towns of southern New Hampshire and northern Massachusetts. Twenty to thirty yards were in operation in the town of Bedford during a single season. The bricks were hauled in oxcarts to Reed's Ferry Landing, and were shipped down the Merrimack River in flatboats to Nashua, and to Lowell and Lawrence, Massachusetts.

Bedford is only one example of a New Hampshire town where bricks were burned by the thousands and marketed in quantities. Farther up the Merrimack River were the rich claybeds of Hooksett, which furnished bricks for the building expansion of the Amoskeag Mills of Manchester. Between 1847 and 1853 brick trains ran continually between the yards of Plaistow and the factory sites of Massachusetts. The Piscataqua Region, also, boasted of its brickyards, some of the finest in New England, which furnished material for the larger markets. As early as 1830 Enoch Pinkham had a yard at the end of Old Dover Point Bridge. He had the great advantage of a location on the Piscataqua and sent his products down the estuary in gundalows, a practice followed by other brickmakers in the locality. Pinkham was the founder of a line of New Hampshire brickmakers, who, like the Parkers of Bedford and the Heads of Hooksett, to mention only two of a long list, were engaged in this business for a number of generations. Today, brickmaking is carried on in eight towns of the State, with Epping taking the lead in the number of local yards.

Although methods of preparing clay for the manufacture of brick have changed considerably with the advancement of science, the process still retains the essential characteristics it had when it was a craft. The early method of preparing the clay for brick burning was to start in the spring and dig out enough material to last through the summer. Clay was wheeled from the pile in barrows and was spread two or three inches thick on dry ground. When it was dry and powdery from weathering, the clay was thrown into pits, and water was poured upon it. Then it was shoveled onto tables, pressed into moulds, struck off with straight edges, and stacked to dry. Sometimes the soaked clay in the pits was spread on a circular plank bed about fifteen feet in diameter and was tempered by the tramping of oxen. The great beasts were hitched by chains to a post set in the middle of the platform, and were managed by a small boy, who kept them treading around and around over the sticky mass. When the clay was thoroughly mixed, it was removed to the moulding table, and another batch was subjected to the same process—a slow, wearisome job for both boy and oxen.

The burning period began early in June and sometimes lasted until Thanksgiving. A "burning" usually continued from seven to ten days, during which time the kilns were fired constantly. While the last firings were under way, the kilns were "dressed" every two hours by filling the arches with fuel. This process required great knowledge and skill on the part of the brickmaker, for the success of the whole undertaking depended upon it.

Usually nothing was allowed to interfere with the constant "dressing" of the kilns, but there is on record one case of a New Hampshire brickmaker who broke this almost invariable rule. Deacon Jesse Morse of Dublin was so strict in his observance of the old Puritan Sabbath that he refused to put wood on his fires after twelve o'clock Saturday night. He thrust upon the Lord the task of keeping his fires going, with the result that he often lost considerable brick over the week-end. The deacon's attitude greatly troubled one of his young employees who decided to save at least one kiln of brick over a long Sabbath. Accompanied by a friend, the young man went to the yards early one Sunday morning and "wooded-up" the arches; for once, the brick burned during the week-end came out in excellent condition. But Deacon Morse did not profit by the experience and continued to follow his old custom; nor did he give any credit to the young men for the assistance he had received. When speaking of the incident later, he declared, "Providence was on my side that time!"

Mrs. Linnie Varney Wyman of Manchester, now rounding out her eighty-second year, remembers the common practice of hiring local help to fire bricks. As a young girl and woman, she lived in Rochester, where her grandfather owned a brickyard. His claybed was a very fine one, but, as she puts it, the supply of material eventually became "used up".

"Most of my grandfather's employees were natives," she says. "Some of them came in from neighboring towns, too far distant for driving with horses to the yard daily. During the burning season they lived all together in the brickyard house. There was a mess hall with long tables, and I remember what quantities of beef stew they ate, and the dippers of water which they drank after a long day's work. When the clay was ready, two or three weeks were employed in burning, and the fires were kept going day and night with the men working in shifts.

"We children loved to go down and watch the burning. We would sit on the woodpiles of the best hard maplewood, cut four feet in length. The men piled the arches full, and kept the fires going all the time. The unbaked bricks were put into kilns and packed in closely. Then the tops of the kilns were sealed over tightly with wet clay. It was quite an art to get everything right and get 'a burn that was perfect', or a 'wonderful burn'. Grandmother used to give the brickmakers a turkey supper at midnight, while the burning was going on. The turkeys were wrapped, feathers and all, in wet clay, and were roasted over the fires. When the clay was removed, the feathers came off with it.

"How good turkeys were roasted this way! We children thought there was nothing better. There was a turkey supper at every 'burning', and I guess there were four or five burnings during the summer. The burners wore little clothing and each had a big rubber apron. They didn't get paid until it was time to go home. Grandfather went out of business when machinery came in. He was just an old-fashioned brickmaker."

There are no records to indicate the exact date when potters started to work in New Hampshire. Perhaps the earliest reference is made in an old deed, in which Nathaniel Libbee of Exeter, who died in 1756, is referred to as such a craftsman. A few potters were working in a small way in a number of towns, but they did not produce wares in any quantity until the Embargo Acts, resulting from the War of 1812, eventually stopped the importation of wares from the famous pottery towns of England. After that time, little potteries started up all over the country, wherever there were good claybeds. Although some of them developed into large manufacturing plants, others had a much shorter existence, for many small kilns ceased burning about 1840, when the arrival of the tin peddler's bright red cart became an annual institution in New England rural towns. Pottery dishes and milk pans were heavy and easily chipped. The peddler's shining tinware appealed to housewives, and soon there was little or no demand for earthenware for kitchen use, except beanpots and storage containers.

The story of early pottery making in New Hampshire centers around the names of a few families like the Burpees of Boscawen, the Lamsons and Dodges of Exeter, the Clarks of Lyndeborough and Concord, the Osbornes of Gonic, and the Crafts of Nashua.

The first member of the Burpee family to locate in Boscawen was Jeremiah, born in Candia in 1748. He was a brickmaker who carried on his trade in Sandwich and Epping before he came to Boscawen in 1792. His son, also named Jeremiah, was born in 1781. He made pottery and bricks until his death in November, 1862.

The earthenware produced by the Burpees was known as "Queens'-Ware". It was a kind of stoneware, more hard-bodied than the red wares usually made from New Hampshire clays. John Ramsay, an authority on early American pottery, says that stoneware was not glazed with slip. While the body was red hot in the kiln, salt was shoveled onto the fire. As it vaporized and settled on the ware, it mingled with the clay, and cooled into crystallized drops that prevented any action of acids on the body.

The Burpees at work were a familiar sight to their neighbors. Charles Carleton Coffin, author of the chatty history of Boscawen, says: "During the bright summer days, travellers on the turnpike were accustomed to see a white horse going his rounds, attached to the sweep of the clay mill, while through an open window of the shop they saw Mr. Burpee and his sons fashioning milk-jars and cream pots and jugs upon the swiftly revolving wheels. Upon long boards on the southern side of the shop were rows of manufactured articles drying in the sun. Later in the season, at midnight, the shop was all aglow with the light of the flame of the kiln."*

As far as is known, the earliest large pottery in New Hampshire was the Exeter Pottery Works, or Lamson Pottery. For nearly one hundred and fifty years it was carried on by four generations of two families, the Dodges and the Lamsons. The business started in a small way in 1794, when Jabez Dodge began making earthenware and advertised for an apprentice. Samuel Dodge, William Philbrick, Oliver Osborne, Samuel Leavitt, and Asa D. and F. H. Lamson were later associated with the business. Asa Lamson was born in 1818. When he died his two sons took over their father's work in the pottery, and later carried on the business with descendants of Jabez Dodge.

According to Professor F. H. Norton, an expert on the subject of ceramics, the ware made at the Exeter plant was typical of America's folk pottery. Red-burning, glacial clay was used to make pans, cups, pots, jars, and jugs, and, later, flower-pots, which were sold to general stores in Rochester, Portsmouth, Hampton, Derry, and in Newburyport, Massachusetts.

The Clarks of Lyndeborough, like the Dodges, carried their knowledge of pottery from one town to another. The first member of this pottery-making family to settle in New Hampshire was Peter, an officer in the Colonial Army. As he records in his diary,

* *History of Boscawen. Charles Carleton Coffin. Concord, N. H. Republican Press Association, 1878. p. 642.*

he "sot out for Lyndeboro", with his family in January, 1775. Peter Clark was a good business man and a public spirited citizen. When he died in 1826 his son, Peter, took over the pottery business and taught the craft to his own sons, Peter and Benjamin. The younger men, however, gave up the trade, and Benjamin became a clergyman in North Chelmsford, Massachusetts.

The Clarks obtained much of their clay from Amherst, ten miles distant. It was of the red-burning variety, with texture and color similar to that of brick. A dark brown glaze was used on the mugs, pots, milkpans, jugs, and beanpots which came from their kiln.

In 1791 Peter Clark's son, Daniel, left home to settle in Concord. He bought land in the section of the town known as Millville, where the clay was good. Within a year, as his "line-a-day" says, he had dug the cellar for his first house, and had started the Millville Pottery by burning six kilns of ware. Daniel Clark died in 1828, at the age of sixty years, but the business was carried on by his two sons, Daniel and Peter, and later by his grandson, John Clark.

William W. Flint of Concord, who has made a study of the Millville Pottery, says that the clay used for the milkpans, crocks, jars, mugs, pitchers, jugs, plates, beanpots, bowls, flowerpots, lard pots, and pudding dishes produced by the Clarks was mixed in a large vat or tub, and was ground by means of a simple pug mill and a plodding horse. The clay, of the red-burning glacial variety, was dug and hauled in late spring. Red lead and bar lead were used for glazing. From this mixture Daniel Clark acquired a type of chronic poisoning, but he continued at his work in spite of it. The pottery grew into a lucrative business, carried on partly by trade and barter at the general store which the Clarks opened for their employees and for the general public.

The Millville Pottery closed when John Clark died in 1885. Now all trace of it has disappeared. The finest examples of the pottery made by the Concord branch of the Clark family are owned by the Society for the Preservation of New England Antiquities. The oldest item in the collection—a red-brown teapot engraved with a decoration of wavy lines—was made about 1800. Another unique

HAND-CARVED CORNER CUPBOARD *taken from an old fort in Canterbury. Property of Mrs. Joshua Higgins.*

WOOD CARVING *of covered bridge by Leo Malm.*

CHARLES CLOUGH *of Bristol, working with wood.*

piece is a light yellow-brown "what not", shaped like a house, with dark brown incised lines representing the boarding and the roof. Besides the usual milkpans, crocks, and jars, the Millville potters also made shaving mugs, pudding dishes, and vases. By 1876, after tinware became common, flowerpots were the chief output.

Elijah Osborne began the famous potteries at Gonic when he transferred his kiln from Loudon, about 1839. His two sons, John and James, kept up the business until about 1875. When they dissolved partnership, James Clark and his son, William, took over the pottery. The red-burning glacial clay used by the Osbornes came from local deposits. While the Gonic kilns were active, two hundred and fifty to three hundred pieces were fired in one burn. Some of the pieces were graceful and beautifully glazed. Potters used so many different glazes that it is impossible to assign definite pieces to the Osbornes. However, it is known that a characteristic glaze used by the Gonic potters was of a mottled yellow and green color. Also they lined some of their wares with a lead glaze, made by grinding sand and red leading together, and adding a coloring oxide. Medium-sized milkpans sold for twenty cents; cups, for ten cents; large jars, from forty to fifty cents each. Because the articles had to be kept cheap, the body and the glazes were fired together in one burn. By applying a second glaze of another color in blotches and allowing it to dry before burning again, the potters achieved mottled effects on their wares.

The Osbornes never sold their wares from house to house, but supplied general stores with their output. The disk of their kick wheel, made of *lignum vitae,* is still in the possession of the family. It has a smooth depression worn in its surface—a surface that has held nearly everything in ceramics from teacups to five gallon jars.

There were other potteries in New Hampshire between 1800 and 1850, but little is known about them today. Sometimes the newspapers announced stands and equipment for sale, as in Alstead when "clay of an excellent quality for manufacture of earthen ware with building and apparatus for that purpose" was advertised.* In 1833

---

* *New Hampshire Patriot and State Gazette.* Concord, N. H. *March 9, 1819.*

Nathaniel Goodhue of Gilford tried to sell a "large pottery for making earthen ware" and a "good kiln on same."* Four years later Charles Stark, "contemplating a removal from Gilford", offered for sale "a shop, kiln, and apparatus for the manufacture of brownware."†

Local histories frequently tell of potteries and potters whose names have been long forgotten. Around 1813, eight or ten shops were active in the section of Dublin called "Pottersville"; and in the neighboring town of Marlborough, business continued in the "Old Pottery" up until the middle of the century. Conditions were far different in Francestown, where a pottery, started in 1800, failed because of poor clay. In 1813 fifteen leading citizens of Jaffrey sponsored a "Crockery Ware Factory" as a war-time enterprise. The wares, of excellent quality, were made of white clay brought by teams from Monkton, Vermont. Potters worked in Bristol and its immediate vicinity. In the neighboring town of Northfield, a potter found excellent clay on the opposite bank of the Winnepesaukee River, but high water washed away the supply of material and he was forced to abandon his trade. Pottery was manufactured in Troy for about seventy years, the first manufactory having been built by Constant Weaver in 1821.

Today there are no manufactories operating in the State. As a craft, however, pottery making has become very popular during the past fifteen years. This seems to be due to three factors: the countrywide revival of interest in American folk arts, the influence of potters of reputation, and the impetus given to the development of the craft through the League of New Hampshire Arts and Crafts and the University of New Hampshire.

The St.-Gaudens family, noted for the contributions various members have made to art, has been an influential factor in developing the creative side of the potter's craft in New Hampshire. The members of the family who have made the most significant contribution are Annetta J. St.-Gaudens and her son, Paul. In 1921

* *Ibid. March 1, 1833.*
† *Ibid. February 13, 1837.*

Mrs. St.-Gaudens, widow of Louis St.-Gaudens and a distinguished sculptor in her own right, began to produce her statuettes, portrait medallions, and modeled vases in terra cotta. This was the starting point of the Orchard Pottery in Cornish. To assist his mother in carrying out her plans, Paul St.-Gaudens studied pottery with Frank Applegate of Trenton, New Jersey. During that spring the first "ground hog" kiln was built in the old orchard behind the sculptors' studio. The young artist then went abroad to study the various types of ceramics displayed in the museums and to study in the art schools of Rome and Paris. Later, for two winters, he worked at throwing and firing in the North Carolina mountains with O. L. Bachelder, son of an early Bennington, Vermont, potter; he gained further technical experience by taking a course in glazing at the School of Ceramics, in Alfred, New York.

Mr. St.-Gaudens says that the policy at the Orchard Kilns was handicraft done the hard way. At first the potters had their full share of discouraging failures and disasters, but as the work progressed they had successes enough to encourage them to continue their work. Annetta St.-Gaudens uses her knowledge of sculpture to make modeled vases, flower holders, statuettes, garden figures, and a number of other forms. Her son produces a variety of ornamental and useful pottery forms, all distinguished for their beautiful glazes. The glazes which the St.-Gaudens have evolved are unlike anything else in the realm of pottery; they are softly lustered and shining from within, and some have an iridescent, wet effect, as if the juice of crushed grapes or fresh limes had been poured over them.

In 1936 another creative artist joined the Orchard Pottery, when Paul St.-Gaudens married the designer, Margaret Parry. She has taken a deep interest in ceramics and has originated a new type of glazed and decorated pottery jewelry. She makes also unusual sculptured pieces, such as candlesticks and vases.

Another New Hampshire potter who is both an artist and a craftsman is Richard Moll of Somersworth. He has a fully equipped laboratory, where he and his wife work and experiment in ceramics.

He grinds his own glazes and uses a mixture of native and imported clays in fashioning his wares. When the Manchester Institute of Arts and Sciences opened pottery-making classes in the spring of 1940, Mr. Moll was engaged to teach them.

Mrs. Carroll M. Johnson and Mrs. William H. Hurlin of Antrim are also outstanding New Hampshire potters. Mrs. Johnson is a graduate of the New York State College of Ceramics. She has taught classes in Boston at the Pottery Workshop and at the Paul Revere Potteries. Also, she organized the pottery classes at the University of New Hampshire, which are sponsored by the League of New Hampshire Arts and Crafts.

With her neighbor, Mrs. Hurlin, Mrs. Johnson is now working at her craft in Antrim. The laboratory where these craftswomen turn out their lovely wares is in the basement of Mrs. Hurlin's home. It is equipped completely with wheel, glazing outfit, and a gas-burning kiln. The Antrim potters do not use New Hampshire clay but send to New Jersey for their material, obtaining a clay with a buff firing body which matures at 2000° Fahrenheit. Their designs are original, unless they are filling a specific order for a customer who wishes an item copied. They make candlesticks, buttons, figurines, book ends, tiles, many kinds of vases, pitchers, and other useful articles for the household. Both women have homes and families, and they work on a part time basis only.

Mrs. Johnson, then Miss Helen Munroe, began teaching the pottery classes at the University of New Hampshire in 1931, and continued until 1936. She was succeeded by Miss Kelsea Griffin and, in turn, by Miss Helen B. Phelps. In the fall of 1939 a master craftsman, William Hallbergh, who is the tenth generation descendant of a line of potters, came from Maine to conduct the Department of Ceramics. He was trained in the finest laboratories of the United States and in Sweden. He is noted for his work with glazes and for his experiments in mixing and handling clay. The pottery classes are elective for sophomores, juniors, and seniors. The University houses the laboratory and provides most of the equipment. The League of New Hampshire Arts and Crafts supplies the in-

GLAZED OSBORN POTTERY, *made at Boscawen Plains about 1815. Owned by Mrs. Mary E. Durgin.*

KEENE POTTERY *owned by Isabel Pennell Marshall of Suncook.*

LLOYD BURT, *student potter at the University of New Hampshire.*

structors. Besides actual work with the potter's wheel, experiments are conducted in the chemical analyses of native clays and of glazes.

The articles which come from the kilns and the wheels at the University have been given the name of "Old Dover Pottery", because Durham once was part of the original town of Dover. "Old Dover Pottery" is a genuine local product, for the clay used in making it is taken from land owned by the University. It is undoubtedly the same kind of material which native craftsmen used in their work years ago.

Most of the early potters prepared their clay by much the same methods as did the brickmakers. But wedging, the process by which wet clay was sliced up and kneaded together to squeeze out bubbles and make the material plastic, was a step used only in pottery making. The early craftsmen did not screen or purify the clay, though they sometimes washed it by hand through a series of tanks, and added modifying ingredients, which they mixed with the material that had settled at the bottom. Then they poured off the water and allowed the paste to dry, so that it could be handled. Modern potters, on the other hand, use sieves or straining bags, which take away the water and leave the clay in the right consistency for working.

New Hampshire clay produced a porus, soft-bodied, "redware" of the same quality as brick and very easily chipped or broken. For this reason a few commercial potters, like the Crafts in Nashua and the Burpees of Boscawen, brought their clay from New Jersey, or, less frequently, from Boston. This imported product was a grey-burning clay that could be fired at a very high temperature, producing a "stoneware" of extremely hard and durable body. Most of the potters working in New Hampshire threw their clay on the wheel, instead of shaping it by pouring slip into a mould.

The years have brought few changes to the potter's wheel. It is still a simple framework, consisting of a heavy bottom disk which, when kicked, keeps going for a time under its own momentum. By means of a connecting axel, it turns a small round plate upon which the clay is shaped. Usually the frame includes a sloping bench, on which the craftsman sits, and a lower shelf, where he rests his feet after he kicks the wheel.

The general method of working is to throw a ball of clay on the center of the wheel. Some potters use a plaster bat, the same size as the wheel, for easier removal of the piece after forming. The bat and the material in it are taken up and set aside for drying, and another bat is put in place for the next throwing. Water prevents the clay from sticking to the potter's hands, which are kept wet during the entire process. Sometimes the clay is worked up into a cone and worked down again to increase plasticity, then held firmly and centered on the revolving wheel.

A piece of rotating clay will assume any desired shape when the right pressure is placed upon it. While the fingers of both hands guide the outside, the thumbs are forced down in the center, until the ball becomes a bowl. The sides of this bowl are then forced upward between the fingers to fashion a cylinder. This is called a draft, and several drafts are sometimes necessary to give the wall its finished height and to form the rim. Finally, by using one hand on the inside and a "rib", or small piece of hardwood, on the outside surface, the correct shape and smooth exterior are achieved.

After wiping his hands, the potter passes a wire between the completed vessel and the wheel top, and transfers the piece to a board in the sun, or to a rack around the kiln. He uses a paddle or a special lifter to handle his unfinished forms, for he must be very careful not to indent or deform the soft, moulded clay.

When a piece is "leather dry", it is fastened to the wheel with soft clay and given the final turning. This is done with a small tool or with bent steel. Sometimes a turning stick, attached near by to project over the wheel, is employed to guide the potter's hand, while he does what sculpturing is necessary to produce the final pattern. The green ware is then allowed to dry thoroughly before it is placed in the kiln.

The kiln is really an oven, in which soft clay is baked into a hard, permanent bisque, or biscuit, and in which later the dry glaze powder placed on the ware is transformed by heat into a brilliant vitreous finish. Kilns are built of all sizes and materials. **Mrs.**

CLAY KILN AND POTTER'S WHEEL

Johnson and Mrs. Hurlin use a cast-iron kiln, made from a design of F. H. Norton, Professor of Ceramics at the Massachusetts Institute of Technology. Modern kilns differ from the old-time models in two ways: they use other heating elements than wood, and they regulate their operations and temperature more scientifically.

Practically all of the early glazes were composed of finely ground clay, diluted with water to the consistency of cream, with an admixture of powdered red lead and coloring oxides. The results were somewhat uncertain, for the chemical impurities in the clay and in the oxides bought at a village store, might cause curious blotchy effects and surprising color combinations. At Gonic, sand and red lead were ground together with a small amount of coloring oxide, and the glaze was fired with the body in one burn. Some of the pieces were reglazed with another color, which was spattered or spotted on with the finger. The mottled ware made by the Osbornes is typical of this method of glazing. The heat of the fire was also important; sometimes a happy accident of overfiring produced ware of unusually brilliant vitreosity. Slip-glazed ware could not be used to keep vinegar, wine, and other foods which are influenced by lead; but it could be used for table dishes and for temporary containers. Though cheaply made, its color was attractive, and it was often very ornamental.

Since stoneware, on the other hand, was used to store preserves and pickles, it was seldom decorated. The jugs and crocks were covered with a plain salt glaze, put on by shoveling common salt onto the kiln fires. When the salt vaporized, it settled like a fog on the ware and formed a hard coating, the roughness of which is similar to the skin of an orange. Pulverized glass suspended in water was sometimes used for glazing; the water was absorbed by the biscuit, leaving a coat of glass dust, which fused into a solid crystal shell upon firing.

Modern potters use three methods of glazing: spraying, dipping the piece in the glaze or pouring the glaze over the piece, and brushing. Today the Antrim potters use an ordinary paint sprayer for their glazing. Mrs. Johnson won her title of Master Craftsman from the Boston Society of Arts and Crafts with an odd blue-black incised milk pitcher. The effect was achieved by incising a pattern on the damp piece before firing. After the initial firing, the pitcher was glazed with three glazes ranging from a pale blue-green at the bottom to a blue-black at the neck. The glaze was then removed from the incisions leaving the red clay exposed. The whole piece was then glazed with a transparent film and subjected to the final fire. Varying effects in color and design evolve through the use of surface treatment, colored clay applied before firing and colored oxide painted on the biscuit ware before glazing. Most ceramic ware is fired twice. The first, or biscuit fire, is to hold the piece in shape and render it porous for glazing; the second, or gloss-firing, is to fix the glaze.

The better glazes of the present time are the scientific results of intensive chemical research and experiment. Finishes of extraordinary brilliance and beauty are produced in the pottery laboratory at the University of New Hampshire. Some of the more recent results strike a new note in color design. This is due to various mineral formulas worked out by the students of ceramics, under the supervision of William Hallbergh. The method of application is remarkably quick and simple: the ware is dipped into a crock full of one mixture, then into another mixture, and perhaps into a third color. The glaze comes from the kiln sometimes a soft blending of three hues, sometimes a lovely green-grey mottle, sometimes a combination of an odd shade of amethyst veined with azure.

Only craftsmen who have thrown pottery on a wheel know how much skill it takes to mould by hand an article of good proportion and artistic quality. In spite of the "surprises, difficulties, and disappointments" of the work, many potters find that their greatest interest lies in experimenting with glazes and lusters. In this part of the craft the scientist must join with the artist, for as George J. Cox says: "The finest work in pottery was not produced by scientists alone and does not depend altogether upon the quality of its paste, its unique colour, or strange lustre. The last word, the form, decoration, and craftsmanship, is with the artist."*

* *Pottery. George J. Cox. New York. Macmillan Co.. 1926. p. 117.*

IX

STONECUTTERS

The American colonists did not make statues or practice the art of sculpture as we use the word today. However, in old graveyards we may still find reminders of the stonecutters who approached the art most closely, slate stones on which painstaking hands carved designs and letters that have withstood more than two centuries of New England weather. Mute testimonials they are to the artisans whose own names were forgotten years ago but whose craftsmanship even now calls to our minds the men and women whose graves they marked.

The burying grounds of the earliest pioneers had no markers of any kind. Instead, crops of corn were planted so that the Indians might not know the number of the dead. Later flat wolf stones were used as a protection from wild animals.

When the colonists began to mark graves, they used field stones, which they placed at the head and foot of each mound. The oldest cemetery in Chester, New Hampshire, has several of this type, without any inscription whatsoever. These are markers. The true memorials, which were inscribed with a name, a date, or both, were a later development.

In Lyndeborough there is a stone that illustrates the transition. This humble gravestone was either naturally of a shape suggestive of a shrouded head and shoulders, or it was carved in that form before being set to mark the grave of a four-year-old child. On the surface of the "head" at the top of the stone, someone knocked out an oval-shaped groove to suggest the outline of a human face, and put the initials "D C" and the year "1785" beneath it. Although this may seem late for such a crude headstone, Lyndeborough, which had been settled only about thirty years before, was still a part of the great wilderness.

The towns in the lower Merrimack Valley, founded much earlier and located comparatively near the urban centers of that day, were more sophisticated. In their old graveyards can be found many examples of rather elaborate designs carved years before the Lyndeborough stone.

These show the influence of Massachusetts stonecutters, particularly of two important families, the Lamsons of Charlestown and the Fosters of Dorchester. They flourished between 1670 and 1770, during which period several generations of each family carried on the trade.

In the Old Burying Ground in Nashua, the stone of Ensign Joseph Farwell (d. 1722) resembles known examples of the Lamsons' work. The exquisitely cut scroll and print design of the border is of the Renaissance style for which the family was famous.

Another design which was distinctive of their early work was a winged death's head with the eyebrows curving upward. Such heads have been found on the stone of John Burns in the Blodgett Yard in Hudson and on that of Mrs. Damaris Dunklee in the cemetery at Amherst Village. After 1750, however, a face was frequently carved in place of a skull, and finally the wings were omitted.

The Foster family included three generations of stonecutters, each of whom was named James. Although genealogical data do not mention that the Fosters were stonecutters, some records of payments for memorials made by the administrators of estates and a casual reference or two in other records prove that these craftsmen really did the fine work attributed to them. Harriette M. Forbes, authority on New England gravestones, who had found many records of payment to the Fosters for stones, says that there are a few examples of their work in Portsmouth.*

* *Gravestones of Early New England and the Men Who Made Them, 1656-1800.* Harriette Merrifield Forbes. Boston. Houghton-Mifflin Co., 1927. p. 62.

One of the very few New Hampshire stonecutters known by name today was John Wight, who carried on his trade in Londonderry, Hudson, Salem, and Derry, between 1734 and 1775. His rough but distinctive products were made from native stone, for slate, the common gravestone material of the times, was not available in the locality where he worked. Because nearly every one of his designs included a coffin and a heart, Wight is known today as the "Coffin-Heart Man".

In his patterns, the space at the top of the stone, ordinarily occupied by a death's head, was filled with a geometric design of circles and semi-circles inscribed in a square. He seems never to have used the same border twice. The stone of Mrs. Jenit Moor, in the Forest Hills Yard at East Derry, dated 1774, is an example of Wight's most elaborate attempt at art; it includes in symmetrical arrangement two rosettes, crossed bones, a shovel, a coffin, a heart, a diamond, and at the bottom another rosette. The last stone made by Wight was cut for his own grave.*

An unidentified craftsman, commonly called the "Circle-Head Man", was cutting crude monuments for the people of Hudson and Londonderry between 1745 and 1759. He kept faithfully to one design, which consisted of a simple circle or oval containing two smaller circles for eyes and two straight lines for a mouth. Sometimes teeth were represented, sometimes a nose, and the figure was always winged. Borders had the same uniformity. The tops frequently had a design which may have been intended to represent a many spoked wheel or a daisy, and the remainder of the pattern was a complicated, modified scroll motif. The lettering was incised in crude Roman capitals, like the inscriptions cut by the Coffin-Heart Man.

Ebenezer Soule, another stonecutter of the period, was born in Plympton, Massachusetts, and worked for some time in that vicinity. Later he moved to Hinsdale, New Hampshire, where there are many examples of his work. In his designs, round-eyed faces stare from circular plaques chiseled at the tops of the stones. The features are

---

* *History of Rockingham and Strafford Counties, New Hampshire.* D. Hamilton Hurd. Philadelphia. J. W. Lewis, 1882. p. 171.

always very flat. The nose is broad and sharply angular at the nostrils, the mouth little more than a shallow groove. The eyes, with their small round pupils, are topped by abbreviated eyebrows that are formed by the upward extension of the lines of the nose.

Soule's work is individual, and easily recognized not so much for the rather ordinary faces as for the unusual snaky hair with which they are surrounded. On each side of the head two heavy tresses curve out and roll into spiral curves. Another distinctive characteristic is found in the borders, each of which represents a tall plant bearing three buds that alternate with bunches of sharp-edged leaves. Examples of such "Medusa" hair and "three-story" floral borders are found on the stones of Sarah Metcalf (1767), Jonathan Metcalf (1768), and Amos Foster (1767), in the Second Burying Ground at Keene.

During this period, when style demanded that the stonecutter place either a death's head or a cherub at the top of the panel, it was natural that the design should become conventionalized. A few of the more skillful craftsmen, however, tried to do work that was less stereotyped. An attempt at realism is found in the Point of Graves Cemetery, Portsmouth, on the tombstone of Captain Tobias Lear, father of George Washington's secretary. It was carved in 1781 by John Homer, about whom very little is known. This one stone proves him to have been an imaginative artist, unhampered by convention. Instead of the customary death's head, he made a realistic three-quarters profile. On the panel below, a flame issues from a round urn upon which the name and dates are cut. To the right a simple, plume-like willow rises to droop above the urn. At the turn of the century this combination became so popular that it practically superseded all other types of ornamental design on New England gravestones, but in 1781 it was distinctly unusual.

Another early stonecutter who did not stick to standard designs was Asa Risley (also written Wrisley), who was born in Glastonbury, Connecticut, in 1754 and came to Hanover during the early 1780's. He settled on a farm in the northern part of the town on what was then "Half-Mile Road", now Route 10. There he built a log cabin, where Asa, Jr., who later became his partner, was born in 1790.

Several manuscripts in the Baker Memorial Library in Hanover list Risley's inscriptions and tell of his work. By means of these, many of the monuments scattered through the neighboring towns of the Connecticut Valley can be easily ascribed to the craftsmanship of father and son. Their refinement of technique and design, as well as their departure from established tradition, make them outstanding. The Risleys favored deeply cut geometric and floral designs with odd treatment of wings, which they combined in various ways with a bold and unusual willow and urn, when that motif became popular. Delicacy and grace was always the keynote of their work.

Many memorials in the older part of the cemeteries of southern New Hampshire are copies of the "Park" type, which originated with the Park family of Groton, Massachusetts. William Park, first of the dynasty, was one of the last men whose work was distinctive enough to be identified by its design. The succeeding generations of Parks, who not only made gravestones but also cut stone and supervised the erection of stone buildings, eventually resorted to a stock pattern as the easiest and most economical way of supplying a large market. Their work became so popular that other stonecutters flagrantly copied this design. Since the time of William Park's son, John, the art of gravestone cutting has never been free from the blight which accompanies mass production.

In the 1760's William Park was carving a peculiar death's head known as the "Bulldog" face. Such a figure is found in the Old Burying Ground of Nashua on the stone of Mrs. Jemima Houston (1762), "ye wife of Mr. Ovid Houston". A favorite Park motto, "From Death's Arrest No Age is Free", appears on the stone of William Adams at Hollis. The Blodgett Yard in Hudson has three stones on which are carved faces whose features, round faces, pointed chins, and scanty hair, are good examples of William Park's style. Another of his designs is illustrated by the double stone of Samuel Leeman (1756) and his wife (1760) in the Hollis cemetery. Above each inscription is a face; Samuel's has wings, but his wife's does not.

William Park's son, John, was a good draftsman and an ingenious mechanic, but his designs had a stereotyped similarity. They had very solemn faces, set in small square niches. A stout oval head with rather dispirited wings, on which all the feathers grew downward, was one of his favorite patterns. Such a head is found on the stone of Abiathar Winn (1783) in the Blodgett Yard, Hudson. In the accounts of the administrator of Winn's estate is the item, "pd. Jno. Park £ 3-12". It is not definitely stated that the payment was made for a gravestone; but the stone of Moses Nichols (1790) in Amherst is similar and is recorded as having cost the Nichols estate the same amount of money.*

The Park family had a profound influence on the art of graveyard sculpture in the latter part of the 1700's and throughout the eighteenth and nineteenth centuries, and the general style of their designs is still widely followed. It was they who inaugurated the use of one stone for an entire family, carving the stone in two, three, or sometimes four sections.

The Treat family of Portsmouth also furnished a number of gravestonemakers of note. Through a period of nearly a century during which father succeeded son in the business, the sign "Samuel Treat, Stone Cutter" dominated the trade. The sign bears the date 1807. The last member of the family, John I. Treat, died in 1898.

Another gravestone business which was carried on by three generations of a family was founded by Moses Davis of Nashua in 1842. Davis is remembered by the older people of the town as a dignified man who wore a long ministerial coat. His advertisement in the *Nashua and Nashville Directory* for 1843 reads:

---

* *Hillsborough County, Records of Probate Office, Nashua, N. H.*

   (a) *Abiathar Winn of Nottingham West; Administrator's accounts, February 17, 1790. Reference: John Park paid.*

   (b) *Moses Nichols, Administrator's account of estate of 1790. Reference: Price of Gravestones.*

STONECUTTERS

> "Moses Davis—Manufacturer of Gravestones from Slate and Italian and Vermont White Marble. Railroad Square, Nashville, N. H."

This advertisement indicates the fact that by 1850 well-established stoneworkers in the larger communities were set up in business.

Davis stones are to be found in nearly all the cemeteries in the southern and central part of the State, cut with the varied designs of the Victorian period. A rose in bud or in full bloom seems to have been the most popular flower, especially on memorials to women and girls; the oak was considered appropriate for men; ivy, lilies of the valley, Masonic emblems, and the well-known open Bible with a hand pointing upward were other common designs. Soldiers' stones were decorated with shields, cannon, rifles, swords, and flags. Besides these, Davis continued the use of the earlier willow and urn motif, which he carved on marble for the memorial to Mary Ada Gould, buried in Nashua in 1856. Previously that design had nearly always been done on slate.

Although Italian marble was advertised for sale in New Hampshire as early as 1807, it did not begin to take the place of slate for gravestones until about 1830. Most of the marble supply came from Vermont and from Stockbridge, Massachusetts. It became increasingly popular, so that during the nineteenth century almost two hundred workers cut marble in various sections of the State.

New Hampshire granite was not extensively used for gravestones until 1885. Before that date many quarries had been opened to supply underpinnings for buildings and bridges and to make millstones; but in 1878, so far as is known, there were only four quarries in which cemetery stonework was done. Monuments cut from one of them, the St. Johnsbury Granite Company's quarry in Stark, took prizes at the Centennial Exposition held at Philadelphia in 1876. They were later shipped to every part of the country.

The beginning of the granite era marked the end of the handicraft period in stonecutting. The story of monument making at the present time belongs to industrial and economic history. There are, nevertheless, a number of fine craftsmen listed among the commercial granite workers of the State. At the age of sixty-seven, Frank Comolli of Milford, an ornamental carver and artist of the old school, continues the craft that he learned fifty-four years ago in a small quarry town in Lombardy, Italy. He has carved the ornamental stonework on a large number of important public buildings in the eastern States. The bas-relief of a woman's figure at the front entrance of the Library of Congress is his work. He has produced a number of figures cut from stone, one of the finest of which is a life-sized cemetery angel, distinguished by the delicate and fragile carving on the wings.

The late Marco Poletti, who, with his brother, Cesare, came to Milford from Italy about 1900, designed and executed a memorial which is considered outstanding. When Cesare died in 1930, Marco at once began working on the design for a memorial to him. He sent his plans and a rough clay draft to his friend, J. Nicolosi, a New York sculptor. Mr. Nicolosi, using his beautiful wife as model, completed a full-sized plaster cast, which he returned to Poletti to be copied in Milford granite. But Marco died in 1934 while he was carving the eagle that was to spread its wings over the top of the stone. Soon after his death, the memorial without the eagle was erected over the graves of the Poletti brothers. A local craftsman later completed the work on the eagle.

Besides slate, marble, and granite, soapstone has been used for gravestone material. It was first adopted by the Risleys of Hanover, who, with their usual disregard for custom, decided that this typically New Hampshire product was well suited to their work.

The soapstone quarry in Francestown probably has the most valuable deposit in the country; some authorities consider it second to none in the world. The story of its discovery has as many versions as it has tellers. According to one, the original owner, Daniel Fuller, found it while he was plowing. Another says that he first noticed that the stone in his pasture was of an unusual quality when he accidentally dropped an axe, edge down, upon a ledge. Seeing that the tool was not dulled by the crash, Fuller bent to examine the rock against which it had fallen. "It cuts like old cheese!" he cried.

The quarry was first worked sometime in the first decade of the nineteenth century. The stone was carried to Boston by oxcart where it was sold in a store on Milk Street. As the product became more popular, people began to travel long distances to obtain it from the quarry. Of greater interest at the present day, however, is its use by craftsmen, who find it an excellent material from which to fashion small decorative or useful dishes.

The Indians were the first to employ it in this way. A number of their shallow soapstone dishes have been found in the region of the Merrimack Valley. One fine example is owned by the New Hampshire Historical Society in Concord. Another, the finest steatite ever discovered in New England, is in the collection of the Manchester Historic Association. An oval bowl about twelve inches long and ten inches wide with four "ears" or handles evenly spread along the rim, it appears shallower than its depth of five inches because of the thickness of the stone. It was found by Isaac Webster in the southeastern part of Manchester.

Modern workmen find soapstone well adapted to making such articles as ash trays, candlesticks, and inkstands. Raymond Baldwin, formerly of Orford but now living on the Vermont side of the Connecticut River, has done a great deal of work of this type, distributing his products through the League of New Hampshire Arts and Crafts. Mr. Baldwin is a cobbler, and works with soapstone as an avocation. With the co-operation of the owner, he gets fragments of soapstone from an old quarry near his home.

Another aspect of stonecutting is the work of the lapidary. Although the cutting of native gem stones may seem far removed from the cutting of gravestones, the two crafts require a similar delicacy and accuracy of touch. An especially high degree of skill is demanded of the lapidary, who uses his tools to cut the facets on a comparatively minute object.

The art of cutting and polishing native gem stones is relatively new to New Hampshire, but local craftsmen believe that it has a great future. The majority of New Hampshire lapidaries are also amateur mineralogists who make frequent trips to the various known localities of gem deposits and to unexplored regions where geological conditions promise rich finds. Percy Leggett of Gorham and Fred Goodwin and J. Philip Morin of Berlin have received prospecting rights over hundreds of acres in Coös County; they hunt for stones during their spare time in the summer, and spend the winter months sorting, cutting, and polishing the specimens they bring home.

The amethyst deposits of Coös County are of superior quality. An amethyst gave Percy Leggett his start in gem hunting. The purple stone, hidden away in gas pockets in the heart of red granite, is one of the most difficult to locate. Yet Mr. Leggett's original find was a huge cluster of amethyst crystals in a sixty-pound boulder lying conspicuously in the open. Fred Goodwin has unearthed many valuable specimens. In 1939, using a stone he had found, he gave his wife for Christmas a large, royal purple amethyst ring.

Garnet of an inferior grade has been discovered in Hanover, Wilmot, and Tuckerman Ravine. Blue and colorless iolite, the opalescent labradorite, and fine specimens of the jasper which has given its name to a mountain near Berlin have been found in New Hampshire. Myer Kassner of Laconia found some phenacite crystals, the gem of which is exceedingly rare, near South Baldface Mountain.

Since good aquamarine (blue-green beryl) is very easy to polish, it is a favorite stone with local lapidaries. Clear green beryl is still among the rarest of New Hampshire gems, but brown, blue, yellow, and white crystals are more common. The belief that there are many pockets of golden beryl and aquamarine in the heart of the ridge between Grafton and Keene, has been substantiated by the discovery of fine beryl crystals throughout that area.

An enormous beryl crystal weighing more than a ton was once excavated near Grafton, but it was of a poor quality, barely translucent, and so brittle that when cracks began to appear soon after its excavation, it had to be bound together with steel bands to prevent its falling apart.

Percy Leggett well remembers the day on which he and a companion were out on what seemed to be an unsuccessful quest through a Kilkenny gully. He grew tired and stopped to rest while his friend went into a neighboring ravine to follow up a granitic vein. As Mr. Leggett sat idly chipping at an apparently solid rock, his steel pick suddenly broke through into a pocket that was heavily incrusted with golden topaz. Amazed at his good fortune, he called to his friend; together, they gleaned nearly one hundred yellow crystals from the cache.

Most lapidaries agree that, while the discovery of crystals in the field is a highly exciting experience, it cannot be compared with the discovery of a gem stone's hidden beauty as it emerges beneath the craftsman's skilled fingers. Mr. Leggett was at first interested in minerals only from the point of view of the collector. When an out-of-State lapidary charged him a rather substantial sum for cutting and polishing a rough amethyst he had found, he began to consider the possibility of doing such work himself. Like Fred Goodwin, who constructed the apparatus for stonecutting from a discarded sewing machine without ever having seen a professional outfit, Mr. Leggett has made his own tools from old belts and motor parts.

Another gem cutter who is self-taught and who makes many of his own tools is John G. Herrick of Hillsboro. At the age of seventy-seven, Mr. Herrick is still a versatile craftsman; he has done cabinetmaking a long time, made violins exclusively for ten years, and is famous for his beautiful work in pewter. Although he has collected minerals as a hobby for many years, he began to cut stones only about two years ago when he read the best books he could find on the subject and carefully applied what he had learned.

Mr. Herrick finds native blue beryl and yellow beryl excellent for mounting in silver rings. Other native stones which he uses for pins, rings, and pendants mounted in silver settings of his own creation are aquamarine, rose quartz, and smoky quartz. He uses fluorite also. This stone is somewhat softer than the others, and is found in Keene and Westmoreland. Mr. Herrick says that one of the fascinations of this work for him is in seeing the beauty of the stone appear as it is polished. He has even polished native granite so that it can be used to advantage in the setting of a dinner ring.

At a meeting of jewelry craftsmen which was held by the League of New Hampshire Arts and Crafts in June, 1940, at the Province Lake home of Miss Laura E. Young, the cutting of this common mineral, gray granite, was stressed. The scope of New Hampshire mineralogy was shown in a display of the collections of private individuals and of Kimball-Union Academy.

Mr. Herrick is one of several gem cutters whose work is handled by the League, which is wholeheartedly sponsoring the development of this craft. Regular classes in native gem cutting are maintained, and from several groups of workers, notably those in Tamworth and Sandwich, there has already come much skillful work.

The first meeting of mineralogists and stonecutters connected with the League was held in the fall of 1939, at the home of the Sandwich Industries in Center Sandwich. Mrs. Iona Kierstead of Lancaster brought to the meeting a bracelet she had made by mounting in silver six vari-colored cabochons cut by her brother from pebbles found among the sands of the seashore. Beryl, tourmaline, and sodalite, amethysts embedded in quartz, crystal topaz, and homely feldspar were presented as the kind of materials, gathered in from the mountain streams and the fields, with which an adventurous enterprise is being built. For with the slackening of the European source of supply, a challenge has been offered the skill and ingenuity of native artisans: to carve from the minerals of their own country, jewels that will compensate, in vigor of execution and originality of design, for the costly brilliancy of foreign gems.

Of all New Hampshire stones, the mythical "Great Carbuncle" is the most famous. Its legend goes back to the discoverer and first explorer of the White Mountains, Captain Darby Field. Returning from his travels, he told fantastic tales of the jewels he had seen in the recesses of the "Crystal Hills", of diamonds and emeralds that blinded the eyes with their mingled light. In the course of

A JEWEL CRAFTSMAN, *John G. Herrick of Hillsboro, polishing native blue beryl.*

A BOTTLE OF LYNDEBOROUGH GLASS *and* INKWELLS *of three-mold Stoddard glass, owned by Isabel Marshall of Suncook.*

time, although Field's story was never confirmed, the legend gathered itself into a single immense stone—the Great Carbuncle.

Neither emeralds nor diamonds have ever been found in the Crystal Hills. The only garnets discovered there have been small and of a poor quality. Nevertheless the quest described in Nathaniel Hawthorne's famous story continues at the present day, for modern craftsmen have revived in spirit the ancient search for the perfect stone.

X

NEW HAMPSHIRE GLASS

In the window holes of the homes of many of the early settlers, diamond-shaped mica panes were placed to keep out the cold and admit the sun's warmth and light, but more often oiled paper or parchment was used. The value of these was negligible, and soon the pioneers began trying to produce glass for this purpose. Glass beads for the Indian trade had been made in Jamestown, Virginia, as early as 1608. A factory where bottles and hollow ware were blown for twenty years had been set up in Salem, Massachusetts, in 1639. Baron Stiegel and Caspar Wistar, in addition to less well-known craftsmen, had been at work before the Revolutionary War. But the first manufactory of glass after the Colonies had declared their independence was erected in the town of Temple, New Hampshire, in 1780.

Robert Hewes of Boston set up this business on a ridge between Temple and Kidder Mountains, a half mile from Sharon and a mile from the New Ipswich boundary. It was a secluded site; the Crown had forbidden all Colonial industry, and secrecy was an important factor. The location was ideal for the enterprise. Land was cheap, living conditions were favorable, fuel and sand plentiful, and hardwood ashes for potash were easily obtained. The building was sixty-five feet square, and approximately the height of the old Temple meetinghouse, which was built about the same time. Francis Cragin was the master builder. By fall the furnaces were ready, but Hewes' limited capital, a legacy from his father, had been absorbed by the many expenses. The Hessian and Waldecker glass blowers, former soldiers of the British army, living in log huts near the works, demanded high wages. Henry Ames Blood, writing in 1860, vividly describes the local situation: "The affair would most probably have succeeded, but before the year was out the entire concern was destroyed by fire. These *thirty-two Dutchmen* were consequently thrown out of employment. The Phlegmatic fellows were lying around the old manufactory, doing nothing but to smoke their kiefekill dodeens, and the vast fuliginous cloud that hung portentously on the skirts of the mountain must have alarmed the people here mightily, for we are told that one Maynard was the first to make a deal of noise about them, and the whole people were at last awakened to the possibility of all these *thirty-two* glass-blowing, smoke-puffing Dutchmen falling on the town for subsistence."*

One of the farmers who lived near the glass house climbed out of a well he was digging one day, his face a "curious mixture of white and green". He had heard loud voices down there in the pit, and "he wasn't going back there again to break through".† Doubtlessly the fun-loving workmen would have had many a hearty chuckle had they known that their guttural German accents penetrating the wall of the well seemed to this good farmer like sounds from hell.

Sympathetic neighbors helped Hewes to reconstruct the razed building, but the furnaces had been exposed to frost, and when they were subjected to intense heat they burst. Hewes was obliged to petition the town for funds to pay his workers. Much correspondence on both sides was fruitless, so he appealed to the General Court. At last this body granted him the right to run a lottery, but he could not dispose of the tickets, and the entire project was dropped.

Hewes returned to Boston where he became a surgeon, a fenc-

* *History of Temple.* Henry Ames Blood. Boston. Rand and Avery, 1860. p. 28.
† *Granite State Magazine.* Volume III (January 1907) p. 21.

ing master, and a manufacturer of patent medicines.* He is listed in the Boston Directory of 1825 as "Hewes, Robert, surgeon, bonesetter, corner of Essex; Poland starch-maker, 372 Washington Street; Teacher of sword exercise, Boylston Market."† He continued to be active in many fields until his death, recorded in the *Columbian Centinel,* July 21, 1830.

Bottles of the decanter type and crude window glass were the only products blown at Temple. They were green, often muddy in tone because bits of earth had been carelessly fused into the blown globes. Authentic Temple pieces are rare today. A gallon bottle, a decanter in the possession of a member of the Hewes family, a tumbler of greenish white, and a three-gallon bottle of cloudy glass are among the relics attributed to the short-lived Temple venture.

A brief glimpse at early methods indicates somewhat the difficulties attendant upon the manufacture of glass. The melting pot, in which the silica, usually in the form of natural sand, and alkaline bases, such as soda, lime, or ashes, were heated to the plastic stage, was made of a special kind of powdered clay, burnt clay, and water. This mixture was kept damp for some time. Then the clay was built up in rings or layers, the workers taking great care to keep it sufficiently moist, and smooth on the sides. When completed, it was put aside for several months to dry. A kiln was prepared, and the dry pot placed inside and heated. After it had become red hot, it was placed in the furnaces.

There were two distinct methods of glassmaking: one used moulds, the second, only blow pipes. Moulds were at first made of clay, but later cast iron, brass, and, in rare instances, steel or extremely hard woods were used. The article to be made determined the type of mould. Bowls and jars, because their tops were large, required the one-part type of moulds. A tumbler usually required only a one-section mould. A flask needed a two-section receptacle. The mould was held together either by hinges or screws

* *Ibid p. 20.*
† *Id.*

in such a way that it could be opened easily and the glass removed. In making the moulded blown glass some of the viscid molten material was gathered on the end of a tube, or blow pipe, and thrust into the mould, where it was blown into shape. Three-mould blown glass is highly prized by present-day collectors.

The joinings of the mould often left seams on the sides and bottom of the glass. Such seams were sometimes minimized or removed by refiring in just enough heat to melt the seam and cause it to disappear; at other times the patterns were so planned that the seam became a part of the design. Patterns were generally cut in intaglio on the inside of moulds, the air from the blowpipe forcing the plastic glass to follow the design. When the article was removed, every line raised on the surface had a corresponding depression inside. During the period from 1825 to 1870, many firms bought their moulds from commercial supply houses, or had them "chipped" by a migratory professional.

The making of blown glass without the use of a mould was a fairly simple process. The molten glass was gathered on the end of a blowpipe, a hollow tapering iron tube from four to seven feet long, and rolled on a polished cast-iron plate or block of wood until the mass assumed an even shape. It was then expanded by blowing and elongated by swinging, after which a solid iron rod, called a *pontil,* was attached directly opposite the end of the blowpipe. A bit of molten sticky glass held the glass fast to the pontil so that the workmen could hold the glass securely while they finished the top. By touching the neck with a wet iron and lightly tapping the glass at the end of the pipe, the glass form was detached from the blowpipe. Later the fractured opening was slightly reheated, smoothed on a block of wood, expanded, and then banded or collared as the style demanded. A "chair man" took the pontil with the glass attached and rolled it back and forth on the arm of his chair while he shaped the glass into its final form with his tools. When the pontil was detached, it left a scar, known as the pontil mark. In some factories this was removed by grinding, or the rough edges were pressed together with pinchers. After 1850 the mark disappeared completely.

The War of 1812 was accompanied by a rise in the foreign tariff, and factories for "homegrown" products sprang up all over the country. In 1814 the first glass factory in Keene was built on what is now Washington Street. Sand for the potworks came from a slope near Beaver Brook. It was first called the New Hampshire Glass Factory, later known as the New Hampshire Glass Company, and finally became the Keene Window Glass Company. Seven men formed the company and Colonel Lawrence Schoolcraft, formerly superintendent of the Hamilton, New York, glass works, was hired as manager. His son, Henry Rowe Schoolcraft, was also employed there. When some of the original incorporators became discouraged, Appleton and Eliott, two of their number, came into full control. Cylinder window glass in small sizes was the only product of this firm, until a later owner added green glass bottles to its output.

In 1815 the younger Schoolcraft, in company with Watson and Twitchell, two other founders of the parent company, started another factory on Marlboro Street. Watson left that same year, and Schoolcraft and Twitchell went on manufacturing. The collaboration lasted less than a year, however. In 1816 Nathaniel Sprague, another member of the original company, became Henry's partner. Under the new agreement they were to ". . . make glass, attend to business, and split investments, expenses, and profits—if any".* All the glass made during Schoolcraft's management bore the legend "H. S."

When Schoolcraft sold the factory in 1817, the versatile Justus Perry became the next owner of the Marlboro Street works. At nineteen he worked in a saddler's shop. In the War of 1812 he was distinguished as Commander of the Ashuelot Cavalry; at twenty-five he became Major General of the Militia. Perry's decanters were geometrically designed, with flat-ribbed, mushroom, or rayed stoppers. Five years later the firm became known as Perry and Wood, then Perry and Wheeler. "IP" and "P&W" are well known trademarks of Keene glass.

* *Ibid. p. 83.*

Flint glass tumblers, decanters, and bottles made on Marlboro Street were of an olive-amber color, running to almost dark brown; aquamarine was rare. During the period 1810-1825, likenesses of national heroes appeared in glass. Andrew Jackson seems to have been the favorite of the Keene flask makers. Masonic flasks, too, were a popular item from 1816 to 1825, when the Royal Arch Masons flourished in the section. These were of greenish amber. The first ones were clear, with delicate impressions, but they became crude when they began to lose favor. From 1822 to 1827 sunburst bottles were made in half pint to quart sizes. These had high shoulders, corrugated sides, sheared mouths, and scarred bases. Some of them were golden amber in color, others came in sea, grass, olive, or sage green. The railroad flask, common at that time, was usually of dark green or golden amber. One of the leading citizens of Keene has in his present collection ". . . one of the original blue bottles with a spread eagle on the outside and a pint of incredibly old port within".*

Collectors' items, however, list few of the products made for distribution. A day's residue of molten glass gave the hardworking glass blower a chance to indulge his creative tendencies, and the canes, "witch" balls, hats in green and amber, and hollow tableware, with which the artisan amused himself and his fellows, are the chief interests of the connoisseur today.

Among the many fine glass blowers of Keene were John Clinesmith, Charles Hirsch, Nicholas Hilt, Henry Lang, and Augustus Smith. After the War of 1812, such men were exempted from military service. They might receive four dollars a day, or, in rare instances, eight to twenty-five dollars when working under high pressure.

About the middle of the century, Joseph Foster bought the Marlboro Street company, where he had been employed as a blower and revered for his extraordinary lung power, and moved the entire works to Stoddard. "Old Bottle", as he was called by his

* *New Hampshire Highways. Pamphlet published by New Hampshire State Highway Department, September 1932. p. 1.*

intimates, failed in his first attempt, but managed to secure enough capital to finance a second venture. Oxteams dragged fuel from the near by woods and transported the finished products to Keene. These articles were of the crudest glass, made of wood ashes, salt, and sand, but the workmanship was excellent. One of "Old Bottle's" books shows accounts of his various expenses:

"South Stoddard, N. H. Thursday June 11, 1848.	
One Master Shearer-board himself	1.50
One wood drier-board himself	1.67
Two Shearers of Furnace, boarded	.67
One material burner, board himself	1.00
One Mix in Maker—$15.00 a month and boarded	.80
One Bottle Packer Ovens	.80
One Empty Ovens	.80
Five Boys to Carry off Bottles	2.50
25 Bushels Ashes	9.00
3½ Bushels Salt	2.62
One Bushel Sand	.75
For—blacksmithing of tools etc.	1.00
For Blowers Work—Blowing 10 Groce Sarsaparilla	16.80"*

Luman Weeks, Almon Woods, Ebenezer A. Rice, Nicholas Hilt, and Fred A. Gilson organized the South Stoddard Glass Company in 1850. In the section of the town known as The Box, they built a glass house, a warehouse, and four tenement buildings. Two years later a store was added to the village. This enterprise prospered on the manufacture of mineral water bottles, for the spas of Saratoga Springs. But southern patronage was a major item at Saratoga, and the coming of the Civil War crippled industry at The Box. Then, too, consumers began demanding clear glass which could not be produced from the impure local materials. Fortunately, the works were taken over completely by Weeks and Gilson, Boston liquor dealers, who had decided to attempt the making of their own bottles. Under the new regime the business pros-

* *Candleday Art. Marion Nicholl Rawson. New York. E. P. Dutton and Co., 1938. p. 319. (Permission of author granted).*

NEW HAMPSHIRE GLASS

pered for a time, turning out a rare quart bottle on the base of which was this inscription, "Weeks & Gilson, So. Stoddard, N. H." Only thirteen of these are known to exist today. In 1873 the warehouse, crammed to the rafters with crates of bottles packed in hay, was abandoned; a grudge bearer or firebug ignited the treasure-filled building some years later, however, four truck loads of perfect pieces were recovered by a collector.

The last factory to be established in the town was built in 1865 by George W. Foster and his brothers, sons of "Old Bottle". George was the manager, Charles and Wallace blew glass, and Joseph made rattan and wicker casings for the demijohns. Many fine golden amber bottles were produced. There has been much controversy as to whether three-part moulds were ever used, but it has been fairly well established that they were not. In 1868 the Foster "flag" bottles had thirteen stars on one side, and "New Granite Glass Works, Stoddard, N. H." on the other. Charles B. Barrett, a liquor dealer in Boston who had long been a good customer, bought the business that year. His advertisement in the *New Hampshire Business Directory* says that he ". . . is the only manufacturer in the New England states who sells his own ware . . . demijohns, flasks, wine, soda, mineral, ale, ink, blacking, baywater, cologne, patent medicine, hair oil, and all other kinds of bottles".* This factory was burned in 1871 and was never rebuilt.

Sand for the Stoddard potworks came from Centre Pond and from pits near Munsonville and Antrim. One farm, owned by John Symonds, in the west part of the latter town, had a large body of sand and from it were carted large quantities of material to be used in the "manufacture of black glass wares".† The dark "ashglass" was made largely from ashes and ground bone. Several types of carboys were made, ranging in size from one-half pint to twelve gallons. Van Rensselaer considers these rich golden amber carboys the most beautiful ones blown in the United States. Many of the wicker covers for the demijohns were woven by a local man, a cer-

* *New Hampshire Business Directory 1868.*
† *History of the Town of Antrim, New Hampshire.* John M. Whiton, Concord, N. H., 1852. p. 85.

tain Jim Smith, who understood the work, and by some of the village women. Among them was the late Mrs. Mary Lane, the last craftworker to practice the trade in Stoddard.

There were several fine glass blowers in the town: the Cutter brothers, the Foster brothers, the McClure brothers, and Horatio Smith. Matthew Johnson ("Mighty Mat") was one of the best. He specialized in "off-hand" pieces: canes, vases, "lily-pad" pitchers, inkwells, cookie jars, glass men, tiny inverted "Uncle Sam" hats, popular as toothpick holders, and other novelties.

The glass houses of Keene and Stoddard were very closely related. But in general, the Keene glass is superior in quality to that of Stoddard. Since the same craftsmen often worked in both communities, and moulds of popular designs were frequently exchanged, it is exceedingly difficult to ascribe certain items to either place. Especially is this true of bottles which have no design or trademark and which have to be identified by color and texture. The most common bottles of the region were cornucopia flasks, those of Stoddard being identified by a cross on the bend of the flowing horn; railroad, eagle, and "flag" flasks; sunburst and Masonic bottles; and whiskey bottles, some of which have small knobs on the sides.

Even before manufacturers inscribed their products with trade names, lips were moulded on the bottles so that a tag tied to the neck could not slip off. One Keene collector has such a bottle with the original label attached; another collector, two pale green pitchers from the Marlboro Street potworks; and a third, a "Keene Green" vase with a quaint pattern worked on the inside. Some Stoddard glass is distinctive because of its quilted and sunburst patterns; many of the amber decanters and jugs extant are fine specimens; and the exceptionally rare, ten-sided, golden amber inkwells prove the skill of the Stoddard plant. Keene and Stoddard glass is to be found in the Metropolitan Museum of Art, New York City, and in the Toledo Art Museum, Toledo, Ohio.

In 1839, because of the scarcity of fuel and good sand in Lowell, Massachusetts, the Chelmsford Glass Company, originally established in 1802, moved to Suncook Village, where the Suncook River joins the Merrimack, and chose a site on what is now Glass Street in Pembroke. In July, 1840, the *New Hampshire Patriot and State Gazette* carried the following advertisement:

<blockquote>

CHELMSFORD GLASS COMPANY
(At Suncook Village, Pembroke, N. H.)

THIS Company having erected new works are now prepared to furnish those who may want, with Window glass of any size from 8 by 6 to 24 by 40; the Glass will be carefully sorted, packed and marked first quality, Chelmsford, second quality, Pembroke, third quality, Suncook. The favorable location of these works for obtaining sand of a superior quality, and other materials for manufacturing Glass will enable them to do it at reduced prices: and they are determined that the quality shall be even better than was ever made by the Chelmsford Glass Co at Chelmsford.

Pembroke will be $1 and Suncook $2, for 100 feet, less than Chelmsford: extra and double thicknesses made to order at same rates. Orders addressed to the Agent at Suncook Village, N. H. will be answered as soon as may be.

WM. PARKER, Agent.
</blockquote>

The company was only moderately successful in its best years. It was located in the heart of the timber country where fuel presented no problem, but it had been misled about the sand supply and some of this material had to be shipped from New Jersey. In August, 1851, the same newspaper which had chronicled the opening of a superior glass house announced its demise.

Some "bulls-eye" window glass is attributed to the Suncook plant. This product was made by cutting a huge globe of glass from the blowpipe, and by rotating it on a pontil until the rapidity of movement caused the globe to open into a large flat disc by centrifugal force. At the center, where the pontil had been fastened, there was a useless lump of glass, the "bulls-eye". Ordinarily, this was thrown into the pot and remelted, but occasionally one of these curious "window panes" was saved and placed in a door or window.

Suncook window-glass was of the quality commonly used in

barns, but now specimens are extremely valuable to collectors because less glass was blown here than at any other single plant in the country. New York and Boston museums and the Currier Gallery of Art in Manchester exhibit "bulls-eye" glass from this factory, and there are pieces in the private collections of Mrs. Wallace P. Hood, Danvers, Massachusetts, and of George S. Mckerin, Hoosick Falls, New York.

An "off-hand" Pembroke piece was purchased in Manchester by the New Hampshire Historical Society in 1927. This item is a hollow cane of light green, open at one end. A similar piece is displayed in the Pembroke Library Collection. Such "canes" served the blowers as flasks in which to tote their applejack.

The Currier Gallery of Art in Manchester has a few specimens of very rare Suncook glass. The largest piece is a pickle jar, blown by Robert P. Colton who came from Sutton to work in this factory. Included in the exhibit are two flip glasses—one with a wide flaring lip—a cane, a small eight or nine inch bottle, and a glass dome. The work was done in greenish glass of various thickness, causing numerous tints and shades in the color effect. The general appearance of the specimens tends to show a not too high quality in workmanship and material.

Two important firms were set up in South Lyndeborough in the late nineteenth century. The Lyndeborough Glass Company was incorporated in 1866 by five men, three of whom formed the New Hampshire Silex Company a year later. The latter factory was to make silex (quartz) into sand, glass, fire brick, and other materials. The field was a good one, and there was quartz in abundance a half mile from the mill, but the business soon failed.

In June, 1868, the main buildings of the South Lyndeborough Glass Company were destroyed by fire. They were soon rebuilt, but continued misfortunes forced the plant to close permanently in 1886. The largest and the smallest bottles were made here; there were never any glass containers blown in America larger than the fourteen-gallon capacity, nor any smaller than the one-ounce variety. The earlier products of this plant were very plain, of a bluish, aquamarine color; the later ones were of amber and different values of green. Fruit jars were a major item. The first Moxie bottles were made here (1875), also the amber and green Simons Centennial Bitters bottles. Lyndeborough glassware was sold all over New England and eastern Canada, for some of the finest quality glass ever made in the country was blown at the South Lyndeborough factory.

The summer months bring glass collectors from all parts of the country to the home of E. R. Guerin on Pembroke Street in Suncook, for his collection has included some of the best of American glass, and at one time was appraised at fifteen thousand dollars. Now it has been broken up. But the fund of fact and anecdote gathered in forty years of collecting is still the property of Mr. Guerin, one of the first men to buy Stoddard glass. He says that while visiting in the country one day, he chanced on a pitcher blown by Mat Johnson for one of the O'Neill brothers who carried Johnson's work to the annealing arches. Guerin paid twenty-five dollars for the piece and thereby gained fame. For weeks afterwards he was pointed out as the man who "paid twenty-five dollars for an old pitcher"; and people of Stoddard thought him the dupe of the century. Guerin then started on the trail of the pitcher's mate, which had been blown for the other brother. The story had reached Wilton, and when the collector located the pitcher there, the price had jumped—sixty dollars! From then on Stoddard glass became steadily rarer.

The experiences of any collector are many and varied. A man once came to Mr. Guerin to sell some real estate. Guerin didn't want any more land, but he said he would take it if the man had anything else for sale that he really wanted. Two Suncook bowls were unearthed and the transaction made. Some time later, as their value rose, the glass collector sold one of these bowls for more than he had paid for land and glass together.

William Pitt, another Suncook collector, has developed a unique hobby. Small balls of glass, chips, and many-faceted pieces have been lying around the neighborhoods of New Hampshire glass factories for years. Boys diving in to the Suncook River have brought up to the surface many a scrap of aquamarine. In the past few years, Mr. Pitt has bought these baubles from the youngsters. He displays his items by first arranging the odd shapes in an artistic pattern and then putting them together with lead, as one would a window pane, to form a window medallion of glowing beauty. One notable example of his work is a piece the center of which is composed of various shades of Sandwich glass, bordered by the pale Suncook aquamarine. The medallions are of interest for their irregular surfaces, which make the fragments of colored glass stand out boldly.

Charles E. Adams of Keene has a splendid collection of early New Hampshire pieces. His flasks include almost every pattern made locally. He has brown amber Marlboro inkwells and Stoddard hats. One lovely piece of Lyndeborough glass is an aquamarine witch ball, with milky white whorls, measuring about eight inches across. Mr. Adams has every type of article from the little pipes, hats, and witch balls to huge demijohns. Among his most cherished possessions are a pair of green six-quart jars, a three-mold pitcher, a flip glass, and a ten-quart bowl, which were blown by John Clinesmith in the Keene window glass factory.

Today, despite their great tradition of pioneer work in the craft, the glassmaking enterprises of New Hampshire are almost forgotten. There is not a manufactory operating at present in the State. Only collectors are cognizant of the fact that glass works throve in the State from late Revolutionary times until after the Reconstruction period.

The men who worked in the old glass factories blew good glass and poor glass; they introduced and developed an art which has made the names of New Hampshire localities known wherever old glass is loved and appreciated. At Lyndeborough, the finest glass was made; at Suncook, about the poorest. But all old glass is so fragile that every year it becomes scarcer; the Suncook product, poor as it was for practical use, is therefore more valuable today than is the fine ware of Lyndeborough; while the mixed earth Temple glass is now even rarer than authentic paintings by Leonardo da Vinci.

XI

WORKERS IN METAL

The smelting of iron, an early native industry in New Hampshire, often escapes the notice of those who explore the folkways. However, in pre-railroad days, ironworks or at least refinery forges for smelting the local deposits of iron ore were in operation in all of the counties of the State except Coös.

Attempts to discover "ironstone" were among the ventures of the early settlers in the Piscataqua region. In 1634 Ambrose Gibbons, agent of Captain John Mason, who directed the affairs of his New Hampshire plantations from England, sent samples across the Atlantic to his employer. The specimens were dug up in the immediate vicinity of Portsmouth, and were, according to Gibbons, "of 3 soartes, on(e) sort that the myne doth cast forth as the tree doth gum. . . ."*

This ore "cast forth" like the gum from a tree, was limonite bog iron ore which is found extensively in New England at the bottoms of ponds and in the low marshlands. An early reference to smelting ore fixes the first date as 1718, with the establishment of the Lamprey River Iron Works. The ambitious fur trader and maritime merchant, Archibald MacPhaedris of Portsmouth, was the driving force behind the enterprise. Tradition says that he rode horseback daily from Portsmouth to Newmarket to superintend the ironworks, and that many of the iron fixtures in his

* *New Hampshire Provincial and State Papers. Volume I. Edited by Nathaniel Bouton. Concord, N. H. Published by the State, 1867. p. 92.*

mansion, the brick Warner-MacPhaedris house, were made at the Lamprey River works.

Captain Henry Lovejoy of Rumford (now Concord) was another pioneer ironmaster. In 1748 the citizens of the town petitioned Governor Benning Wentworth to furnish a company of soldiers to protect the Captain's ironworks, located on a branch of the Turkey River, from Indian depredations. But the story goes that this military protection was not necessary; the rude smelter produced such a display of fire and smoke, and the triphammer gave out such awesome sounds, that the Indians fled from the region in terror.

Up until the early 1800's, New Hampshire ironmasters were concerned mainly with bog iron. It was taken from Ossipee Lake for the use of three forges. Moses Morrill of Gilmanton, where the memory of this industry is preserved in a place name, the *Iron Works Village,* got his ore supply from Lougee Pond. At Kingston, long tongs were used by the local men for fishing bog ore from the bottom of Great Pond. Ore dug from the swamps of old No. 4 (Charlestown) on the Connecticut River was carted by ox teams to the ironworks of Benjamin Tyler at Claremont. The Cram brothers at Lyndeborough shared their supply of meadow ore with the operators of a refinery forge at Temple. Daniel Ladd of Deerfield, who grubbed sulphur-laden ore from a pocket at the base of Saddleback Mountain, never made iron that was really satisfactory, although he did the best he could. Both Colonel John Goffe and James Martin, at Bedford, secured the bog ore for their forges from the sedgy banks of Crosby's Brook, which empties into the Merrimack River about two miles south of the Piscataquog. The ore must have been abundant, for in 1775 James Martin offered to supply the Continental Army with any amount of cannon shot that might be needed.

It is probable that the little bog ore furnaces produced only bars or billets of wrought iron, to be hammered out later by local craftsmen into useful implements, and that it was not until 1795 that a plant capable of refining iron ore into cast iron began working

ROSCOE GRANT, *a Dover blacksmith.*

WALTER ROGERS *working with copper.*

WORKERS IN METAL

in New Hampshire. A group of men from Rhode Island started up the smelter at Winchester. They produced the first cast-iron kettles, pots, and fireplace utensils ever made in the State.

New Hampshire's largest and best-known commercial venture in the field of ironworking was at Franconia. The deposits of ore in Iron Mountain, just over the Lisbon town line, at one time were regarded as the richest in the United States, and in 1805 the New Hampshire Iron Factory Company was incorporated to exploit them. The wealth taken from the mountains made other promoters desire a share, and in 1808 the Haverhill and Franconia Iron Works Company was formed. The newcomers built a smelter just north of the New Hampshire Company's works, but it was not nearly as large. In 1827 the plant of the Haverhill and Franconia Works was destroyed by fire, and was not rebuilt. The older company, on the other hand, continued to prosper, and for over half a century successfully produced hollow ware of various kinds, and also the famous "Franconia Stoves". But eventually, with the changing times, the ironmasters of New Hampshire were forced to sell their lands to meet pressing obligations, and around 1865 the fires in the smelters and forges went out. The only marker at the place where once a busy community carried on a profitable, if noisy, industry is a part of the former furnace, the picturesque "Old Stone Stack" on Gale River.

Although iron was produced at many local furnaces, besides those at Franconia, examples of the work of the early ironmasters are difficult to find. Most of the tools and utensils produced were picked up very cheaply by a type of collector who had no appreciation of the antiquarian value of his accumulations. He was the junk dealer of the latter part of the last century, whose only interest was the scrap-metal value of old iron. Almost any man who was a country boy in the 1890's can remember rummaging through barn, shed, and attic in search of odd bits of discarded iron to sell to the junk man; thus, hinges, door latches, pots, skillets, and all other sorts of ironmongery, which today are treated as venerable antiques, were hastened off to the scrap heap.

"Native" iron came into use much later than bog iron. Early settlers, such as the proprietors at Hampton, brought bars of iron with them to their plantations as part of their equipment; but they lacked a skillful hand to fashion the iron for use. In 1639 William Fuller was voted full planter's privileges, with the liberty to "sit down here" as a smith.* This was not in the least unusual, for the people of the newly settled plantations had to offer tangible inducements in order to secure a blacksmith. Nearly a century later, the grantees of Penacook on the Merrimack River were eager to bargain with a man who could "up wi' the hammer". They voted, in 1730, to give Cutting Noyes fifty acres of land if he would agree to "hammer iron" for at least ten years. At Lancaster, the settlers gave David Page two hundred acres of land "as a reward for bringing a set of blacksmith's tools and maintaining a shop in town".† At Keene, the town fathers made no offer of land, but they did vote to procure an anvil, a bellows, a vise, a hammer, and tongs, for the use of a blacksmith.

The trite phrase, "a man of parts", aptly describes the old-time village blacksmith. From his forge came every type of iron utensil needed in the ordinary routine of home and farm life. The fitting of horseshoes, really the work of a farrier, was but a part of his labors. There were tires to be forged and fitted to wagon wheels; iron edges must be made with which hardwood shovels were "shod"; chains of many kinds, welded; hoe blades and pitchfolk tines, hammered out; and fireplace outfittings and a hundred and one useful household gadgets, pounded into shape. Lieutenant Josiah Underhill, a noted smith and toolmaker of Chester, once made a *turnkey*, "an instrument to haul teeth".‡ Also, like all early anvil artists, he fashioned *loggerheads,* ornamented iron rods, which, when heated red hot, were plunged into mugs of flip to

* *History of the Town of Hampton, New Hampshire. (1638-1892.) Volume I. Joseph Dow. Salem, Mass., 1893. p. 17.*
† *History of Lancaster, New Hampshire. A. N. Somers. Concord, N. H. Rumford Press, 1899. p. 98.*
‡ *History of Old Chester—1719 to 1869. Benjamin Chase. Auburn, N. H., 1869. Published by the Author. p. 442.*

warm the liquor and make it foam. All of the iron gear of the famous Concord Coaches was made by blacksmiths. In fact, all of the builder's hardware used by the carpenter, such as hinges and door latches, carpenters' tools, and the nails which he drove, were fashioned on the anvil.

In the days when they were hammered out one by one, handmade nails were never thrown away but were always straightened out for further use. And in one instance, at Exeter, nine hundred and one of them were actually counted for the inventory of the estate of a deceased person. After the Revolutionary War, the State of New Hampshire offered bounties for nailmaking. Three pounds sterling was given for one hundred thousand four-and-a-half-penny nails, and greater amounts for larger nails. The bounty was paid not for nails by weight, but by number. Many farmers as well as blacksmiths increased the family income by hammering out wrought iron nails on rainy days, or at other times when outside work was impracticable.

No artisan in a community of hardworking people performed more strenuous labor than did the blacksmith. He needed prodigious strength and great endurance to cope with the heavy tasks which fell to him. In one year alone, Elder Nathan Jones, Canaan's blacksmith from 1855 to 1880, made with his own hands six hundred and ten hammers, and this was only a small part of his annual output of iron products.

Blacksmithing was, without question, a man's work, but at least one New Hampshire woman is said to have "faced the anvil". Lydia Stevens of Weare, daughter of the town smith, was a "very skillful artisan" who forged the "handsomest door handle of any one in town".*

The blacksmith and his forge are fast disappearing from New Hampshire. According to Cornelius Weygandt, author and summer resident of Sandwich, only one anvil was ringing in 1934 in the town where thirteen formerly sounded.

* *The History of Weare, New Hampshire, 1735-1838. William Little. Lowell, Mass. Published by the Town of Weare, 1888. p. 544.*

Among the few blacksmiths working in New Hampshire at the present time are two, at least, who are adapting their skill to the reproduction of old door hinges, latches, pokers, andirons, sconces, and other iron articles in domestic use, and to the creation of iron ware for what might be termed a "luxury trade".

When the shoeing of his neighbors' horses ceased to be profitable, Elmer Spencer of Orford mechanized his blacksmith stand. He mounted his forge on a truck and fitted up a traveling blacksmith's shop. Thus equipped, he carried to distant farms the latest fashions in fancy iron hoof-ware for horses. Besides his itinerant farrier's work, Mr. Spencer makes faithful reproductions of Colonial hardware. He reproduced the door latches, fireplace irons, and other pieces for "The Old Settler's House" in Orfordville, to match specimens which the owner furnished for patterns. Mr. Spencer hopes to develop this artistic feature of the blacksmith's craft to a point where he can discontinue his traveling forge.

Converse Purington Trufant, of the little Monadnock village of Francestown, is probably one of the most widely known blacksmiths in the United States. His renown brought him an invitation to attend the New York World's Fair in 1939 to demonstrate his anvil technique. There, his anvil and forge in the workshop of Electrified Farm became a center of great attraction.

Mr. Trufant was apprenticed to his trade when he was fourteen years old. Since 1908 he has had a shop in Francestown. He says that his wife has been of great assistance to him in developing the line of ornamental ironwork which has established his reputation as a craftsman. Mrs. Trufant assists with the designing and frequently draws plans to scale from pictures which she finds in books and magazines.

People who are restoring old houses often bring broken hinges, a foot scraper, or a simple andiron to the Francestown blacksmith to be duplicated or repaired. A common saying in the town is, "Take that to Con Trufant, and he'll make you one to match so good you'll never know the difference."

Not all ornamental ironwork, however, comes from the hand

of the village blacksmith. A notable example of a New Hampshire craftsman who has taken up the work is Sylvester Rinta, a native of Finland, who is responsible for the artistic masonry which adds to the charm of the campus of the University of New Hampshire. He has a shop near his home in Newmarket, where he makes andirons, hunting knives with handles of bone, hard rubber, or granite, toasting forks, pipe cleaners, pipe lighters, and other novelties of iron. The pipe cleaner and lighter, an old Finnish hearth implement, is a long slender tong, made of hand-hammered steel. In describing it, Mr. Rinta says: "With it, all you need to do when your pipe goes out is to reach into the fireplace, snip up a live coal, and relight your pipe. Then flip the coal back into the hearth, tamp the tobacco a little with the lighter, and sit back and enjoy your smoke."

Town histories contain the names of many ironworkers, but practically no names of early New Hampshire pewterers have been recorded. One exception to this general statement is found in the *History of Old Chester,* which says, "Robert Leathhead, who lived where Matthew Dickey lately lived, used to *itinerate* with ladle and spoon-mould to *run* pewter spoons".*

*   *   *   *   *

The story of early silvercraft in America centers around the towns along the Atlantic seaboard; workers in gold and silver gathered in these centers in numbers proportionate to the prosperity resulting from maritime trade. Portsmouth was an important and wealthy shipping point, but in the art of silvermaking it was nearly a century behind Boston, which was only a few years its senior in time of settlement. As far as proven records go, except for a possible brief interval, there was not a single silversmith working in the Piscataqua region in the seventeenth century; and the first third of the eighteenth century had passed before the accomplished William Whittemore turned out his first piece of ecclesiastical

---

* *History of Old Chester. Benjamin Chase. Auburn, N. H. Published by the Author, 1869. pp. 413-414.*

silver. After that time, as the files of the historic *New Hampshire Gazette,* founded in 1756, show, many silversmiths, goldsmiths, and jewelers plied their craft constantly, to supply treasures for wealthy merchants and ship owners.

These merchants had very little security for the surplus money they acquired through the shipping industry. If stolen, there was no way of identifying the coins which bore the stamps of many nations. Moreover, there was no standard of monetary value set, and paper currency was equally unstable. Therefore, it was a very common procedure for a prosperous man to take his surplus money to a silversmith to be made into spoons, porringers, and tankards, which were carefully marked to identify the pieces in case of theft.

The first New Hampshire silversmith of which there is any record was Robert Sanderson, a highly trained English "goldsmith". In 1638, at the age of thirty, he took up eighty acres in the town of Hampton and lived there for four years. Then he went to Boston, where he became associated with his friend, John Hull, silversmith and master of the mint which was established by the General Court in Boston, 1652. There are no proofs that Sanderson ever worked at his trade in Hampton. The only evidence of his New Hampshire sojourn is found in the neglected grave of his wife, Lydia; in the tradition that his daughter, Mary, was the first white child born in Hampton; and in the positive record that he owned property on the plantation.

William Whittemore, nephew of Sir William Pepperell, conqueror of Louisburg, was the earliest local silver craftsman to leave a signature on the pieces he made. He is famous for his ecclesiastical silver. Whittemore was only twenty-three years old when he finished three fine and graceful communion cups, dated 1733, for the First Congregational Church of Kittery, Maine. Three years later he made a tall chalice of exquisite proportions and form, which is still in St. John's Church in Portsmouth; and in 1740, a beaker for the Newington church. A few years ago the beaker was purchased by a collector, and its present location is unknown. Whittemore was generally supposed to have died in 1770, but it

WORKERS IN METAL 139

has been definitely proven that he was living with his mother in Kittery in 1775, to which town he had returned after working for years in Portsmouth.*

Besides Whittemore, William Cario, David Griffith, Benjamin and Samuel Drowne, and Martin Parry were engaged in silverwork in Portsmouth, living as close neighbors on Queen Street.

For some years a question has come up among silver collectors as to the exact location at which the distinguished Cario worked at his trade. Tradition has assigned him at various times to New York, to Philadelphia, and to Boston, instead of to Portsmouth where recent research has placed him. The confusion is explained by the fact that there were two William Carios, probably father and son. The elder Cario doubtlessly was the goldsmith of that name who was in New York in 1721, and who advertised in 1738 in the *Boston Gazette*. A small obituary notice in a *New Hampshire Gazette* of 1809 throws considerable light on the situation. The inconspicuous lines state: "Died: At Newmarket on the 20 of July, very suddenly, Mr. Wm. Carrio, formerly of Portsmouth, age 75, leaving a wife and one child".† This was the death notice of the younger man. The documents of the administration of his estate, found in the probate records at Exeter, give an inventory including both tools and considerable material, and indicate that he was actively engaged in his vocation until the last of his life.

The younger Cario was married twice. Abigail Peavey, whom he married in Boston in 1759,‡ died eight years later and was buried in the Point of Graves in Portsmouth. An inscription on her gravestone identifies her as Cario's wife. Seven months later, the silversmith married Lydia Croxford of Portsmouth.§ Since Cario signed the Theatrical Protest in Portsmouth in 1773 and the Association Test in Newmarket in 1776, he evidently changed location in the interim.

* *American Collector. Volume V (November 1936). "Early Church Silver of Kittery, Maine." Stephen Decatur. p. 3.*
† *New Hampshire Gazette. Portsmouth, N. H. August 1, 1809.*
‡ *30th Report of Commissioners—Boston Marriages. Document 101. p. 32.*
§ *Records of South Church, Portsmouth, N. H. Rev. Alfred Gooding. pp. 32 +384.*

Few examples of the famous craftsman's work are found in New Hampshire today. In the collection of the New Hampshire Historical Society at Concord is the Joseph Judkins communion cup, made in 1770 for the church at Newfields. The famous "Atkinson Waiter" with its mortuary list of forty-eight names and death dates, falling between 1740 and 1771, is in the same collection. The list was engraved and signed by "W. Cario, Sculp." The waiter may have been made out of the silver funeral mementoes which it was the fashion to give to close friends and relatives in the eighteenth century.

The Sign of The Goldsmith Arms, in the heart of the old silver colony on Portsmouth's Queen Street,* was a thriving center of a silvermaking industry, which was already established and required apprentices in 1757. David Griffith, the proprietor, was a silversmith of evident skill and, from his advertisements, used a great deal of silver. He was a contemporary of William Cario, but died much earlier. He was taken prisoner in the ill-fated expedition against Quebec, the last day of December, 1775, and was not heard of again.

There were three other members of the Griffith family who were in the goldsmithing business: Samuel (1729-73), like David, a general merchant, and two Nathaniels, one of whom was David's brother. Both of these latter men were manufacturing jewelers and important watchmakers. There is no silverware of the three last-named Griffiths extant; that they actually made it is established by their own words and by obituaries and inventories designating them as active silversmiths and goldsmiths.

Samuel Drowne and Timothy Gerrish were identical contemporaries, both of them coming into the work in 1749 and leaving it in 1815. Their careers were so parallel, their silver so alike, their political sympathies and achievements so similar, that where research encounters one, it may expect to find the other. Timothy was deputy sheriff and gaolkeeper during the last fifteen years of his life, to counterbalance Samuel's term in the Legislature.

* *Queen Street was later called Buck Street and is now lower State Street.*

Through all their civic activities, they continued to make silver, until the advent of the "fiddlehead" handles for spoons, and the general decline in demand for genuine craft skill.

Captain Martin Parry (1759-1802) succumbed to the call of maritime trading and turned over his shop to his young brother-in-law and apprentice about 1795. He became wealthy as a merchant and ship owner, but, according to the *New Hampshire Gazette,* his death from yellow fever cut short his career "in his forty-fourth year".* Evidently, his talents lay in trading rather than in silvermaking, for the style of his spoons is archaic for the period in which he worked, and, though well made, they show no special genius. Only their scarcity makes them prized.

Benjamin Drowne, brother of Samuel, and born the same year as Parry, died at the age of thirty-four. He was a very distinguished citizen of Portsmouth, and married into the prominent Gardner family of Revolutionary loyalties.

There was a second group of silversmiths, who might be called the "second flight" of craftsmen. They were inheritors of the fame and skill of the older men, who very likely had trained all of them, although Stephen Hardy finished his training with Paul Revere after previous apprenticeship with William Simes.

In this group were Joseph Clark, William Simes, Stephen Hardy, John Abbot, Daniel P. Drowne, and Thomas Pickering Drown, who never used the final *e* in his name. Abbot, who usually signed one *t,* must not be confused with John W. Abbott, who always used two.

Joseph Clark (1774-1838) never succumbed to the "new style fiddlehead". He made only spoons, and though a much younger man than any of the "old guard", he adhered to their technique and to the 1780-1800 spoon type, until he sold out to T. P. Drown in 1811.

William Simes (1773-1824) was also a specialist in spoon-making. Indeed, his fastidious manipulation of form gave his spoons a subtle distinction. He yielded to prevalent style so far as to make

* *New Hampshire Gazette. Portsmouth, N. H. August 3, 1802.*

flatware in the 1805 manner; even to that he lent distinction. His odd pieces—tongs, mustard spoons, and ladles—are all different in design and of superior quality.

Of the two sons of Samuel Drowne; Daniel, the younger (1784-1863), opened a silversmith shop in 1806, and seems to have advertised for but three years; he then followed other occupations.

Again, two silversmiths seem to parallel each other in this second generation. Thomas P. Drown (1782-1849) and Stephen Hardy (1781-1843) were persistent advertisers and often in the same paper. Both carried large mercantile stocks in addition to that of jewelry and silver, and both had several apprentices.

Thomas P. Drown, so far as is known, was trained by his father, whose business he took over in 1804, a few months after Stephen Hardy had returned from Boston, where, working with Paul Revere, he had perfected himself in the making of hollow ware. There are extant a greater number of pieces exhibiting highly skilled technique that are attributed to Hardy than to any other New Hampshire silversmith. Members of the Hardy family esteemed them very much and have passed them down as heirlooms to the present day.

The Historical Society of Portsmouth holds, as a loan, some fine examples of T. P. Drown silver which has come down to a great-great-granddaughter. It is strongly reminiscent of Samuel Drowne's work.

Near the close of the War of 1812, T. P. Drown went into banking, and Stephen Hardy became a commission merchant. With the passing of these men from the craft, New Hampshire silver-making declined rapidly. Inartistic, mediocre handmade silver became popular—it was the era of the fiddlehead spoon. From then on, Portsmouth silversmiths became simply spoonsmiths.

An exception may have been Robert Gray (working 1813-1851), greatest of the last of the silverworkers using hand technique. Young Gray came from Salem, Massachusetts, to Portsmouth immediately after completion of his apprenticeship in 1813, and set up on the corner of Market Square where Daniel(s) Street opens into it. He sold out to John Abbot in 1817 and moved down the Square to No. 9, opposite the old State House; a few years later he located at No. 7, where he conducted the largest store in town.

Since this craftsman's death in 1851, the original Gray corner has been continuously occupied by jewelers, a record of one hundred and twenty-seven years of constant endeavor in the craft of silver and gold. Succeeding Robert Gray were John Abbot, Jr., John W. Abbott (who took over the site in 1819), John H. Clark, and Ira Haselton, all engaged in making fiddlehead spoons, which lie about the town as thick as leaves.

Much is known about John Davenport (1753-1842) as a man, a great patriot, a distinguished townsman, a pious churchman, and the very genial host of Noah's Ark Tavern; but little is known about him as a silversmith. There are records of his fine cellar; but of his fine silver, nothing is known except the fact that he was famous for his shoe buckles.

This is true, also, of several other silversmiths; no pieces of their work are in existence to bear out the claim that they were major craftsmen. There were the very prominent Nelsons, John (working 1759-1774) and Mark (1734-1787); Clement Jackson, Jr., who told his public in 1762 that he could make any kind of hollow ware; Stephen Morse, who assured his customers in 1771 that he would "use them with fidelity and dispatch"; Samuel Place, who came from London prepared to do fine goldsmithing and who brought with him a "small assortment of watch furniture"; and the two Ponds, a generation apart, makers of fine jewelry and watches. It is a surprise to find that Andrew Gerrish (1784-1835), son of Timothy, who advertised consistently as a brass founder, is called *silversmith* in the Probate Order making him administrator of his father's estate.

Out of the level of mediocrity into which silvermaking had fallen by 1860, there appeared another outstanding craftsman. For some reason not known to us today, William B. Durgin, born on a Campton, New Hampshire farm in 1833, selected Concord as a place to start his work with silver. The young silversmith had served an apprenticeship with Newell Harding of Boston, and was excellently prepared to carry on the work when he opened his shop near the Free Bridge Road in 1853. Humphrey Nichols, Ivory Hall, L. R. Henderson, and Seth Eastman had been making spoons in Concord at intervals before Mr. Durgin settled there. The last named craftsman once advertised for two thousand five-franc pieces, old crowns, and silver dollars, for which he offered to pay the highest prices.*

When Durgin came to town, at least one silversmith was well established, besides a retail jeweler who called himself a silversmith. According to Captain John B. Abbott of Concord, young Durgin purchased the tools of these two competitors; by so doing he bought out their businesses, and thus had a clear field for himself. Mr. Abbott also says that the silversmith contacted his customers in their own homes, taking his pay, whenever possible, in old silver. When he returned to his shop from one of his sales expeditions, he would strip off his coat, lay aside his tall beaver hat, and begin at once to make new stock. He took in a number of apprentices and gradually built up an important and nationally known business, in which he was engaged personally until his death in 1905.

In the meantime, a company had been formed with Mr. Durgin as president. After his death, this company was reorganized several times; today the Concord Silversmiths, Inc., under the direction of John D. Murphy, are producing seven distinct flatware patterns in the Durgin factory. Fifty-three of the men who were formerly with W. B. Durgin Company are now employed here. Among them is Frank A. Leavitt of Concord, who learned his craft under the personal supervision of Mr. Durgin, who thought very highly of him. The late James Harriott, one of the most distinguished engravers and all-round silver craftsmen in the country, was employed there for forty-eight years and taught his art to many apprentices.

On one of his annual trips to England to visit experienced crafts-

* *New Hampshire Patriot and State Gazette. Concord, N. H. Monday, September 30, 1839. p. 2.*

men, Mr. Durgin met the late Rowland Rhodes at the British Museum. He persuaded Mr. Rhodes, then only twenty years of age, to return to Concord with him, where the young man became one of the company's foremost designers. Rhodes made a number of outstanding contributions to the craft of silvermaking, but his best known design was the Davis Cup, the world's most coveted tennis prize, which was made by the Durgin Company. Every tennis champion in the world has played for it; it was last awarded to an Australian team, late in 1939. The cup was spun by the late William Rowan who was descended from a family of English silversmiths.

Another English craftsman working for Durgin was the late Frederick W. Greene, who was very expert in the art of engraving silver. Charles F. Simms is an exception to this practice in the Durgin Company of employing English talent; he is American-born and was trained in the Rhode Island School of Design. His practical experience was gained by work in well-known silver companies. While employed by the Durgin Company, Mr. Simms designed all the hollow ware and many fine patterns for flatware. His most popular achievements, however, were the various trophies which the company has made; he designed all of them except the Davis Cup.

The famous silver service of seventy-one pieces which the citizens of the State gave to the United States Battleship *New Hampshire* in 1908 was designed by the late Fred R. Roberts and Burton P. Jenks; the latter was the designer of the "Fairfax", the largest selling flatware pattern ever produced in the country. When the battleship was scrapped with others, to carry out the terms of the Versailles Treaty, the superb silver service, though still owned by the United States Navy, was taken to Concord for display in the collections of the New Hampshire Historical Society.

Andrew Nicoll of Bow, one of the most versatile New Hampshire craftsmen working with metal today, started his career as an apprentice in the Durgin Company. He remained in Concord for about five years and then went to Gardner, Massachusetts, where he was associated with David Carlson in producing hand-wrought spoons and hollow ware. Mr. Nicoll has not restricted himself to silver. He is equally proficient with pewter; while at David Carlson's he worked with it extensively, duplicating the work of Paul Revere in the way he finished his pieces. Mr. Nicoll later returned to Concord to work in the plant where he had served his apprenticeship. From 1927 to 1936 he was an instructor in metalwork at the Manchester Institute of Arts and Sciences. He was the first instructor of his craft in the League of New Hampshire Arts and Crafts, and still continues in this position.

For twenty-five years Wayne Griffin of Manchester made a hobby of metalworking; now his hobby is a full-time vocation. He works in a shop in one of the old Stark Mills, Manchester, where he produces beautiful articles made of copper, pewter, and silver. Lately, he has added aluminum to his list of materials.

Although Mr. Griffin has done some jewelry work in silver and copper, he prefers to work on larger articles. He teaches his craft in private classes, and for the past two years has been an instructor in metalwork for the League of New Hampshire Arts and Crafts.

In perfecting his craft, Mr. Griffin has had instruction from some of the most competent and distinguished American artists and craftsmen in his field. He believes that silverworkers owe much to the late George E. Germer of Mason, New Hampshire. Germer absorbed the traditions of his trade from his father, a noted jeweler of Berlin, Germany, and then was apprenticed to the famous Otto Geriche, from whom he learned chasing and modeling. In 1893 Germer came to America and worked at his craft in New York, Providence, and Boston. After 1912 he worked independently, devoting himself to the making of ecclesiastical silver from his own designs and those of prominent church architects. His designs for silver panels, altar crosses, chalices, and offertory plates were based on the traditions of both the Catholic and the Protestant churches. In 1917 the artist bought an old farm in Mason; in his workshop in the old farmhouse, he turned out each year one or two pieces of silverware.

Silversmithing is more than an exacting craft, it is also one of the greatest arts in the world. Collectors eagerly seek examples of the pieces produced by early American craftsmen. It is regrettable that so few early silver pieces remain in New Hampshire, and that many are not more accessible. Unless some person, or organization, takes up the collecting of early New Hampshire silver, as was done in the State of Maryland by Mrs. Miles White, the "tender grace of a day that is dead" will never come back to us.

XII

SPINNING WHEEL AND HAND LOOM

The picture of a spinner at her wheel has come to symbolize a Colonial woman at work. But spinning and weaving became home crafts in New Hampshire about twenty years after the first settlement was made, when the General Court of Massachusetts Bay Colony first ordered the manufacture of woolens and linens, in 1640. At that time New Hampshire was under the jurisdiction of the Bay Colony; so the magistrates' orders to investigate the number of spinning wheels, the operators available, and the number of young people who could be taught the craft, were applicable both to the people of the Piscataqua settlements as they were to their neighbors to the south. By 1703 spinning and weaving had developed into important home industries in the frontier towns. From that time on, the sad moan of the great wheel, the whirr of the little wheel, and the click of the clock reel were familiar sounds, which ceased only after the establishment of New Hampshire's cotton and woolen mills in the mid-nineteenth century.

Hand spinning continued to be carried on in the northern rural districts much later than in southern New Hampshire. Today there are people living in the hills and mountains who remember their grandmothers walking back and forth before their wool wheels. One of them, Mrs. Joseph Sherburn of Franconia, knows how to spin, and brings her old spinning wheel down from the attic to prepare yarn for Christmas mittens.

LOOM *designed by the League of New Hampshire Arts and Crafts, and* CLOCK REEL *in the collections of the Manchester Historic Association.*

THE WEAVER, Mary Jones Smith of Epsom at her flax wheel.

SPINNING WHEEL AND HAND LOOM

There are few spinners like Mrs. Sherburn in the State, though recently there has been a movement among craftsmen to revive the old art. Also, New Hampshire numbers among its residents women who were brought up in sections of Europe where textile crafts are practised extensively. One of these, Mrs. Anna L. Ploof of Nashua, New Hampshire, came from Norway, where, in her childhood days, practically every girl was taught to weave and to spin. Mrs. Ploof says the Norwegian girls of her former home followed an ancient tradition in their spinning at Christmas time. They put their wheels away for a twenty days' holiday; when they brought them out again after Christmas the first young man to pass a girl's wheel was recognized as her sweetheart for the following year. Mrs. Ploof, who is an expert craftworker in many lines, recently purchased an old New Hampshire wheel and has returned to the art of spinning for her own amusement.

For years sheep raising was an important part of New Hampshire agricultural life, and practically every farmer had his own flock to supply wool for the family needs, and later to meet commercial demands. But during the eighteen years prior to 1900, the local business of sheep husbandry decreased from one thousand sheep per each New Hampshire town to an average of less than two hundred and fifty. Sheep, however, continue to graze on certain New Hampshire hillsides, as they do in Randolph at Broad Acres Farm which has never been without a flock to supply wool for the Wood family's blankets.

All through the nineteenth century shearing the home flock was as important an annual event in rural New Hampshire as haying or husking. Sheepshearing called for skilled workers who knew exactly how to use the large, sharp shears to the best advantage. In May, when the sheep were to be shorn of their thick winter coats, experienced shearers went from farm to farm to exchange work with their neighbors, or to earn a little hard money. These men were very handy at their work. According to Reverend John Hayley of Tuftonboro, who was very familiar with the work, "An expert shearer would peel off the fleece from a sheep almost as easily and quickly as one would peel an onion."*

After the laborious work of shearing came the very tedious process of preparing the fleeces for home use and for market. When these fleeces were opened to remove tarred locks, every cutting of the precious wool was saved. The wool was carded before it went to the spinner, and this task usually was given to the young people or to men and women too old for hard manual labor. Sometimes in rush seasons everybody in the family had to take part in the carding. It is said that Dr. Samuel Wood of Boscawen, a noted clergyman and tutor who prepared young men for Dartmouth College, constantly used the cards as he studied his Sunday's sermon. The Chester people often held carding bees, or wool breakings as they were called, when all the people in the community got together to help one another with the work.

Before the wool was carded, melted hog's fat was worked into the fibre, in the proportion of three pounds of grease to ten pounds of wool. The cards, used in pairs, had long wire teeth set in foundations, or "cards" made of wood. In manipulating them, the worker, holding one card with her left hand on her knee, drew a tuft of wool across the comb with her right hand, until a mass of fibres was caught upon the wire teeth. Then she drew another warmed wool card across the first one, working it until the strands of wool became parallel to each other.

Using wool combs (shaped like the letter "T", with long steel teeth ten to eighteen inches long set in at right angles) required more skill than did carding and was accomplished by the expert manipulation of the two combs.

When the wool finally reached the hands of the spinner, it was spun on a big wool wheel. To operate the wheel, the worker leaned slightly forward with her weight on her left foot, and, picking up a roll of carded wool, wound the end of it on the point of the spindle. A wooden peg, held in her right hand, started the wheel rotating.

* *History of Tuftonboro, New Hampshire.* Rev. John W. Hayley. Concord, N. H. Rumford Press, 1923. p. 19.

SPINNING WHEEL AND HAND LOOM

The roll of wool had to be held at a correct distance from the spindle to permit it to be "drawn" out. As the wheel hummed, the spinner stepped back and forth, holding the yarn as it twisted and quivered and wound on the spindle; then, taking another pinch of wool roll, she gave the wheel a new turn and started the process over again.

A clock reel or triple wheel was used to wind the yarn. Forty threads made a knot; and seven of these knots made a skein. In measuring linen, however, twenty knots made a skein. The woolen yarn was spun twice when a hard-twisted thread was desired, but one spinning was enough for knitting material. If the operator were adept at the work, it took her about six hours to walk far enough to spin the average stint of five skeins a day. She lightened her work frequently by singing to the accompaniment of the moaning wheel. One New Hampshire woman still remembers a great-aunt who walked back and forth at her spinning, humming one line over and over again: "Tumpty-tumpty, let's be walking; tumpty-tumpty, let's be walking."

Girls were taught to spin as soon as they were old enough to stand at the wheel. But in large families, even with maiden aunts and grown-up daughters to lighten the burden, extra workers were often hired in to prepare enough thread and yarn for weaving and knitting. Female labor was very cheap in the first half of the nineteenth century; and in Barnstead, girls who went out to spin usually received three shillings and board a week, if they produced a regulation day's work of five skeins.

The little wheel upon which flax was spun differed in many ways from the great wool wheel. The driving wheel of the former was about twenty inches in diameter as compared to the fifty inches of the larger one. No treadle motion was used in the large spinning wheel; it was rotated by hand, with motion transmitted by a band attached to a small countershaft at the opposite end of the machine and then to the real spindle. The flax wheel, on the other hand, had a wheel hung on an iron crank, and was operated by the spinner's foot placed on the treadle as she sat before it.

The flax wheel came from Ireland to America with the Scotch-Irish immigrants, who brought with them their skilled knowledge of flax raising and the manufacture of linen. Because of famine, taxes, warfare, and religious persecution, these Scotch Presbyterians found living conditions very hard in Ulster. In America they settled in Pennsylvania, in the mountain districts of the south, and in New Hampshire, where about 1719 they established a community, which they called Londonderry after their old home in Ireland. New life came to the linen industry in America from these Londonderry people, for their knowledge of the craft was unexcelled and their linens were of such superior quality that they were in great demand. From Londonderry the original settlers and their descendants spread out to surrounding towns, such as Chester, Bedford, Antrim, and Peterborough, where they began at once to raise flax, produce their wares, and sell them.

New Hampshire people quickly adopted the Scotch-Irish linen wheel and the Irish methods of flax raising. Soon patches of blue-eyed flax grew on every New Hampshire farm. Preparing the flax for the spinner was a long process of nearly a year's duration. Harvesting usually took place in June, when the flax was pulled and allowed to dry in the sun for a day or two. The next step in the work was "rippling", when the seed-bolls were broken from the stalks by means of a large wire comb. The succeeding process, "retting", softened the woody part of the plant, and the flax either was spread out to rot in the dew and sun, or was lowered into running water and left to soak for four or five days.

After the fibres had turned dark and had become very pliable, the material was removed from the water and stored away to dry all winter. About the first of March, "at the end of sledding", the flax was taken out and made ready for "breaking"—the first step in its final preparation—which cracked the woody part of the plant into small pieces. The flax break was a strange looking implement, set upon legs, with hardwood slats, and sharp upper edges inserted edgewise. Benjamin Chase, historian of the town of Chester, who was familiar with this work, says: "To match this were another set of slats, one end inserted in a block called a 'head', and the other in a wooden roller hung to the back part of the body of the break. The operation of breaking was to raise the top slats with the right hand, by means of a pin or handle in the head, and with the left hand put the flax into the break, and it was operated until the woody part of the flax was broken fine, and most of it fallen on the floor."*

Next the flax was "swingled", by a heavy wooden knife on a block, to separate the finer "shives" and the coarser tow. On a good dry day, a man could swingle forty pounds of the material. The clean fibres, or "strikes", were swingled again, and then were combed, or "hatcheled", by pulling the fibre through a wire comb until the short or imperfect strands were drawn out. The fineness of the linen thread depended upon the number of hatchelings, the fineness of the combs, and the dexterity of the worker.

Spinning flax differed in many ways from spinning wool. The operator, sitting in front of her wheel, moistened her fingers in a gourd shell of water, and with her left hand drew off a heavy strand of the linen fibre which was wound around the distaff. Her foot moved the treadle which rotated the small wheel and flyer attached to the bobbin, and her right hand fed the strand to the eyelet of the flyer and down one arm of the flyer to the bobbin within. This rotation twisted the thread into a strand which the spinner skillfully drew out to a fine texture. It required much practice to twist the threads to a uniform size.

Sometimes neighbors got together and made flax-spinning a community event. In Henniker, for instance, the women put their wheels and their babies on the family horses and cantered away to have a "dish of gossip" with their friends while they were spinning, and frequently they held bees to help neighbors with their work. When Ephraim Goss married Ruth Campbell, the wives of her brothers, David, John, and Phineas, and four neighbors set a day to take their wheels to the bride's house to help her get a start with her spinning. They laughed and gossiped, but they did a tremendous

* *History of Old Chester.* Benjamin Chase. Auburn, N. H. *Published by the Author, 1869. p. 420.*

amount of work in spite of the fun. Skein after skein was finished; and when they were counted at the end of the day, it was found that the three Campbell women had spun eleven double skeins of linen thread and were the champions.

Weaving linens and woolen fabrics for clothing and household outfittings was a continuous and a continuing process, and the sound of the batten was heard from daylight till dusk in practically every New Hampshire home. Five or six yards of weaving was considered a good day's work for a weaver, but Mrs. Moses Rowell of Andover once broke the record by producing fifteen yards of flannel between dawn and bedtime. New Hampshire's champion weaver was Polly Locke, whose name as an expert craftswoman comes to light in the records of a number of towns. She was living in New Ipswich when her sixteen-year-old brother, John, was suddenly called to service in the Revolutionary War. He had no suitable pantaloons in which to set out on the expedition, and his mother knew no way by which he could get a pair. But his younger sister was determined that John should leave for war in fitting attire. The story goes that she cut fleeces from a white sheep and a black sheep, cleansed and carded the wool, spun the yarn, and washed and dried it. Then, since the family loom was full with a partly completed web of linen, she wove the cloth on a loom owned by a neighbor. When the web was completed, she cut and made the trousers. Forty hours after she began to shear the sheep, she had her brother decked in his new outfit, all ready to join the Continental Army.

As she grew more experienced in weaving, Polly became famous for the variety of her weaving patterns, and for the beautiful colorings of the coverlets which came from her loom. Coverlets were used as bedspreads as late as the mid-nineteenth century. Some of them were made by professional weavers, but many were of home manufacture. At the Agricultural Fair held in Concord, coverlets "direct from the looms and hands" of the farmers' wives were exhibited, and received considerable publicity in the local paper.*

* *New-Hampshire Patriot and State Gazette, Concord, N. H. Thursday, October 21, 1841.*

SPINNING WHEEL AND HAND LOOM

The women of early New Hampshire seem never to have been daunted by an emergency. Like the mother in *Swiss Family Robinson,* they were able to produce almost anything their families needed at short notice. Madam Mason, wife of Colonel Stephen Mason, wove the sail used on the boat in which the Hampton people who settled the town of Tamworth crossed Lake Winnepesaukee. A Northfield housewife was even more ingenious: when she had no wool to weave a sadly needed muster day suit for her son, she patiently prepared bears' hair and thistledown to make the material from which she cut the pantaloons and jacket.

Every hamlet in the State boasted at least one woman weaver— usually a widow obliged to earn her own living—who could be called upon to fashion webs of homespun and linen on a home loom. Some of them built up very good businesses. Mrs. Sally Tenny of Francestown, assisted by her mother, made a comfortable living by weaving cloth for her neighbors at four cents a yard. A Windham woman, Agnes Hemphill, mother of eighteen children, set her ten daughters to spinning after her husband died. Each of the Hemphill girls had her own wheel upon which she spun yards of linen thread during the three months her mother spent weaving cloth for market. When the webs were bleached and whitened, Mrs. Hemphill saddled the family horse and started out at two o'clock in the morning for Salem, Massachusetts, to sell her wares. Margaret Hills also of Windham, widowed in 1817 and left with six sons and two daughters dependent upon her, turned to weaving to support them. She made all kinds of table linen, bedspreads, carpets, and woven blankets to sell. She taught her little boys to fill spools and quills; her daughters, to weave. Two or three times a year she journeyed to Salem and Danvers, Massachusetts, to dispose of the wares made by her energetic family.

"Widow" Bussiel wove web after web of cloth, rag carpets, and bedticks for the Hillsborough people. Frank French, painter of rural New Hampshire folk scenes, who saw her at work when he was a boy, says: "There was a mystery about the ponderous machine that excited our boyish imagination, and responsive sympathy in the face of the weaver that appealed to our hearts. As she sat upon her rude bench her head was silhouetted against the light of a cob-webbed window and framed in by the shadowy posts, beams and braces."*

Many professional men weavers from Scotland, Ireland, and England came to New England during the eighteenth century. Probably more of them settled in the towns colonized by the Scotch-Irish than in other sections of New Hampshire. There were several among the pioneers of Antrim and Gilsum. One was James Campbell, who had been apprenticed to a weaver when he was fourteen years old. When he first came to Antrim, he offered his neighbors one day's work in weaving in return for two days of felling trees. His proposition was accepted immediately.

The Londonderry weavers had more than local fame. They got their looms in order as soon as their houses were built, and began at once to produce wares for the Boston market. As early as 1748 they were taking steps to protect themselves from competition by calling a town meeting to consider the appointment of "proper and fit persons to survey and inspect linen and hollands made in this town". They finally voted to have their linens sealed officially by the selectmen before they were put on sale.

Professional weavers worked from drafts, as their patterns of dots and dashes were called. Many experienced home weavers used them when they were weaving linens of such intricate designs as the American Beauty and the Orange Quarter. In describing these old-time drafts, Mary Jones Smith, an experienced weaver, says: "When I see the intricacy of some of the old patterns, I am amazed that our ancestors accomplished so much that was beautiful and frequently fine in texture, with their crude, cumbersome looms, and with yarns of their own spinning and dyeing."

Mrs. Smith, working today on her modern forty-five-inch, six-harness loom, uses Colonial patterns—rarely in their original form, but arranged and adapted to present-day use. She says: "Few, if

* *History of Hillsborough. George Waldo Browne. Published by the Town, 1921. p. 322.*

any of these old patterns belonged solely to New Hampshire; identical or similar drafts were found wherever weaving was done by the early settlers in America."

A vigorous campaign to promote the home manufacture of silk was also carried on in the southern part of the State. Cocoon-raising and silk spinning and weaving appealed especially to women; and a number of well-known New Hampshire residents took up the business with great enthusiasm. The Misses Stark of Dunbarton, granddaughters of the hero of the battle of Bennington, were among the earliest raisers of silkworms in New England. Mrs. Theodore A. Goffe of Bedford was another well-known woman who was interested in the work. She spun considerable thread from the cocoons she raised, and knit silk stockings for members of her family and for friends.

The most prominent name among New Hampshire silkmakers was that of Mrs. Betsey Kimball of Hopkinton, who raised over 20,000 cocoons in 1836. During that same year she invented a spinning machine to "aid the common spinning-wheel for the formation of the ordinary single silk thread from several fibres of cocoon."* In 1837 the committee on silks for the Merrimack County Agricultural Society commended her "industry, ingenuity and perseverance"† in the production of silk articles, including gloves, stockings, a striped vest, and dresses; and on several occasions she appeared in public attired from head to toe in silk articles of her own manufacture.

People interested in silk raising used every method and pulled every political wire possible to boost the business in New Hampshire. To bring attention to the industry's needs and to get helpful legislative action, Amos Little of Newport, wearing silk garments of home manufacture, appeared before the General Court of 1843 to present a petition asking a bounty and protection for the silk manufacturer. No action resulted from his visit; eventually, in spite

---

* *New Hampshire Patriot and State Gazette. Concord, N. H. Monday, October 31, 1836.*
† *Ibid. October 23, 1837.*

of all efforts to save it, the industry died out in New Hampshire. In the rural towns, after weaving had ceased to be a home craft, the cumbersome hand looms were often used to weave strips of rag carpeting and rugs in prodigious quantities. Ella Aldrich of Franconia, who, until 1934, made woven rugs for her neighbors on her mother's old loom, often declared that she had produced enough carpeting to encircle the globe. The Canterbury Shakers were particularly adept at rug weaving, making their products from wool sent in by their customers. Shaker woven rugs were distinguished for their lovely colors and intricate patterns, which gave them the appearance of tapestry of rich needlework.

Rugmaking was an important factor in the revival of modern hand loom weaving. A number of weavers say that they started weaving simply to make rugs for their homes, and then became so interested in the craft that they branched out into weaving fabrics on their looms.

The present interest in the craft in New Hampshire is due to a great extent to the weaving classes started in 1918 at the Manchester Institute of Arts and Sciences and to the state-wide impetus given to it by the League of New Hampshire Arts and Crafts. Weaving was one of the first crafts undertaken by the workers at the Sandwich Industries, which was the starting point, as far as work is concerned, of the League as it operates today.

Two well-known and experienced modern weavers who feel that they owe much of their success both to the Institute and to the League are Mr. and Mrs. John W. Blake of Plymouth. The Blakes have been weaving for twenty-five years, and their North Country studio is one of the finest equipped of its kind in New England.

For Mrs. Blake, weaving was the result of a real creative impulse. When she first started her work, she had never seen anyone weave, knew nothing about looms or weaving; she simply realized that she wanted to take up the craft. She studied with well-known American weavers, among them the master craftsman, Mary Meigs Atwater. Mrs. Blake says her first dream was to reproduce old-time patterns, such as "Orange Peel", "Double and Single Snowball", "Four

O'clock", "Indian War", and "Pine Bloom". After she had produced her first thousand yards of pattern weaving, she felt that she wanted to make her own designs, so she turned her attention to "Lain-In Weaves", which she studied first under the direction of the late Cecelia C. Willard. This venture led her to take a three-year course in design at the Manchester Institute of Arts and Sciences. Mr. Blake also studied weaving under Mrs. Atwater, and he, too, took up various courses in craftsmanship at the Institute.

The Blakes opened their studio in Plymouth four years before the League of New Hampshire Arts and Crafts was organized. Mrs. Blake has taught classes for the League ever since its first director asked their co-operation. Twenty-four looms are in use in their studio; pupils work on two-, four-, and six-harness looms, but only experienced craftsmen like Mr. Blake use the eight- and ten-harness looms.

The products of Mr. Blake's eight-harness loom have been shown in many places; they were included in the exhibit sponsored by the American Federation of Art at the International Exposition held in Paris in 1937.

Robert F. Heartz of Brentwood had his work displayed at the same exhibition. He is a very experienced weaver who has worked at his craft and taught it since he graduated from high school in 1917. For some years he worked on power looms of various types, but eventually he began to weave on hand looms, ranging from simple weaving frames to the complicated hand-Jacquard and draw-looms.

Mr. Heartz has built and rebuilt various looms, including a hand drawloom of the type on which handwoven brocades, velvets, and Paisley shawls were made. In his work he uses all kinds of designs and all known and available materials. Among his most distinctive products are the window draperies which he made for the New Hampshire Exhibit in the Custom House Building of the New England Group at the New York World's Fair, in 1939. The design was adapted from a wedding dress worn by an Epping woman in 1779. He says his longest day's work of weaving was the twenty-three and a half hours in which he produced a nine-yard length of material for a special order.

There are other notable and experienced weavers in the State. Special interest in the craft is demonstrated by the individuals who have taken up the work as a hobby or as a spare time industry. Mrs. Mildred P. See of Manchester says she started weaving for that reason. But she became so interested in developing the craft that she studied and experimented, until at the present time she has built up a fine home industry of making beautiful woven yard goods. Like many others of the younger weavers in the State, Mrs. See feels that she owes part of her success to the instruction she received in the classes directed by Mrs. Louise C. Martin at the Manchester Institute of Arts and Sciences. Mrs. Martin, who has taught at the Institute for the past ten years, also gives much credit to this art school, where she first began to weave under the supervision of the late Mrs. James Dodge. Mrs. Martin first took up weaving as a pastime, but became so proficient in the art that her teacher, on resigning, suggested Mrs. Martin take over the classes. She has supplemented her knowledge and practical experience in the studios of some of America's finest craftsmen. Mrs. Martin is experienced in all types of Colonial weaving—tapestry, laid-in, Spanish, and shadow weaving—but she is interested especially in plain weaving, for she believes that some of the most beautiful and distinctive examples of the weaver's art are found in plain, fine-textured linens.

Like Mrs. See, Mrs. Burton Seavey of the Keene Home Industries is a typical example of a woman who has learned to weave in her own home, and who has kept up this work for her own amusement as well as for a source of income. She has a four-harness loom in her kitchen on which she weaves rugs and luncheon sets. She studied under a Swedish instructor of weaving sent out by the League of New Hampshire Arts and Crafts. Mrs. Edith Burt of Laconia is another home weaver who says she does her own housework and weaves in her spare time. She uses table looms of two sizes, upon which she produces bookmarks, luggage-straps, runners, bags, luncheon sets, and scarfs. Her favorite weaving material is linen.

In Laconia also lives a young girl who has established a real reputation as a weaver. When she was only twelve years old, Elizabeth E. Marsland began weaving under the direction of her mother, Mrs. Hila Marsland. Now the young girl, who was graduated from high school in 1940, is so proficient in the art that she maintains her own studio and shop, located in the old barn which once housed the family horse and buggy. Here she produces hand-woven fabrics of her own design, table scarfs, luncheon sets, and mats. Elizabeth has the good fortune to belong to a family in which the members are all interested in craftwork. Her mother and younger sister weave and her father makes looms and paints landscapes as a hobby.

Even the master weaver, Mrs. Mary Jones Smith, started her work on a table loom in a very simple way, but after a few months' work she found it inadequate for her needs. A long time elapsed, however, before she purchased the six-harness loom upon which she now weaves all kinds of articles, ranging from luggage-rack straps to coverlets.

Mrs. Smith has very definite ideas about the creative side of weaving. She believes that the art in handweaving lies in its flexibility, which permits each piece woven to be a finished unit and not one of hundreds of articles all made alike. And she maintains that the weaver, if he has the soul of an artist, is able to express himself in line and color, as the power loom operator cannot. If a man is a true weaver he puts as much of himself into his work as a master of painting puts into a creation on his canvas. She says: "It is a fallacy that 'anyone can weave'. Anyone can throw a shuttle, but weaving is more than that. It demands accuracy in planning, painstaking care, concentration in the doing, and endless patience. Given these, together with a sense of color, line, and proportion, the finished fabric that grows under the flying shuttle truly deserves the name of art, as well as craft."

XIII

WITH THREAD AND NEEDLE

Drive along any country road and you will see, hanging from porch railing or clothesline, rugs and quilts whose "hit or miss" design indicates the economy that inspired them. Then visit the New Hampshire Historical Building, Park Street, Concord; on the second floor there is a piece of handiwork which called for a lavish use of material and time. It is a needle-point portrait of Benjamin Franklin, made in 1850-1851 by Mrs. Crosby Kimball Haines, a native of Concord. This ambitious piece closely resembles tapestry in the even perfection of the tent stitch in which it is embroidered; and it has a rich appearance resulting from the fine material with which it is made.

The embroiderer could scarcely have made a clearer, more lifelike portrait had she used the more facile medium of paint and brush. So skillfully has she managed the shading of the forms that her subject sits there almost lifelike: benign countenance, ruddy cheeks, blue-gray eyes, and fluffy gray hair falling to his shoulders. His costume is just as clearly delineated: jabot and cuff frills of white lace; long blue stockings; black knee breeches with buckles at the knee; black Colonial shoes with large buckles; and buttoned vest of a henna shade, topped by a knee-length coat of black velvet, held together by one button.

The Currier Gallery of Art in Manchester owns a similar needle-point portrait of General George Washington which was worked in 1852-1853 by the daughter of Governor Noah Martin. Like the

Franklin portrait, this embroidered representation of the first President of the United States is worked in materials which obviously were not taken from the family attic, but which were acquired at some expense to the needleworker.

By the mid-eighteenth century, American women had acquired more leisure time for decorative needlework than had been possible for them in the first hard years of colonization. This interest in the art of stitchery has continued up to the present time. Almost every New England household treasures some bit of needlework which was diligently stitched by an ancestor. Many specimens are preserved in New Hampshire collections of early Americana. A study of the miscellaneous articles which have come down to us—embroidered portraits, waistcoats, party slippers, wedding veils, christening blankets, purses, table and bed linens, and wall hangings—helps us to reconstruct the social scene of the day when they were used.

The waistcoat presented by General Lafayette to Major General John Sullivan of Durham is preserved in the New Hampshire Historical Building, Park Street, Concord. It probably was worked in France; but similar pieces of finery, cut from rich white taffeta and elaborately embroidered in satin stitch, were made occasionally by American women.

There are specimens of fine needlework which are equally interesting to New Hampshire people because they were made or were owned by someone historically prominent. The needlebook made by Sarah, Countess of Rumford, containing needles purchased in England in 1796 by her father, Benjamin Thompson, who was made a Count by the Emperor of Bavaria, are notable examples. These pieces are now on display in the New Hampshire Historical Building in Concord.

In the matter of design, American women have not only adapted patterns from England and from Europe, but also have made use of their own original ideas. A disposition to model from nature and actual objects prevails among New Hampshire needlewomen of the present day. Recently Mrs. C. R. Whitehouse of Manchester, noted as a versatile and expert needlewoman, decided to work a picture of the old family homestead, to be used as a covering for an antique footstool. Imprinted indelibly on her memory was the Currier and Ives grouping of the saltbox house under sheltering trees, the path, the huge red barn. An old pump had stood between the house and the barn. As a child visiting her paternal grandfather, it had been a joy to work its long arm up and down and to bring water of cool deliciousness from its subterranean depths. Try as she might, she could not bring her recollection of the old hand pump into focus sharp enough for reproduction. There must be such an old pump somewhere, she thought, and set forth to find and copy it. She traveled the length and breadth of the State before she discovered one.

Mrs. Whitehouse is an instructor in embroidery and needlepoint tapestry as well as an able craftsman. It was under her guidance that Mrs. Walter M. Africa of Manchester worked an exquisite sampler based on an old design called a Persian Flower Garden. This piece of embroidery carries out traditions of fine stitchery and design which have been handed down from one generation of needleworkers to another; faggot stitch forms the paths in the garden; birds and rabbits are portrayed in satin stitch; gay little flowers in *petit point*; and a margin of double stitch filling surrounds the lovely scene.

All stitches in use today are of ancient origin. The exhibit in the Rochester State Fair, 1939, which bore the coveted blue ticket reading "First Prize, Professional Class", included a luncheon cloth worked in the same simple stitch found upon embroideries taken from the ancient tombs of the Pharaohs. The designer and maker of this effective piece of needlework, Mrs. Rose Mangano of Portsmouth, worked a five-inch border of full-blown roses around a fifty-four-inch square of linen. The work was done with a blue thread in cross-stitch, simplest and most primitive of stitches, and the first stitch ever used on woven material. A narrower band of rose buds in the center of the cloth was developed in the same

DOLL DRESSED IN 1852 CLOTHING, *originally owned by Ann Page of Gilmanton and now the property of Miss Ruth Whittier of Concord.*

EMBROIDERED PANEL *worked in a variety of colors and stitches on a black background. It was made about a hundred years ago in Webster, by the mother of the present owner, Austin Smith of Laconia.*

stitch. Another admirable piece in this collection was done in the ancient stitch, called *intaglio,* or cutwork.

The modern woman's cleverness in adapting the stitches of other countries and other days is seldom more clearly brought out than in the display of bags made by Mrs. Mabel F. Ames of Somersworth, exhibited at the Rochester State Fair, 1939. Cards beside the bags indicated that the design of one was of Greek origin; another, Czechoslovakian; another, Moorish; still another, American Paisley. One had taken its design from a pattern emanating from Perugia, Italy; and another, perhaps the most appealing of the whole collection, had utilized a design taken from an old French hand-woven towel, showing three figures worked in blue tufting thread on a gray linen background.

In 1937, stitches and needlework designs adapted from the early Colonial embroidery of New Mexico were introduced to eastern craftworkers by Mrs. Martha S. Watson, an instructor in the art department of the Manchester Institute of Arts and Sciences. On a return trip from California, Mrs. Watson, who is always looking for new ideas in handwork, visited a vocational school in Taos, New Mexico, to study the embroidery first produced in the region during the period of Spanish colonization. The unusual needlework patterns which plainly show that the embroidery of Spain was influenced by Oriental, Persian, and Moorish designs, were developed later by women of culture during the Mexican occupation (1821-1848) and probably were taught to the Indians by them. The tradition of this beautiful type of American Colonial needlework has been preserved and is revived in experiments in industrial education carried on in certain towns in northern New Mexico. The finest examples of this embroidery are preserved today on old bed coverings, or *colchas,* made of homespun woolen cloth, on altar cloths, and on ancient Spanish shawls. The distinctive designs which Mrs. Watson brought East to enrich the traditions of New England embroidery have been received enthusiastically by craftworkers at the Institute and have been applied to forms of craftwork other than embroidery. A study of this needlework reveals one important fact: the stitches which have reached New Hampshire through this long and devious journey are basically the same ancient types which came to America from Europe by the shorter way of England.

While modern teachers do not throw all tradition overboard, they do believe that embroidery should declare both in design and technique, the age in which it was developed.

A search for a better means of rendering perspective and a stitch which would permit broader scope to their choice of patterns caused some early workers to combine two sizes of stitch and two kinds of thread in the same piece. Such a combination of *gros* and *petit point* and of worsted and silk thread may be found in a needle-point picture at Hill Acres near Suncook. This picture is English in appearance, its embroidered roses especially connecting it with the reign of the Stuarts. The name of its worker is not known.

Couching, a type of needlework popular in England in the latter part of the seventeenth century, was used by American women in the eighteenth to adorn bed coverlets. Various methods were employed in this work, but in one type a pattern was traced on the cloth and outlined in over and over stitch, a slender twig being used to keep the threads loose. This work was very much like the candlewicking done on bedspreads today. When the twig was removed and the threads cut, a lovely fluffy, feathery effect resulted.

Any discussion of old coverlets would be incomplete without mention of that rare kind, known as "wool-on-wool", a specimen of which is in the collection of Americana in the Currier Gallery of Art in Manchester. The date (1771) stitched into it proves that, among the few extant, it is next to the oldest. The embroidery has been done with thread made of the same wool used in weaving the foundation, and with a coarse needle carrying several threads at a time. A simple running stitch fills in the pattern detail, and the resulting effect shows a close kinship to crewel embroidery. The pattern is a vigorous adaptation of scroll and flower design, with possibly an affiliation to the Tree of Life pattern so widely used by early needlewomen. The huge carnation-like flowers are saffron in color; the stems, green; and the deeply serrated leaves, blue-green. The homemade dyes are clear and fast after nearly two centuries of exposure. The welcome comfort of such a bedcovering—soft wool yarn closely stitched through coarse homespun woolen blanketing—can easily be imagined, but it is much more than just a practical blanket. The nimble fingers of the unknown needlewoman have worked into it something of her own independent creative spirit, something of her pleasure in the task.

A coverlet of entirely different technique and of especial interest to New Hampshire people is the one which hangs in the Museum of the Society of Daughters of the American Revolution in Washington, D. C. Although the card attached to it classifies it as a rug, it is not one in the present-day use of that word. It is one of the very few bedcoverings which have survived of the many made between 1773 and 1802. Its interest does not entirely lie in the fact that it is an outstanding piece of handwork, in the robust vigor of the design upon it, in the quiet beauty of its colors, and in the perfection of the stitching in which the pattern was carried out; it has the added interest of having been worked by Elizabeth Stark, who was renamed "Molly" by her famous husband, hero of the Battle of Bennington. In 1773 General Stark's niece, Polly, married James Lathrop and went to live in Bennington, Vermont. This coverlet was a wedding gift to her from her aunt and uncle. The wool of which it is made came from the backs of sheep which grazed along the banks of the Merrimack near the Amoskeag Falls; and the butternut, hemlock, and maple trees which suggested to Molly the beautiful, quietly cheerful colors—creamy tans to deep-red browns—in which she developed her pattern, still lift their tall heads above her grave in Stark Park in Manchester.

Several pieces of coarse homespun wool blanketing were sewed together to make the foundation of this heirloom, which is something over seven feet long and nearly as wide. After the bold pattern of carnations, buds, berries, and acanthus leaves had been drawn on with a piece of charred wood from the hearth, the whole piece was sewed into a quilting frame and was rolled and unrolled so that the proper amount of working surface was exposed at a time. The same wool of which the blanket had been woven was loosely spun and dyed, and several strands at a time were pushed and pulled through the meshes of the foundation with an implement called a crotchet, first used for "turkey" work. The smooth beauty of the finished work is due to the even precision with which the loops of fluffy yarn were pulled in and out.

Fifty years after Molly Stark made her coverlet, American women were engaged in a quite different kind of needlework. They were making wool embroidery executed in cross-stitch called "Berlin work", because the materials and the patterns were imported from Germany. By the middle of the nineteenth century, the long list of "ladies ornamental work" in the *Ladies Manual of Fancy Work* included antimacassars, bookmarkers, cushions, doilies, foot muffs, lambrequins, mats, mitts, penwipers, sachets, shaving books, smoking caps, tobacco bags, and slippers. They were decorated with highly colored designs which vied for honors with the outsize lilies and plump roses embroidered on fire screens, chair seats, footstools, sofas, and bell pulls. Practically every woman and girl in the country who could afford to buy the materials was engaged in this kind of work.

Needlework in New Hampshire has developed as a definite art form since 1904, when embroidery classes were opened at the Handicraft Society of Peterborough. It received added and permanent stimulus in 1911 when the Manchester Institute of Arts and Sciences started embroidery classes, under the supervision of Mrs. C. R. Whitehouse. Since 1929 these classes have continued, with Miss Elizabeth M. Christophe as instructor. Miss Christophe also conducts classes under the sponsorship of the League of New Hampshire Arts and Crafts. Examples of work shown at the Annual Institute Exhibitions have received favorable comment from many out-of-State experts. In 1927 the display included forms of Italian embroidery and Roman cutwork, shawls of heavy silk embroidered in wool, bedspreads of embroidered lace, cross-stitch and tufted work, and a particularly beautiful wall covering showing a Tree of Life design worked in thirty different stitches and the same number of colors.

Needleworkers in the League of New Hampshire Arts and Crafts owe much to Mrs. Foster Stearns of Hancock. Mrs. Stearns, an expert in needlework form and design, was trained in the Continental traditions of the art, but has gone a step farther in her adaptations of purely local forms in embroidery designs. A moss rosebud on a child's gravestone in a New Hampshire cemetery, an apple from a Hancock orchard, the silhouette of an oak leaf by the wayside furnished her with inspiration. As she says: "If we are looking for design, we see it everywhere; and after a time those who really train themselves discover that all forms of art have a relationship to each other, and the laws that govern line and balance and color in one apply to all. It gives us a new love for the whole creation with which we are surrounded."*

Lacemaking is an exception to the trend of American needlework toward originality. Like embroidery, this art came to America by the way of England and the Continent, but it has taken on no definite American characteristics.

Every piece in the valuable and extensive array of lace made by Mrs. Claude Crafts of Grasmere, a noted and skillful lacemaker, is a reproduction of some old design. In fact it was a collection of very old Point de Venise pieces in the Museum of Fine Arts, Boston, Massachusetts, some eighteen years ago, that started Mrs. Crafts on her lacemaking career.

It takes Mrs. Crafts only a few moments to enumerate and briefly demonstrate the steps taken in making one of her complicated pieces. So readily and obediently do the tiny stitches fall into place as she plies her fine tapestry needle, carrying "No. 70" linen thread, that the admiring onlooker is scarcely prepared as she refers to her long apprenticeship. "Yes", she notes, "It takes ten years of weekly lessons under a competent instructor to get a working knowledge of lacemaking."

* *Bulletin, No. 54 (November-December 1939). League of New Hampshire Arts and Crafts. Mrs. Foster Stearns, Editor.*

Mrs. Crafts' lace is of the type known as "point" or "needle-point" because it is made with needle and thread without a cloth foundation. There are three forms of this lace: Venetian Raised Point, sometimes called Rose Point; Venetian Flat Point, which includes the famous Coralline pattern and has no *cordonnet;* and Venetian Grounded Point. Mrs. Crafts' collection includes many exquisite pieces. Notably handsome is a piece fifteen by twelve inches which reproduces the much-used medieval design of Adam and Eve. Another piece of the same size shows two dragons facing each other with an urn of fire between them. A slightly smaller piece depicts two doves of peace facing each other, between them a fruit-filled urn of peace.

"Cutwork" and "reticella", the first needlework to venture away from the long-established rules of embroidery, employ the buttonhole stitch. The lace which is the outcome of this experiment uses buttonhole stitches on top of cloth, since it was discovered that it was not necessary to fasten down any but the first row of buttonhole loops. This discovery was the initial step toward the art of making lace. These rows of free loops at once were called *punto in aria,* and there was but one step to be taken for this "stitch in air", which was a form of embroidery, to become point lace, which is entirely distinct from all other forms of needlework. It was not long before some Columbus of needlecraft found that a framework could be temporarily fastened to a background material and filled in, after which it could be cut free with the design intact.

Making the mesh or background was naturally the least interesting and most tedious part of lacemaking, and a machine that could make this was hailed as an aid to the art. Most of the lace made fifty or sixty years ago made use of a machine-made foundation. The filmy white veil worn by Mrs. Moody Currier when her husband was inaugurated Governor, and now displayed at the Currier Gallery of Art, Manchester, was made by hand on an exquisitely fine machine-made net, imported from Belgium.

In 1905 the art of making the intricate bobbin, or pillow, lace was introduced to New Hampshire craftworkers through classes at the Manchester Institute of Arts and Sciences. Instruction was given by Mrs. Henry Lundberg, a native of Sweden, who had learned all the steps of the delicate operation from European lacemakers. This craft was wholly unknown in Manchester until Mrs. Lundberg brought her pillow and bobbins to the city. Since the work was tedious and the equipment somewhat expensive, the number of pupils was not large; however, people who saw samples of the lace produced under Mrs. Lundberg's supervision say that they were extremely beautiful. A display of bobbin lace shown at the Annual Institute Exhibition of June, 1909, particularly impressed a local journalist, who said: "It is hard to believe that these beautiful laces, having great commercial value, are the product of those who a short time ago knew absolutely nothing of the art of their making."*

Far removed from the intricacies which distinguish the making of pillow lace are the rapidity and ease with which crocheted lace is produced. Probably no implement employed in ornamental needlework and lacemaking has been used more extensively than the slender steel, wooden, or bone needles, or hooks, which turn lengths of fine and coarse threads into lace. It is believed that the art of crocheting was developed first in the early convents of Ireland and France, and quickly spread over Europe and America. The late Mrs. Charles Jepperson of Franconia, who was very proficient in this type of lacemaking, often said that she did not remember when she could not crochet the filet, or square-mesh, picture antimacassars of the type seen in all New Hampshire parlors during the 1860's and 1870's. She added that the older girls of her day carried their crocheting to school, and spent their long recesses comparing patterns and making tidies.

In decorative lacemaking, knitting needles have been close rivals of the crochet hook; in work of a practical nature, they have surpassed it in quantity of output. Before knitting machines were first used, in the early 1800's, all New Englanders were wearing stock-

* *Daily Mirror and American. Manchester, N. H. Wednesday, June 2, 1909. p. 7.*

ings of home manufacture. Knitting needles clicked through the day and far into the evening. As the hosiery business developed into one of New Hampshire's largest industries, women of the rural districts were kept busy working toes and heels into the machine-knit stockings. Each completed bundle of wares sent back to the mills meant ten to twenty-five cents in pin money for the housewife. In 1873 nearly 200,000 pairs of stockings were sent out by three manufacturers of Newport to local women for toeing and heeling. This industrial custom was in existence until a little more than fifty years ago.

During the period when stockings were made entirely by hand, old people and children did a large share of the family knitting. It was not uncommon for children as young as four years of age to knit their own stockings. As soon as they had enough skill, both girls and boys made their underwear, mittens, mufflers, caps, and the suspenders which held up small boys' trousers. The experience made the girls, at least, experts in the craft, when they were older.

Practically all New Hampshire communities can boast of at least one old-time knitter who is remembered for her ability to manipulate knitting needles. One of the best-known folklore stories of Shelburne is concerned with the renown of such a craftworker; she was Peggy Davis, famous for being able to knit the letters of the alphabet into the texture of her mittens. Barker Burbank, a neighbor, showed a pair she had knit for him to a man who remarked that he knew an old blind woman in Gorham who could do the very same thing. Burbank said he would wager twenty-five dollars that there was not a woman in New Hampshire besides Peggy who could do it. Peggy heard of the argument, and for several nights thereafter her family noticed that, instead of going to bed at the usual time, she sat up in the dark—knitting.

In a few days she sent a new pair of perfect mittens to Mr. Burbank. The letters of the alphabet undeniably appeared in them, but not in the usual order; they were neatly interknit in the form of a four-line verse which might have been used more conventionally on an embroidered sampler:

"Money will make you many friends,
But do not praise them high;
For should misfortune make you poor,
Such friends will pass you by."

In the early nineteenth century, men also did considerable knitting. To earn a little tobacco money, they sometimes helped their wives with their "feeting" for the stocking manufacturers. John Lougee, who was born on the Isle of Jersey in 1700 and who settled in Exeter when he came to America, was a knitter by trade all his life.

In 1827 a hundred Saxony sheep were brought to Walpole from Boston by a sixteen-year-old German lad, John F. Kraetzer, for Major Samuel Grant and William Jennison. Young Kraetzer became Jennison's shepherd. In his spare moments, he knitted socks in the German fashion he had learned in his own country, and thus introduced the method to the region.

The fleece of the Saxony sheep was well adapted to knitting, for it was exceptionally fine and light; but merino was the fleece which most commonly furnished yarn for New Hampshire knitting. After 1810 cotton yarn was spun in factories and could be bought very cheaply by the farmers' wives. A good yarn for making durable stockings consisted of a thread of cotton twisted with a thread of wool.

In the nineteenth century, knitting, like many other homely crafts, became more of a social art than a means of filling domestic needs. In 1807 the *Concord Gazette* advertised a "school for the instruction of young ladies" in Boscawen, and knitting was an important and typical course in the curriculum. Eight years later some of the women of Keene decided to form a Reading Club, but the following year changed the name to the more practical "Ladies' Charitable Society". One of their first activities, after the change, was to buy a quantity of wool and have it carded and spun. During their meetings, they knit the yarn into stockings for the needy.

The mood of the Victorian Era directed the knitting impulse into other forms, such as purses of silk net decorated with beads, flowers with petals in different colors, and ornamental berries and fruit; huge enveloping shawls; and long scarfs of fleecy wool known as Nubians. Knit hosiery continued to be made by ladies in the 1850's from silk, worsted, and linen and cotton threads. Around 1870 there was a vogue for knitted quilts, and for bedspreads of a lacy pattern. At one of the State Fairs, held in New Hampshire during that year, there were on display fifty-eight varieties of knit edging for bedspreads.

Fashion has played an important part in the revival of the knitting craft in New Hampshire, just as it has in other parts of the country. Locally, too, there has been another strong factor influencing women who had put their knitting needles aside to bring them out again. The popularity of winter sports has made knitting a source of income to a number of craftworkers who can produce socks, bonnets, caps, and sweaters for skiers. But the most important products from New Hampshire's knitting needles are the beautiful double mittens which are made in quantities in some communities.

Whitefield, located in the center of the northern winter sports area, is noted for mittens which are made in the Norwegian manner. Mrs. Frank S. Dodge of the Mountain View House has organized and maintains a project in which twenty women are engaged at the present time. She has developed a series of charming designs which are knit into the mittens to form patterns of unusual beauty. The Whitefield craftworkers have spent four years perfecting their technique, and at present they are knitting constantly to fill the orders. Two kinds of patterns are used: one is the heavy double Norwegian sort in two or more colors; the other, the "spectator winter sports" type, single knit with Swedish embroidery. One woman has set a record for rapid production by knitting six pairs of mittens in a week. The Whitefield project is unique in this respect: all profits from the sale of these articles go to the knitters themselves.

In describing the work Mrs. Dodge says: "Such a project exemplifies the influence of present European conditions on American handicrafts; for the goods produced by the Whitefield knitters will replace those formerly imported from Scandinavian countries. This industry has grown from a hundred pairs of mittens the first year to over a thousand items including socks, caps, and scarfs made during 1939. More knitted articles are made in this village at the present time than in any other in New England."

Needlework, in all its aspects which have been discussed, is the one craft that belongs essentially to women. In lonely farmhouse kitchens and in luxurious city drawing rooms, they have made needle-point pictures, embroidered linens, glorified coverlets with fine stitchery, produced exquisite laces, and knitted sturdy woolen garments which have kept countless children warm. It is one of the mediums by which many women have helped to pass down to the future the culture that has come to them from the past. By combining stitches and designs of generations of women of the old world, she has woven into the pattern of American life the color and drama in the lives of European and Oriental peoples. As they have patiently plied their needles and made from fluffy woolen yarn and shiny silken thread as much beauty as they knew how, women have also been taking fine, but determined, stitches in time.

XIV

SAMPLERS AND QUILTS

In tracing the development of American needlework, the craftworker soon discovers that samplermaking and quiltmaking stand out from the other subjects in the same category, for samplers and quilts have universal appeal and human interest not found in more formal examples of needlework. For over two hundred years, practically every woman who could thread a needle produced at least one of them. Into these commonplace and homely pieces of handwork were stitched the hopes and the disappointments of their makers. Every old sampler, every cherished family quilt, is a record of homely happenings. Each has its own story, handed down by anecdote or family legend.

The word sampler, the "ensempler" of Chaucer's day, referred originally to the fact that these pieces were a means of recording needlework stitches for future reference. All seventeenth-century samplers, both English and American, had this purpose. They were made by experienced needleworkers, and the stitches worked on them were elaborate and intricate in design. Like English samplers of the period, American specimens were rich with drawnwork, cutwork, and lace stitches which the owners intended to use in the adornment of bed curtains, petticoats, and other household and personal finery. Few of them are in existence today. An exhaustive search conducted by the Society of the Colonial Dames of Massachusetts in 1921 revealed only seven American samplers of the years 1600-1700. One of these is the well-known Anne Gower sampler (actually made in England), embroidered by the first wife of Governor John Endicott of Massachusetts Bay Colony. None of the seven was of New Hampshire origin.

These early samplers were worked on the narrow, coarse linens produced on the hand looms used at the time. The embroidery threads were linen or loosely woven silk strands, usually no coarser than present-day sewing silks. "Sam-cloths", as they were called, could be easily rolled up, tucked into a bag or an apron pocket, and then brought out at an instant's notice when the needleworker wished to study a stitch or to add a new one to her collection. Sometimes they were a yard long and only eight to twelve inches wide. Even after wider linen became available, they held to this convenient, longer-than-wide form during the years when samplers were used simply for pattern purposes.

The oldest New Hampshire sampler of which we have record was worked by Mary Wingate of Hampton, probably in 1719, and is nearly twice as long as it is wide. Besides the pattern stitches, it is ornamented with designs of animals and birds and has two sets of alphabets. Another example of these longer-than-wide samplers is one made in 1731 by Lydia Hart. It is owned by the New Hampshire Historical Society.

Besides the rows of stitches with colorful names, like trellis stitch, hollie stitch, fern stitch, queen stitch, and fisher-stitch, all of which John Taylor immortalized in verse in 1640, samplers were adorned with alphabets and numerals, as patterns to mark household linens and to keep track of the number of pieces turned out. They were also embellished with embroidered portrayals of "Flowers, Plants, and Fishes, Beasts, Birds, Flyes, and Bees" as Taylor, in "Needle's Excellency", pointed out three hundred years ago:

"There's nothing near at hand, or farthest sought,
But with the needle may be shaped and wrought."

Many of the motifs were executed in that oldest form of needlework decoration, the cross-stitch, which is still one of the best liked of stitches. Arranged in double lines, blocks, and borders, the tiny crosses make perfect frames to enclose embroidered verses and pictures. After 1740 few samplers were made which did not include such frames.

On a sampler embroidered in 1729 by Polly Eppes of Francestown, and now owned by Mrs. Orpha Durgin of Manchester, the border appears only as a frame around the verse, but it anticipates the general use of borders by a number of years. This piece of New Hampshire needlework, next in age to the Wingate sampler, is worked on two layers of linen. On it Polly inscribed this couplet:

> "This needle work of mine doth tell
> That the child hath learned well."

When the sampler advanced from the sam-cloth stage to a status where it was displayed as a certificate of merit for ability in needlecraft, the name of the work, the date it was finished, and an inscription, became part of the design. Many of the inscriptions of eighteenth and nineteenth century work were moral mottoes, often designed to instruct the young needlewoman in the precepts of daily living. Mrs. Mary Thompson of Troy says she was brought up on the principle expressed in a verse on her grandmother's sampler, and that she, in turn, impressed the thought upon her own children. When one of them started to complain of another's wrongdoing, Mrs. Thompson quoted the first line and asked the child to complete the quatrain which little Ruth Aked embroidered in 1811:

> "How soon our watchful eyes can view
> The smallest faults which others do
> Yet to our own we're ever blind
> And very few or none we find."

The stanza worked by Sarah K. Little in 1827 is more sombre in its feeling and quite similar to the melancholy lines which were inscribed on samplers made during the years when the followers of Jonathan Edwards were hurling their threats of damnation at the New England people. Fourteen-year-old Sarah embroidered a design of pink roses and green leaves with feathery edges on her sampler, but she enclosed in a black-bordered frame the following verse:

SAMPLERS AND QUILTS

> "As summer flowers fall to rise no more
> As billows rise and die upon the shore
> So generations live and pass away
> They sleep in silence till the Judgement Day."

This sampler hangs in the Manchester Historic Association Building.

Even more lugubrious is the inscription on a sampler owned by Mrs. Eaton Sargent of Nashua:

> "Let me in life prepare to die
> That I may live with God on high,
> With Saints and Angels let me be
> And dwell with them eternally."

The saddest note of all the words enclosed in the beautifully embroidered border is found in these words: "Elizabeth Gage wrought this in 1822 in the 10th year of her age."

Among the definite changes which took place in the evolution of the American sampler during the eighteenth century was the decrease in the ages of their makers. The samplers of the seventeenth century were embroidered by mature women; by the 1780's they had become the prerogative of girls around thirteen years of age and younger. Every well-brought-up daughter of the family made at least one, to show that she had served her apprenticeship in an important branch of work which for centuries has been allotted to womankind.

According to the investigation of the Colonial Dames of America, twenty-four samplers of the period between 1700-1800 are credited to New Hampshire. A late eighteenth-century sampler made by a little New Hampshire girl is displayed in the Manchester Historic Association Building. Betsy Fletcher was fourteen years old in August, 1797, when she held the nine-by-twelve-inch piece of homespun linen up before her and decided that her sampler had been completed. Betsy probably was much younger when she began the piece, for the work in the upper half is more childish than that in the lower section, where a bird seems to sway on the top of a tree. It is easy to picture Betsy as being distressingly indifferent to book learning; several letters are repeated in her cross-stitch alphabets, probably for the purpose of bettering her knowledge. It is easy, too, to guess that Mistress Betsy was pretty and aware of that delightful fact. Else why was this verse from Congreve's "The Mourning Bride" selected for her?

> "Beauty soon grows familiar to thee
> Virtue alone has charms that never die."

Another interesting New Hampshire sampler of the late eighteenth century is owned by Mrs. Edith Durgin Johnson of Boscawen, the granddaughter of the maker, Hannah Pearson of Haverhill. Hannah was nine years old when she embroidered the basket of flowers and the bird of the design, and set the stitches of the alphabet and of numerals up to seven on the piece of coarse linen. No one knows what young Hannah's thoughts were when she was doing her daily sampler stint. She may have been proud of her accomplishment; more likely, however, her reactions were similar to those of a Maryland child who signed a sampler: "Patty Polk did this and she hated every stitch she did in it."

The period between the close of the Revolutionary War and the beginning of the Civil War was the great era of American samplermaking. Nineteenth-century samplers are distinguished for their original designs, which include birds of a coloring and shape Audubon never catalogued, and animals of strangely mixed characteristics. Pictorial samplers portraying Biblical scenes, like the tempting of Adam and Eve, and the spies returning from the Land of Canaan, or showing representations of patriotic symbols, public buildings, and dwelling houses, were all popular.

Death, never far distant from the minds of early New England settlers, left a definite imprint on needlework designs. Memorial samplers,

> "Each with its urn and stiffly-weeping tree
> Devoted to some memory long ago
> More faded than their lines of worsted woe,"*

* *James Russell Lowell.*

SAMPLER *made by Fannie Wilkins of Merrimack in 1819. Now owned by Miss Hazel V. Dodge of North Conway.*

LOG CABIN QUILT *made by Mrs. Betsy Colby of North Sutton about 1894. Now owned by Mrs. A. E. Chadwick of Bow.*

SAMPLERS AND QUILTS 181

often were worked at girls' schools as a part of the assigned courses in needlework for all young gentlewomen. In 1802 Sarah Catherine Moffatt of Portsmouth, twelve years old at the time, embroidered such a piece at "Miss Ward's School, New Hampshire". The upper section of the sampler is quite gay with its vines, flowers, sprays, and birds enlivening the Ten Commandments, but the lower half is extremely funereal in effect. A looped and tasselled band frames an urn under which is inscribed the words: "In Memory of Mrs. Catherine Moffatt, Obiit December, 1802."

In 1810 another Portsmouth girl embroidered a similar memorial to her "affectionate mother, aged 40 years". According to the inscription, Sarah Fitzgerald worked her designs of small trees, a dog, a bird, a large basket of flowers, and a basket of fruit "under the supervision of Mary E. Hill". Supervision was not confined to the needlework curriculum of girls' schools. Most children made their samplers under the keen eyes of their stern elders. But they did not always note the fact, as did little Mary Hudson who, in 1828, stitched the information that she was bound out to Miss Kelly and that the sampler was made under that lady's directions. The indentured child was most industrious, for besides the verse and design on her masterpiece, she carefully wrought three alphabets, numerals to the usual number of fourteen, the vowels, *a, e, i, o, u, y,* and many cross-borders. This sampler, distinguished for the symmetrical balance of the design and the meticulous stitching of the border, is also owned by Mrs. Durgin of Manchester.

Genealogical samplers, which appeared just before the Revolutionary War, read like pages from the family Bible, and provide a valuable historic record of births, marriages, and deaths. They continued to be made for years. A genealogical sampler gains an added interest when shown by the maker, as did the one fashioned by the late Mrs. Roanna S. Eaton of Hollis, who lived to see her hundredth birthday. Mrs. Eaton said she remembered working the design when she was a fourteen-year-old girl living in the town of Hollis. Besides the family record and a memorial verse, this sampler is decorated with an anchor and a harp in the upper corners, and with large crosses embellished with a design of flowers and vines in the lower corners.

Some samplers, like the one made by Rebecca Fletcher, who later became the sister-in-law of Daniel Webster, have a supplementary interest derived from their association with the lives of famous New Hampshire people. Such is the Caroline Langdon sampler, made in 1780 by the daughter of Woodbury Langdon, the brother of New Hampshire's famous patriot and statesman, John Langdon of Portsmouth. The New Hampshire Historical Society owns another, an unsigned and undated sampler which was worked by Sarah, Countess of Rumford, the daughter of a former Concord resident. A sampler which hangs in Stark Cottage in Manchester is interesting because it was designed and executed by a member of the family who sold the land on which the house stands to Major General John Stark's father. This piece of needlework was presented to the Daughters of the American Revolution, Molly Stark Chapter, by Miss Mary Jane Wellington, the niece of the maker.

One of the most interesting samplers in this category was displayed among the Washingtonia exhibited in the summer of 1939 in the Tobias Lear house in Portsmouth. It was worked with the hair of General and "Lady" Washington by Mary Lear Storer, who, as a child, sat upon Washington's knee when he visited Portsmouth in 1789. There are two inscriptions, one dedicated to the national hero, "entolled among the dead", and the other to his "relict".

In its essentials the art of samplermaking has changed little since Colonial days. Like Cynthia Locke of Sullivan, who wrought her sampler about 1816, the modern needleworker

> "Inserts the curious lines in proper ground
> Completes the work and scatters roses round."

She is faced with the identical choices the Colonial women must have made. Shall she make a stitchery sampler, a pictorial sampler, or try her hand at combining the two forms? What size is best? What colors shall she use? What shall she work it on?

Two projects in needlework have been promoted by the New Hampshire Federation of Women's Clubs, and in both of them the sampler has been used as a medium for teaching stitches. The first of these, made in 1927, was of the genuine stitchery type and had no ornamentation other than panels filled with line and composite stitches, and with squares of darning and lace stitches. The stitches which were placed on the sampler, as soon as they were learned, were worked in blue and gold linen threads, as were the alphabet, the name and insignia of the club, the name of the maker, and the date. The sampler was designed by a needlewoman of note who had studied at the finest schools of art in England and Austria. The actual work was supervised by the chairman of the art department of the federation, and the classes in local clubs were directed by leaders who demonstrated the stitches by drawing them upon a blackboard or working them out on burlap with coarse thread.

In the spring of 1934 Mrs. Foster Stearns of Hancock designed a pictorial sampler which had special appeal for the clubwomen of the State; the top border of rosebuds, the center composition of a small farmhouse with a hemlock tree standing beside it, the lower border of lilacs, and the sentiment of the verse were typically New Hampshire in feeling. For the needleworkers among the New Hampshire clubwomen, Mrs. Stearns has also designed a wall hanging, featuring the lilac, which is the State flower; the design is a vase of lilac sprays and around the border is introduced a quotation from Amy Lowell's poem, "Lilacs". The plan for the wall hanging was presented at the annual meeting of the State Federation of Women's Clubs in 1940 by Mrs. Fred Wilman, the art chairman.

* * * * *

For many years patchwork, like samplermaking, was part of every young girl's education. According to Lucy Larcom, almost every New England girl learned to make patchwork at school while she was learning the alphabet.

Patchwork bedcovers were divided into two groups: the "comforter", made with a thick interlining, and the quilt, in which the interlining was much lighter. The top and under covers of the "comforter" were held together by strands of worsted pulled through them and the interlining and then tied or "tacked" together, while the coverings of quilts were fastened by means of fine patterns done in running stitches.

Quilting was an art in itself, and needleworkers were proud of their ability in this line. Sometimes they "quilted by the eye"; again they used the edge of a saucer or pan to make patterns of scallops or circles. Sometimes a string was chalked and stretched tautly across the quilt top. It was then snapped to impress the lines of the design on the fabric. A Nashua woman says that one of her earliest recollections was watching her grandmother mark a quilt in this manner. "Snap it again, Grannie!" she always cried as her grandmother completed each step of the marking process.

Another method of marking patterns was by means of carved wooden blocks which were heavily chalked and then pressed firmly against the upper side of the coverlet. Mrs. R. P. Peabody, a native of the Androscoggin valley town of Shelburne, wrote in 1882 that in her girlhood pressed quilts were part of every bride's marriage outfit. She recalled a number of pressed quilts of unusual beauty made by her mother's friends. One was bright green, lined with straw color, and quilted in inch squares with blue thread; another was blue, quilted in little fans; a third was quilted in feather work with a border of sunflower leaves, and then cross-quilted in straight lines. The patterns for these, like most others made in this vicinity, were pressed and marked by Mrs. Ezekiel Evans, who was famous in those days for her designs.

In the nineteenth century, needlewomen who were expert quilters were the queens of the quilting bees. All the women in the neighborhood were invited to these social gatherings, which combined business and pleasure, to quilt or tack the patchwork tops made by the hostess during the winter. Probably no other festival is more fundamentally a part of early American folklore than is the quilting bee. Customary thrift and industry imposed traditional restrictions on gaiety unless it was for a practical purpose, but a day busily spent over a quilting frame provided that justification.

The men folks came to the bee, the village parson rendered thanks for all material benefits, and then merriment reigned. The hostess prepared stewed chicken, smoked hams, beans and Indian pudding baked in brick ovens, pies, cakes, jams, preserves, and pickles. After the evening meal, in communities where such amusement was permitted, the floor was cleared for games and dancing.

The more ambitious quilter was not always content to use a single quilting motif on a coverlet. In one case, a pieced top in star pattern, made of red calico with border and intersecting strips of pale lemon yellow, showed alternating blocks of cross and star designs in quilting. This was the handiwork of a Nashua woman over eighty years old who decided, at that advanced age, that she wanted to leave a patchwork quilt as a legacy to each of her daughters. The finest type of quilting is found in the padded designs, where bits of wadding are inserted to raise the motif so that it "stands out", giving the effect of a bas-relief. Beautiful examples of this treatment are shown in the all-white coverlets which were once so popular. Such a coverlet, with an exquisitely quilted pattern made by Eliza Carter, a niece of Dr. Amos Twitchell of Keene, was displayed at the New Hampshire Historical Society quilt exhibition held in May, 1939. Another, equally beautiful, quilted in the Tree of Life design, was stitched in Nashua over a century ago. Two other quilted spreads of unusual beauty were shown at this exhibition. One was made of rose-glaze chintz; the other, of red figured material. Both of them were backed with homespun of butternut brown. Near them hung a copperplate tied quilt.

Copperplate "chince", often found in antique quilts after 1758, was widely used for bedcoverings by those who could afford to import this material. Two specimens, said to have come from homes in Hampstead, were found in Nashua. One, an all-over coverlet, in mellowed bronze, green, and rose, was made for a large four-poster bed, and is reputed to be one hundred and fifty years old. The other is a patchwork quilt with ten-inch squares of copperplate alternating with equal squares of white cotton, and hand-embroidered in poppy design. The quilting is beautifully done in a small diamond pattern, and the colors in the chintz are as fresh as when first printed despite its alleged age of one hundred years.

The terms "pieced" quilt and "patchwork" quilt have become synonymous through common usage, despite the fact that to *piece* means to *join by seams* and to *patch* means to *sew a smaller piece of goods onto a larger one.* Strictly speaking, the appliquéd quilt belongs in the latter category.

The pieced variety is the more common, and nearly all the quilts made in America before 1750 were of this type. The pieced squares of geometrical figures, based on the square, the rectangle, the diamond, the circle, and the hexagon, were made by sewing together vari-colored pieces of cloth, usually combining an equal number of light and dark pieces. Quiltmakers were proud of the fine stitches they used in joining these myriad bits of fabric. A quilt of this kind, composed of four triangular pieces in the inch block pattern, the whole containing 42,568 pieces, was completed by a young girl of Bow when she was only ten years of age. It, too, was displayed at the New Hampshire Historical Society exhibition of 1939.

In making appliquéd or laid-on quilts, flowers, leaves, wreaths, and similar motifs were cut from colored fabrics and sewed with small stitches to a neutral background. The one well-known deviation from these two standard groups is the crazy quilt, in which odds and ends of cloth were put together hit-or-miss "crazy fashion", and which was probably the earliest type of American-made quilt. In its simplest form it was designed to use up scraps of worn-out clothing; the more elaborate type, which was very popular in the late nineteenth century, consisted of "boughten" pieces of cloth and was adorned with featherstitching, herringbone, and other examples of line stitches.

Mrs. Anabel Glines of Haverhill owns two of these elaborate crazy-quilts, made of silk and velvet pieces. One was made before 1880 by Mrs. Glines' grandmother, who was born in 1818. Thirty-two different fancy stitches were used in sewing together the pieces of varied shapes. Garden and wild flowers, no two alike, are embroidered on the plain blocks. Scattered among the embroidered flowers are appliquéd designs, one of them showing a fat red velvet bird perched on a brown velvet branch. In the second quilt, which was made by "Grandma Susan's daughter", born in 1839, the pieces are arranged in a definite pattern, and the edge of the quilt is finished with pointed strips arranged to form a scalloped border. During the last seven years, Mrs. Glines has made two hundred quilts, fourteen of which have been crazy quilts.

Every quilt block, from the simple pieced-up "four-square" and "nine-square" to the intricate laid-on "Rising Sun", has its own individual name. To the imagination of our feminine ancestors, we are indebted for the variety given the designs of their handicraft. Living experiences, involving history, religion, politics, romance, and nature, were reproduced through the creations of their fingers, and christened "Log Cabin", "Star of Bethlehem", "Tree of Life", "Jacob's Ladder", "Rose of Sharon", "Whig Rose", "Yankee Pride", "Fifty-Four Forty or Fight", "Lincoln's Platform", "Air Castle", "Lovers' Links", "Orange Peel", and other picturesque names.

Variations of the "Log Cabin", "Star", and "Basket" designs are perhaps the most popular with modern quiltmakers. One elderly New Hampshire needlewoman confided to a visitor that there was "an awful lot of sameness" in her quilts because she loved the basket pattern. She said: "When I'm making patchwork, I think of all the baskets I've had. One I used to put apples in, shiny red Mackintoshes, one for flowers, and then my old work basket—I sort of miss my old work basket, it got lost someway. But I do like baskets."

One of the most ornate designs ever used by American quiltmakers is the "American Eagle", which was applied to many forms of arts and crafts during the first part of the last century. Mrs. Mabel F. Ames of Somersworth displayed a quilt decorated with this symbol at the Rochester Fair in 1939. The quilt was made approximately one hundred and fifty years ago. In the center, narrow red, green, and gold bands, shaped like elongated leaves, form a circle. These are enclosed in a narrow band of crosswise stitches, arranged to form a sort of frame to the first picture. Around this circle are placed four eagles with heads and tails of green, bodies of deep gold color, and spreading red wings. A four-inch band of needle scrollwork, finished with a band of red, encircles the four eagles. The quilt is finished with a narrow band of green.

Like the sampler, a quilt was often used as a memorial piece. Friends and neighbors of the deceased would reverently open her scrap bag and stitch together bits of dress materials she had worn into a "Memory Quilt", reminiscent of her life and the qualities which endeared her to them.

A near relative to the "Memory Quilt" is the "Memorial" coverlet. At first the names were interchangeable, but later the term "Memorial" came to mean the work of living persons to perpetuate their memory for posterity. An illustration of this type of bedcovering is found in the rooms of the Milford Historical Society at "Lullwood", ancestral home of Colonel Oliver W. Lull. It is made of unbleached cotton, each block bearing the embroidered name of some person prominent in the life of the community. The writing was all done in the same fine hand, that of the late Mrs. Arthur W. Howison, during the first World War. The embroidery is beautifully executed, and the brilliant colors of the material make the quilt a valuable memento of which the town is very proud.

Out of the autograph album with its varying sentiments both wise and maudlin, emerged the "Album" quilt, each block bearing an embroidered text or verse and signed by the donor. Sometimes the inscription, written in indelible ink in a bold masculine hand, gave evidence that men were not averse to joining in these testimonial tokens. To be the recipient of an "Album" quilt was considered a distinguished honor.

Similar to the "Album" was the "Friendship" coverlet, often more interesting than beautiful because of the latitude allowed in both design and coloring. The finished product was a medley of patterns and fabrics, since each block, including material and workmanship, was the contribution of some friend.

The autographs of women who were prominent in Concord during the mid-nineteenth century appeared on a "Friendship" quilt shown at the New Hampshire Historical Society Exhibit in 1939. Sentiments also were inscribed on some of the white centers of the cross-pattern blocks which formed the design. Clara A. Foster wrote: "The Lord deal kindly with you, as ye have dealt with the dead & with the living. October 4, 1850." Hattie Gibbs Brown's inscription was: "From her Mother—L. G. Brown—June 5, 1886."

The names of New Hampshire quiltmakers are legion. Many of them are elderly women who, as a pastime for unaccustomed leisure, revert to a form of handicraft which they learned in their childhood. One of them said recently, "Yes, indeed, I sewed patchwork from the time I was five years old. Used to have to piece so many blocks as a stint before I could play. And I couldn't hurry it either for if it wasn't done just so, I had to rip it out and do it all over again. Oh, we were disciplined in those days." Another chuckled when a friend brought her a book on the subject, "So they write books about patchwork, do they? Well, I never could write a book, but I sewed a heap of bed quilts in my day."

Collecting quilts is the hobby of Mrs. Frank P. Ayer of Chichester, who often exhibits her quilts publicly in pageants and gives talks about quilt patterns. And a pageant revived an interest in quilts for a woman who probably is New Hampshire's outstanding authority on the subject. Mrs. Ellen Emeline Webster of Franklin, at the time she was a member of the staff of Wheaton College, was asked to take charge of a faculty club program. She wished to make her program a very different one, less formal if possible. So she decided to have an old-time party and show the audience how people entertained in the 1860's and 1870's. She borrowed the choicest old quilts which various members of her family owned, and hung them around three corners of the hall.

Meantime she had written a pageant, arranged the music, and trained a group of the faculty club to perform in it. During the presentation Mrs. Webster, assisted by four or five members of the club, attired in costumes which were cherished family heirlooms, actually worked at a quilting frame and explained the craft in a conversational way. The pageant was a tremendous success, and even the men in the audience evidenced an extraordinary interest in the subject of old-time quilts and the patterns used in making them.

Starting at this point, Mrs. Webster began a piece of research which she believes will have great historical value to quilt lovers. She made a miniature chart of many of the interesting quilts she has seen, reproducing the pattern as accurately as possible in scale and color. These charts are made on white cardboard about two feet square with pieces of cloth pasted over the preliminary sketch. Usually, the charts show only one motif of the quilt pattern. Some of them, however, are whole miniature quilts, especially when the all-over pattern is the outstanding feature of the quilt. She has over one hundred and sixty of these charts, all designed from quilts she has actually seen, and all reproducing old-time patterns. In one or more of her charts she has used over a thousand pieces of cloth to make the reproduction.

She says her favorite quilts probably are those of the appliquéd type, particularly one which has an early chintz flower appliquéd onto an unbleached cotton background. She thinks that color selection is one of the most important points to be considered in judging a piece of this type of needlework. Mrs. Webster is interested in quilts from all sections of the country; she owns several early New England specimens which she intends to describe in detail in a forthcoming book.

She was born in a small New Hampshire town where quiltmaking was a necessary chore in every household. Her mother taught her to piece and quilt meticulously, and there was a family "piece-box" of odds and ends of material, kept handy for idle fingers to cut and stitch into "tops". She made a dozen or more quilts in her girlhood, all of them carefully planned, but none of them was regarded as a show piece.

At the time that Mrs. Webster and her sisters were making quilts for the family bedsteads, the "Charm" pattern became popular. This piece of needlework is composed of hundreds of pieces of cloth with no two in the whole quilt alike. In a small New England town of the late nineteenth century, one would think it would be quite impossible to get together one thousand different patterns of cloth; yet it was done. For in time the odds and ends cut away from garments, the scraps left from dresses and aprons, and the bits "swapped" with neighbors, mounted up, and blended together into "a mosaic of hallowed memories."

XV

HOME RUGMAKING

Home rugmaking was not a Colonial craft; "ruggs" are mentioned in early New Hampshire inventories and in old wills, but in the seventeenth and early eighteenth centuries the word referred to bedcoverings, not to mats or carpets.

It is not known who first had the idea of using worn-out clothing and old blankets to make rugs. Most authorities agree, however, that the earliest rag floor coverings were put together by sewing pieces of cast off clothing onto lengths of homespun and by overlapping the edges of the patches to give the rug greater warmth and durability.

From such simple beginnings came the patchwork or appliquéd rug, which was followed by the braided rug (made by plaiting long strips of discarded cloth into braids and then sewing the edges of the braids together to form a round or oval mat), and by the hooked rug, with its gay design, formed by pulling bits of cloth in loops through a coarsely woven foundation material.

The hooked rug is, perhaps, the most popular and most publicized type of all the modern handmade rag rugs. Probably more of them were produced in New Hampshire during the two decades following the Civil War than at any other time except the present. The craft owes much of its popularity at that time to Edward Sands Frost, a tin peddler from Biddeford, Maine, who, in 1868, designed and sold the first commercial rug patterns in America. These patterns, which he carried over the countryside in his peddler's cart, sold like "hot cakes" when he showed them to his customers, the rural women of northern New England. Eventually, the enterprise proved so profitable that Mr. Frost opened a salesroom in Boston, where he continued in business for about six years.

Frost's patterns included varied designs composed of floral motifs set in borders of elaborate scrollwork, animals framed with wreaths and sprays of flowers, and an assortment of conventionalized units, strongly Oriental in character. The floral rugs showed the influence of the Aubusson carpets which were imported from France and used in the homes of well-to-do Americans in the nineteenth century. An excellent example of Frost's style of pattern-making, of interest to collectors, is shown in the "White Frost Rug", which hangs on a wall of the second floor of the New Hampshire Historical Society building on Park Street, Concord.

Popular as hooked rugs were at the time when the former tin peddler was selling patterns, women began to lose interest in them during the 1890's. The time came when rugs which had once been treasured possessions were transferred from places of honor before the haircloth sofa and the square piano in the parlor to humble spots in front of the wood range and the cast-iron sink in the kitchen. Some years later, however, a revived interest in early pine and maple furniture brought the gay drawn-in mats back to their rightful positions in livingroom and guest chamber. This was due in a great degree to the influence of the "city folks" who were buying backroads property to turn into summer homes. Following their lead, New Hampshire women unearthed the rug frames stored away in the attic, and spent long winter evenings cutting up discarded clothing for "hooking". These women soon discovered that there was a market for the products of the rug hook and piece bag; they learned also that the old rag rugs which had been used as a cover for the apple barrel or as a bed for the tortoise-shell cat might be salable.

At first the rug industry was carried on intermittently by a few isolated workers and by one small rural community group. But the popularity of the work has increased steadily during the past quarter of a century, until today it is one of the major home crafts, engaged in by both men and women.

Interest in rugmaking as a community project owes much to the background laid in the early twentieth century by the late Helen Rickey Albee, who acquired a national reputation as the organizer of the first American rural industry using this craft as a neighborhood business. Mrs. Albee, who owned a home at Silver Lake, a crossroad corner of the mountain town of Madison, had been trained in design, but knew very little about actual handicraft work when she bought her New Hampshire property. While furnishing her house, she found that "a strange glamour hung over work done with the hands".* This discovery was the cornerstone upon which she built her plans for finding some kind of home work which would give employment to the women of the neighborhood in which she lived.

Mrs. Albee felt that a rural industry such as she visualized must be built around a craft somewhat familiar to the workers. As practically all the women of Silver Lake knew how to "draw-in", she decided on the hooked rug for the medium of expression. Her neighbors understood little about design and the correct use of color; she, on the other hand, was wholly ignorant of the technique of rugmaking. This lack of practical knowledge did not deter her when once she had decided to undertake the task. As she says: "That I had never seen a rug executed, and had merely heard the process described, seemed of no consequence; nor did my absolute ignorance of dyeing daunt me."†

One day, after weeks of hard work and constant experiment, she was rewarded by finding that she actually had completed a rug, a fact so surprising that she has described it by saying: "So long was the way and so slow the ascent, I scarcely recognized it when the supposably worthless hooked rug proved itself an en-

* *Mountain Playmates. Helen R. Albee. Boston, Mass. Houghton, Mifflin and Company, 1900. p. 56.*

† *Mountain Playmates. Helen R. Albee. Boston, Mass. Houghton, Mifflin and Company, 1900. p. 242.*

chanted carpet that had lifted me into a new world, where I not only had an enlarged outlook on many things undreamed of before, but where it gave me extended opportunities . . . to serve others."*

The making of this "enchanted rug" was the beginning of the Abnakee Rug Industry. The rugs produced and sold under this label differed in a number of respects from those which the women had made before they worked under Mrs. Albee's directions. Abnakee Rugs were made entirely of wool, and were hand-dyed; their bold, effective, and varied designs were worked in tones of terra cotta, old rose, old pink, tans, dull yellows, rich old blues, olive, sage green, and old ivory. The technique of hooking varied somewhat from the old-fashioned methods; instead of being of even height, the loops were pulled up a trifle unequal in length, and the higher loops were sheared.

The first exhibition of the Abnakee rugs was very modest; but it attracted so much attention that plans were made to show the rugs in various large cities. The rugs were described in metropolitan newspapers and in magazines; art schools investigated the technique of their workmanship; interior decorators recommended them to their clients.

Eventually, for personal reasons, Mrs. Albee gave up the work at Silver Lake; but she continued to teach rugmaking and to lecture on the subject. In 1918, through a special arrangement, the Manchester Institute of Arts and Sciences acquired the rights to her designs and to her dye formulas. Later, the technique used in fashioning Abnakee Rugs was taught in the Institute craft classes by Miss May Davis, who had studied with Mrs. Albee in her Washington winter home, and by Mrs. Maud Briggs Knowlton, instructor of design and art.

This rug class was the first step in the development of the craft as it was taught at the Institute. The technique of rugmaking in this class has changed from time to time, but the use of artistic color combinations and fine designs is maintained as faithfully today as it

* *Ibid. p. 244.*

was when Helen Albee first planned her "Enchanted Rug". For some years, the rug class at the Institute has been directed by Mrs. Martha S. Watson of Manchester, who is an authority on all kinds of rugmaking. Mrs. Watson also supervises craftwork at the NYA Resident Center in Berlin.

The Extension Service of the University of New Hampshire promotes classes in rugmaking as part of its county program for rural women. Lessons are not restricted to the hooked rug, however, but include instructions for an assortment of easily and quickly made varieties of rugs. The home demonstrators are constantly looking for new ideas for their classes. Recently, under the supervision of Mrs. Alice Goodrum, a group of women met in Marlboro to learn how to make rugs constructed of squares, woven on small handlooms and crocheted together, which the instructor had seen while traveling in Tennessee.

Hooked rugs were very important in establishing an interest in the Sandwich Home Industries, a New Hampshire community project, which was the forerunner of the League of New Hampshire Arts and Crafts as that organization operates today. Like Mrs. Albee, the late J. Randolph Coolidge and Mrs. Coolidge of Sandwich were interested in helping their neighbors find some way by which they could make use of handicrafts to supplement their incomes. Working with a committee from the town historical society, Mr. and Mrs. Coolidge developed a plan to stimulate interest in the idea. They invited everybody in the community to the village library to view an exhibit of locally owned hooked rugs, and to hear a talk by a craftworker.

From that time on until the present day, rugmaking has been part of the League program. The rugs are designed to meet the requirements of workmanship established by a jury on craftsmanship and the products turned out are of the finest types.

Rugmaking in New Hampshire owes much of its present popularity to certain local collectors who have preserved rare rugs which otherwise would have been destroyed. Prominent among them is Robert P. Peckett of Sugar Hill, one of the first persons in northern

CONCORD WREATH HOOKED RUG, *pattern adapted by Mrs. Josephine Driscoll of Manchester from a rug owned by the New Hampshire Historical Society.*

WHEAT PATTERN HOOKED RUG *designed by Mrs. Josephine Driscoll of Manchester.*

MRS. ELVIN PRESCOTT *of Hampton Falls, hooking a rug.*

New Hampshire to recognize the historic and the artistic value of the old-time floor coverings. Mr. Peckett's rugs, which include every variety of design known to the hooked rugmaker, are displayed on the floors of his inn overlooking the Franconia valley. Another New Hampshire inn noted for the homemade rugs used in its interior decoration is the Ellis House of Keene, where over one hundred rugs cover the floors of both public and guest rooms.

Designing rug patterns and teaching the craft of rugmaking, rather than producing marketable rugs, is a form of home industry developed during the past few years by a Manchester woman. Mrs. Josephine Driscoll is one of the best-known teachers of rugmaking in the State, and she has a large number of pupils in numerous towns and cities. As a background for her present work, she has studied applied design, theory of color, dyeing, water color, and oil painting.

Although Mrs. Driscoll is a competent hand-hooker, most of her own work and that of her pupils is done with a mechanical hooker, which she recommends enthusiastically. This gadget is worked with a reverse push-and-pull action, and, contrary to opinion, is not a new thing by any means. A similar device was used as far back as 1891, and, according to William Winthrop Kent,* many of our grandmothers' rugs probably had their backgrounds filled in by this method. Following this technique, the craftsman works from the wrong side of the rug, and pushes the cloth strips through the background by means of a prod, or a mechanical hook, which is threaded with the material.

As far as is known, Mrs. Driscoll can be accredited as the first person in recent years to make extensive use of a foundation material other than burlap. She noticed that the foundations of the old rugs often wore out before the designs, so she experimented with fabrics to discover one that would have more lasting qualities. Her final choice was a cloth which is soft and pliable to work on, and which has extraordinary long-wearing qualities.

Mrs. Driscoll's rug designs are patterns copied exactly from old

* *The Hooked Rug. William Winthrop Kent. New York. Dodd & Co., 1930.*

rugs; and the rugs which she has completed herself are hooked with old colors. She has an 8' 6" x 10' 10" hand-hooked rug, the design for which she copied from an old rug, which was priced by a New York City dealer at $10,000. Mrs. Driscoll's copy is hooked almost entirely with old materials—with paisley shawls and old blankets. She dipped and dyed the new cloth to match the colors and shadings of its model. In addition she has copies of three patterns taken from rugs in the Metropolitan Museum in New York City; two, from the collection in the New Hampshire Historical Society in Concord; and one, from the Currier Gallery of Art in Manchester.

There are a number of well-known rugmakers in New Hampshire who have developed the art to a point where the products of their rug hooks meet the rigid demands of workmanship required by the League of New Hampshire Arts and Crafts, or who dispose of their wares in markets which they have built up through their own initiative. Other artisans, equally as proficient as those who sell their rugs, make rugs solely for their own pleasure. So many fine craftsmen are perfecting the technique of the handmade rug at the present time that only a few typical examples can be selected for description.

The hooked rugs made by Mrs. William T. Gardner of Nashua are distinguished for their hand-hooking of incredible fineness and even texture. Mrs. Gardner learned to handle a hook when she was a girl in Newfoundland, and many of the designs which she works out have been in her family for several generations.

One particular pattern used by this expert craftworker is a simple "S" scroll, which was originally copied from the carved paneling in the cabin of a boat wrecked many years ago off the coast of Newfoundland and washed ashore. An oak leaf was worked into this scroll, giving it the proper balance so that it can be used as a border design, or can be enlarged and used as a central theme. One of the most noticeable things about her work is the manner in which she handles the coloring in the backgrounds. She seldom uses a solid color, but dyes and colors the rug material she hooks in, and creates a mottled effect, which from age and wear takes on a streaked and marble-like appearance.

This marbled effect in backgrounds has also been perfected by Mrs. Marion M. MacLean of Hopkinton, an indefatigable worker who has made and sold over a hundred hooked rugs. Her products resemble the "White Frost" patterns, and feature designs of roses on light groundwork. Mrs. MacLean, like many New Hampshire rugmakers, uses a hook manufactured at home. Ingenious workers have adapted a variety of implements to rug hooking. Mrs. MacLean's hook is made from the discarded piston rod of a Model T Ford. Mrs. Nellie French of Manchester, who, like Mrs. Gardner, learned the technique of hooking in Newfoundland, and Mrs. Nellie Runnells of Hopkinton use hooks of old kitchen forks; and one of the hooks owned by Mrs. Charles R. Corey of Manchester was fashioned from the tine of a pitchfork.

Mrs. Corey is interested particularly in copying old designs and reproducing patterns in exact replicas of the originals. Among her adaptations are designs taken from an early hooked rug. Her method is characteristic of local rugmakers, who generally make use of motifs which follow the traditions of New England or the maritime provinces of Canada.

A notable exception to this general rule is found in a set of rugs, each six feet by two and one-half feet in size, which are being made at the present time by Mrs. Elvin J. Prescott of Hampton Falls. The rugs were ordered by a client living on Long Island, New York, and are intended for wall hangings rather than for floor coverings. They are proof of that statement made by Dorothy Drage in her book, *Rug Making:* "Architecture has been described as History writ in stone: the art of making carpets might equally be called History writ in wool."* These rugs depict an historical event executed in needlework rather than in carpetwork, for the designs are replicas of the famous Bayeux Tapestries, those ancient masterpieces of needlecraft which tell the story of the coming of William the Conqueror to England.

* *Rug Making. Dorothy Drage. London. Isaac Pitman & Sons, 1937. Introduction—p. v.*

A number of New Hampshire men have gained publicity in local papers through their interest in hooked rugmaking. In a few instances the work is simply a hobby which a craftsman, though adept in another line, has taken up. Robert F. Heartz of Brentwood, well-known weaver and teacher, makes hooked rugs in his spare time. His ideas are unusual, and are distinguished for the modern manner in which they are carried out. He says: "In my hooking I use old patterns as well as my own designs. I weave my own foundation fabrics and dye all my materials, both rags and yarns." Mr. Heartz's work has been exhibited in several of the large art museums in the United States. One of them, hooked through a hand-woven canvas with specially spun and hand-dyed yarns, was hung in the exhibit at the International Exhibition held in Paris in 1937. Several of his rugs were shown at the International Rug Exhibition at the Metropolitan Museum of Art in New York City.

Starr K. Verge, Sr., of Derry makes hooked rugs purely as a hobby. In this avocation, however, he carries on a family tradition. In their home town of Liverpool, Nova Scotia, members of the Verge family gained considerable reputation for their products in a community where rugmaking was the rule rather than the exception. Mr. Verge had his first lessons from his mother when he was only seven years old. For over thirty years he has devoted his spare time to this hobby. He is a versatile and rapid worker; his prized Log Cabin rug was completed in the record time of six days. He adapts his patterns from old tapestries and original sketches, drawing the designs on the burlap foundation after it has stretched in the frames.

George Chandler, a well-known cabinetmaker of Concord, does not make rugs, but he is noted for the original patterns which he draws with great facility at almost an instant's notice. In this line of work he carries on an old New England custom; for in each generation there usually was some person in every community who had an eye for form and line and the manual dexterity necessary to block out a pattern when his neighbors needed one.

Students of design have discovered that environment has played an important part in the evolution of rug patterns. They have noted that along the Atlantic coast, hooked rugs are decorated with representations of ships, marine life, and other nautical subjects. Inland, garden flowers, field flowers, and domestic animals are used for models. Among the domestic animals, the family tabby and the pet dog are most often represented; in wild life designs, lions, tigers, tropical birds, and deer are very popular.

A rug in the collection owned by the Currier Gallery of Art in Manchester is adorned with a stag and doe picture, reminiscent of the period when a Landseer painting hung in almost every American home. There are other rugs in this collection which are also typical of the fads and fancies of the days in which they were made. One of them which attracts much attention is a Bride's Welcome Mat, of the 1880's, with the initials of the contracting parties appearing at opposite ends. Sentiment rugs were very popular at the time when the bride's mat was designed; they included hearth rugs of all kinds, made in half-circles to fit against doorsills, and often bearing the slogan, "Home Sweet Home", and Welcome Mats, with their words of greeting hooked in gay colors. The Welcome Mat in the Currier Gallery appears to be the ugly duckling of the collection; nevertheless, its very ugliness, exaggerated by its lopsided shape and its crudely made cabbage roses, has an odd charm and an endearing appeal for recognition.

The braided rug is the hooked rug's greatest rival. It is favored by many craftworkers because it can be so easily planned to carry out almost any designated color scheme in interior decoration. Mrs. Ralph Parsons of Manchester is particularly adept at braiding rugs to match hangings and wallpapers. Mrs. Parsons has the knack of combining colors in a way that makes her rugs resemble those her grandmother and great-grandmother braided years ago. She has built up a fair-sized home business which started in a small way; one of her small braided rugs was displayed in a country store in Northwood, where its beautiful colorings and exquisite workmanship were admired by many tourists. This "one-rug show" brought Mrs. Parsons a number of orders; they have increased steadily, until today her rugs are found in homes as far west as California.

Mrs. Anabel Glines of Haverhill started a little rugmaking industry in a different way. She began by braiding chairmats and table covers, and was so successful in her venture that she branched out into rugmaking. Her wares have sold well. She says, "I have made so many rugs that I have lost actual count of the number I have braided up to the present time."

In Epsom, Mrs. Mary Curtis of "The Cobweb" spends all the time she can spare from her duties in her antique shop braiding large rugs. Recently she made a nine-by-twelve oval rug, containing six hundred and fifty running yards of handmade braid, which she completed in three months and three days. The colors used were rust, brown, gray, and dark blue, with each braid showing one strand of black throughout the pattern, which is bordered by ten rows of solid black braids. Mrs. Curtis prefers the darker shades of colors for her wares; she claims that they harmonize better with the varied color schemes in interior decorating and that they follow the genuine traditions of the old-time rugs. She says she began making rugs of this type about ten years ago, when she bought an early house whose floors needed traditional coverings to fit its style. After she had covered the floors of her own home, she began to make rugs for her relatives and friends, and later produced them on special orders from clients outside her immediate circle of acquaintances.

The technique of braided rugmaking is especially adapted to group work. In Portsmouth the craft has been a source of revenue to the women of the Baptist Church in earning money for the church missionary society. The chairman of the committee in charge assigns parts of the work to each member; some of them do the braiding, while others, seated comfortably around a low table especially constructed for the work, sew the braids together. The rugs are made on order, and the demand for them far exceeds the supply.

A variety of homemade rugs, other than the hooked and braided types, have been and still are made by local craftworkers. Contrary to general belief, they are not entirely of New England origin; in some form or other practically all have been produced in rural sections of this country and of Europe. For example, patchwork rugs of soft, pliable leather were made in Spain; tufted rugs, in Brittany; the button rug, known in Scandinavia as the rosette rug, was a common form of handwork in Norway; and needlework rugs, developed in *gros point* and in cross-stitch, have been made in England ever since the late eighteenth century, and continued to be turned out by both English and American needleworkers far into the nineteenth century.

Some ambitious women even went a step farther than embroidering small rugs: they made carpets adorned with a varied number of needlework stitches and of such a size that they completely covered the floor upon which they were spread. Examples of these carpets are extremely uncommon and are relatively valuable. According to the magazine *Antiques,* the embroidered carpet is considered the rarest type of early American textile.*

Probably the best known embroidered American carpet still intact is the Caswell Carpet, made early in the last century by a young woman of Castleton, Vermont. At least three carpets of this type are known to have been embroidered in New Hampshire. The first one was probably manufactured in Lancaster in 1805, to adorn a bedchamber in the home of Richard Claire Everett, the first attorney in Coös County, and later a justice of the Supreme Court.

According to a description written by Persis F. Chase, Squire Everett's great-granddaughter, forty pounds of wool from the backs of the home flock of sheep were used in making the floor covering. Nancy Greenleaf and Lucy White, experts in their line, were hired to spin it into good strong yarn, four skeins to the pound. Then the yarn was taken to Eunice Stockwell, champion weaver of Lancaster. It came home again a great roll of white flannel, which, in turn, was carried on horseback fifty miles down the reaches of the Connecticut River to Haverhill to be fulled and colored.

When the actual work of making the carpet began, the three great rolls of dark brown cloth were cut into breadths, the length of the room. Each breadth was marked off into blocks a foot square, ar-

* *Antiques. Vol. XIII (April, 1928). The Editor's Attic. Homer Eaton Keyes.*

ranged so that they would match when the breadths were sewn together. In describing the embroidery on the squares, Mrs. Chase says, "In each square was a large star. It was worked in what you call Kensington stitch. . . . The squares were worked in green, the stars in yellow, and in each point of the stars were little stars, worked in different colors; and so the whole carpet was made by hand. It was real handsome when it was done. Folks came from all around to see it."*

The second carpet of which there is a written record is in point of chronology the last of the three to be made. In 1850 Mrs. M. J. Otterson exhibited a floor covering of over thirty square yards at an agricultural fair held in Concord. According to a local journalist, it was "tufted and wrought by hand, a fine thing, which must have cost much labor."†

The third New Hampshire embroidered carpet, more than the others, has attracted the attention of collectors of early Americana. It was designed and executed by a young girl of West Rumney, who made it for her "setting out". Although Lucetta Smart stitched her name exactly in the center top of her masterpiece, she made no record of the date. Certain facts, however, prove that the carpet probably was completed in the year 1820.

The foundation of the rug, which measures about five feet by seven feet, is made of two lengths of white wool stitched together. The embroidery, executed in chain stitch, is carried out in three shades of blue, in varied browns, in reds shading from vermillion to pale pink, and in gray-green to form a pattern around which a border of flowering vines surrounds a flowering tree growing from a basket.

Some years ago this extraordinary rug, which antedates the Caswell Carpet by some years, was sold to a resident of Rumney who

---

* *The Lancaster Sketch Book. Persis F. Chase. Brattleboro, Vermont. Frank E. Housh and Co., 1887. pp. 104-105.*

† *Transactions of the New Hampshire Agricultural Society for 1850, 1851, and 1852. Concord, N. H., 1852. p. 111.*

used it as a floor covering for the parlor bedroom. Thence it passed to a dealer in Manchester, and eventually it became the property of a famous collector of Manhassett, Long Island. This carpet, embroidered by the deft fingers of a New Hampshire girl, is preserved as a priceless piece of art and is a memorial to the State's needleworkers and rugmakers.

XVI

ART AND NEAR ART

In the middle of the eighteenth century there came from Bermuda to Boston an artist who acquired a notable reputation for his portrait painting. It was the fashion around 1760 to have one's portrait painted by Joseph Blackburn, and many of the well-known New England men and their wives sat for him in all the splendor of their rich brocades, lace ruffles, and jewels. Blackburn painted in Portsmouth as well as in Boston, and certain Crown officers, ship owners, and other nabobs of wealthy Old Strawberry Bank came to life on the artist's canvas before 1763, when his name disappeared forever from contemporary records.

Blackburn, like many less successful artists, began his career in New England as an itinerant portrait painter. Before the days of the daguerreotype, the tintype, and the cabinet photograph, these traveling artists went from one New Hampshire town to another, set up their easels, and painted well-to-do residents and members of their families. Although only a few of the names of the men who engaged in this occupation are known to us today, many examples of their work are owned privately and others hang in local museums.

Numerous portraits of local personages, painted during the late eighteenth and early nineteenth centuries, are well preserved. A large collection of them is displayed in the Manchester Historic Association Building. Others, painted during the first half of the nineteenth century, are owned by the Currier Gallery of Art in Manchester. The likenesses of Benjamin and Diadamia Gooden, painted in 1824, are hanging in the Colonial Room of this Gallery. Other portraits, part of their permanent collection of American antiques, are kept in the Gallery vaults. One of the oldest of these pictures is painted in water colors rather than oils, and shows a young girl holding a rose and a basket of flowers.

The survey of American portraits painted prior to 1860, which is being made at the present time by the Historical Records Survey of the Work Projects Administration, reveals a collection in the William Long Memorial Building in Hopkinton, covering approximately a period of one hundred years (1750-1850). Among them are the pictures of the Reverend and Mrs. Broughton White, presented to the museum during the 1820's.

Although these early portraits are without doubt excellent likenesses and serve as authentic sources of data for costumes, many of them are not works of art, in the ordinary sense. In many instances the men who painted them were untrained. They depended on native skill and facility with brush and pencil to achieve craftsmanship.

There was a general similarity in the methods which itinerant artists employed. During the winter months they blocked out their canvases and painted in figures of men, women, and children. Then, in the spring and summer, they went over the countryside seeking customers. To the figures which they had previously outlined on canvases or pieces of board, they added faces painted from life, and such individual touches as a lace collar, a treasured brooch or ring, or the usual hair style of their models.

Occasionally an itinerant artist would settle down for a time and open a studio in one of the larger towns. In the early 1830's, A. W. Ingalls and P. Hewings "took rooms for a short time" in Concord. The name of the latter crept into the records set down by the Reverend Nathaniel Bouton in Concord's first history. The clergyman noted that, when President Andrew Jackson visited the town in 1833, Hewing made a sketch of him, while attending services held in the Old North Church. From this sketch he painted "one of the best likenesses ever taken of the General".

Probably the best known of the itinerant artists who worked in

New Hampshire was Samuel F. B. Morse, inventor of the electric telegraph, who came to Concord early in the nineteenth century and painted five portraits for fifteen dollars each. According to the "Recollections" of Deacon Asa McFarland, Morse treated the town to three great surprises: first, by painting portraits of its inhabitants which could be recognized at sight; second, by courting and carrying off the prettiest girl in town; third, by bestowing the largest marriage fee on record up to that time. But in spite of the degree of success which he later attained in art, Mr. Morse's chief interest was science.

It was not expensive to get one's portrait painted in Concord during the 1830's. D. G. Lamont of Scotland, member of the Royal Academy of Arts, London, "artist, profile and miniature painter", while visiting the town in his professional capacity, gave his customers their choice of profiles executed in colors for three dollars each, and miniatures painted on ivory "in elegant style" for five dollars and upwards.

In 1841 William B. Hoit of Concord, who had formerly advertised that he was a "Portrait and Ornamental Painter", announced in the local paper that he had added daguerreotype miniatures to his line of work. In doing this Mr. Hoit was simply following the trend of the times, for he foresaw that the invention of the daguerreotype in 1839 would play havoc with the portrait business of the minor portrait painters.

Daguerreotypists, like portrait painters, often traveled about from town to town. An historian of Candia recalls that the first of these itinerant artists to visit the town arrived with "a large saloon, or operating room, on wheels,"* and located on the common near the Congregational Church; there he waited for customers, each of whom sat six minutes for a likeness.

The cutout paper profiles fashionable during the eighteenth and early nineteenth centuries were called *silhouettes* after Etienne De Silhouette, Minister of Finance to Louis XV of France, who imposed

---

* *History of Candia. J. Bailey Moore. Manchester, N. H. George W. Browne, 1893. p. 370.*

the rigid economies which made the use of cheap materials necessary for such work. The craft of cutting silhouettes spread to England and then to America.

The most important name linked with silhouette making is that of Edouart, a French master, who had great success in the line. He came to America in 1839, and before he returned home in 1848, he had cut the profiles of many famous men, among them Daniel Webster and his brother Ezekiel, the handsome and prominent Boscawen attorney.

Silhouettists sprang up all over the country; they used all kinds of methods. The simplest form of silhouette was the one cut out of paper or thin silk with an ordinary pair of scissors. Not all silhouettes, however, were cut with scissors.

Jacob A. Potter, artist and inventor who lived on the shore of Turtle Pond on the east side of the Merrimack River, invented an instrument for cutting these profiles. Similar instruments were invented by other men, but all of them followed the same general idea—that of a small rod about four feet long, hung horizontally on a pivot about five inches from one of its ends. J. Bailey Moore, author of the history of Candia, and a portrait painter of local reputation, minutely described a similar instrument as follows: "A pencil was inserted in the short end of the rod and when the long end was passed carefully over the features of the sitter an excellent profile likeness in miniature was traced by the pencil upon a piece of paper attached to a board standing in a perpendicular position."* Silhouettes were sometimes touched up or improved with ornaments placed in the hair or dress by means of the pen; again the head might be cut from paper and the body indicated by pen and ink drawings. Frequently silhouettes were painted on glass, ivory, plaster, paper, or cardboard.

Local silhouettists did not usually sign their names to their work and must be traced through their advertising in local papers. One of them, William King, who was in Portsmouth in 1805, called

---

* *History of Candia.* J. Bailey Moore. Manchester, N. H. George W. Browne, 1893, p. 370.

himself a "physiognitrace". He put a notice in the *New Hampshire Gazette* saying that he was ready to cut profiles at the reasonable price of twenty-five cents for two profiles of one person. His advertisement stated that he had already made over eight thousand of these pictures in Salem, Newburyport, and the adjoining towns. Furthermore, he said that he could cut a silhouette in six minutes. King was evidently an itinerant artist, for he announced during the next year in the *Dartmouth Gazette* that he intended to stay at Mr. James Wheelock's in Hanover for one week.

William Chamberlain of New London, a little known profilist of the 1820's, usually made his silhouettes in duplicate, keeping one copy for himself. A collection of eighty-nine of his silhouettes is now in the possession of the American Antiquarian Society. When Chamberlain's granddaughter presented it to the organization, she said that the silhouettist did this work while he was on tour through New York and New England, particularly in New Hampshire and Massachusetts.

Martha Ann Honeywell, born in Lempster about 1787, is one of the few New Hampshire women silhouettists whose names have been recorded. In spite of the physical handicap of having been born with abbreviated arms and a single foot, the girl became quite proficient in the use of needle, brush, and scissors, which she controlled with her mouth. From 1808 to 1848 she was carried about the country and exhibited. According to the advertisements circulated about her, she cut paper portraits, flowers, landscapes, and "even the Lord's Prayer". Examples of her work are rare, but a number of her portrait silhouettes survive and are shown in *Shades of Our Ancestors,* Alice Van Leer Carrick's book on the subject.

By 1850 New England women were able to turn their attention more to home arts and decoration than had their mothers and grandmothers, and were plying their brushes and needles busily in these attempts. Painted forget-me-nots, brilliant carmine roses, and idyllic water scenes appeared in unexpected places all over the house. Practically every aspirant to the estate of gentlewoman learned how to paint. The staff of Atkinson Academy, which opened in May, 1805, notified parents and guardians of prospective pupils that "Young Ladies may there employ a portion of the day in acquiring the refined arts of Embroidery and Painting";* soon afterwards art was taught in all girls' schools and in the "female departments" of the new academies being established in various towns.

A "flowing script" was considered as important an accomplishment for a young lady to acquire as painting and crayon drawing. Sometimes such work with the pen was used to decorate family trees and genealogical registers. Making wax flowers and fruit was another kind of art work enjoyed by the young ladies of the 1870's and 1880's. The craft was frequently taught in local classes by an instructor who had become proficient in the work. Mrs. Ella Kimball of Troy says she joined such a class sixty years ago when she was a young girl of eighteen. The teacher was a visitor from the West. Mrs. Kimball says that her own efforts were not wholly successful and she never felt that her flowers were good enough to be preserved under a case. Mrs. Loren Talbot of the same town owns an example of this work in the form of wax flowers and leaves on a base of princess pine, kept intact under a glass bell.

Wool and hair were also employed for making pictures and household decorations in the mid-nineteenth century. Mrs. Carl R. Converse of East Rindge owns a typical example of woolwork in a wreath of pulled wool flowers in red, purple, orange, and pink with framed green leaves. It was made by Nellie H. Hadley about fifty years ago. Mrs. Talbot, who owns the wax flowers previously described, remembers seeing girls braiding tiny strands of hair to be used in various forms of decoration. Sometimes they asked their friends to contribute little wheels made of braids of their own hair, and when they had enough assembled, they arranged them into wreaths which they framed.

An unusual wall decoration, executed by Sophronia Whitney of Rindge, commemorates General Lafayette's visit to Burlington, Vermont, in 1825. Miss Sophronia was twenty-two years old when

* *New Hampshire Gazette. Portsmouth, New Hampshire. Tuesday, January 29, 1805.*

she danced with the General at the ball given in his honor. She worked her commemorative piece during the following year. A picture of Lafayette is mounted on the center of a piece of cream-colored velvet with the words, "United We Stand" and "Divided We Fall", written in ink in a semicircle across the top. The picture is framed with a deep blue and green embroidered border from which radiates a wreath of embroidered leaves. This unusual combination of needle and pen is owned by the maker's grandniece, Mrs. Ella Kimball of Troy.

Fred W. Lamb, Director of the Manchester Historic Association, has made a representative collection of these feminine efforts. Among the objects he has assembled is a group of wax fruits elegantly reposing in a basket made of beads; a delicately tinted wreath of feathers; and examples of wax, worsted, shell, and hair work.

Painting on glass was sometimes done by young ladies, but usually this art was carried on by professional decorators. First practiced in this country by the Germans in Pennsylvania, it soon spread all along the Eastern seaboard. Paintings on glass were largely used for the tops of mirrors and the lower panels of shelf clocks. In the 1840's, according to the *New Hampshire Patriot* and *State Gazette*, S. G. Sylvester of Concord was painting tablets for "Looking Glasses" and "Time Pieces" at his shop which he called the "Looking Glass Manufactory":* Some of the craftsmen who painted pictures for clocks and looking glasses also did sign and ornamental painting. There are also a number of cases on record where such craftsmen, with an especially keen eye for line and color, studied art and became portrait and landscape painters.

A sign painter who achieved recognition in art circles was John Rand, born in Bedford in 1801. Young Rand was apprenticed early in life to the well-known cabinetmaker, Robert Parker, and later opened his own cabinet shop. In his spare time he painted houses and tavern signs. When Rand's cabinet business failed, he began to devote more time to portrait painting, supporting himself mean-

* *New Hampshire Patriot and State Gazette. Concord, N. H. Monday, August 24, 1840. p. 3.*

ROCKING CHAIR *with original stencil,* HAND PAINTED TINWARE, *New Hampshire Historical Society and* HAND PAINTED WINDOW SHADE *owned by Mrs. Mary E. Durgin of Boscawen.*

HAND PAINTED WALL in a house in Lyme, by courtesy of Mrs. O. Wittenborn.

while by his sign and ornamental painting. His portraits attracted considerable attention, and he moved to Boston and opened a studio in the Cornhill section. He continued with his art while traveling abroad; for twelve years he was located in London, where he painted portraits of members of the British royal family.

Elder John Gillingham, Freewill Baptist clergyman of Bradford, never achieved the reputation Rand had, but he did furnish an idea which enjoyed considerable recognition in the field of art. This was a design for a sign which he painted over a hundred years ago for a tavern in Sutton. On the sign "which was painted in colors, richly arrayed",* appeared the figure of the Goddess of Liberty. It was seen and greatly admired by a little girl who later became a well-known artist of the nineteenth century. Mary Pillsbury Weston used the good clergyman's "Goddess" as a model many times in her own work, which was very popular during her lifetime.

Ornamental signs which formerly swung above New Hampshire tavern doors are eagerly sought by present-day collectors of early Americana. Their decorations vary from designs of a most primitive nature, often executed by mine host himself, to the very elaborate ones which were made by expert ornamental painters. There is a vast difference in technique between the simple sign made by Deacon Frederick Fitts when he opened a tavern at his residence in Candia in 1828, and the sign, adorned on one side with a view of Keene's Main Street and on the other with a picture of the tavern, which Charles Ingalls painted when the Eagle Hotel in Keene was remodeled in 1826. Among the old tavern signs still in existence in New Hampshire is one which was painted for the first inn in Bristol and inscribed with the words, "Entertainment by P. Sleeper, 1802". It is displayed in the William Long Memorial Building in Hopkinton.

The most famous of all New Hampshire's painted tavern signs, however, is preserved only in a written description. This is the sign of the Old William Pitt Tavern in Portsmouth, described by Charles

---

* *History of Sutton. Vol. 2. Augusta H. Worthen. Concord, N. H. Republican Press Association, 1890. p. 875.*

Brewster and other writers. The face of the great friend of the American Colonies looking down from the sign seemed strikingly like the face that had preceded it, that of the Earl of Halifax. The inn was the rendezvous of the Loyalists until the Sons of Liberty rebelled against these meetings. A minor fracas between the factions took place in the ancient hostelry; when the damage to the inn was repaired the sign was repainted and the name was changed from "The Earl of Halifax" to "William Pitt".

The ornamental painter had various other outlets besides signs for his creative abilities. One of the most lucrative was ornamenting sleighs and wagons. In this line the Burgums, father and son, stand out preëminently. John Burgum, a young Englishman, came to Concord in 1826 to work in the painting department of the shop operated by J. S. and E. A. Abbott. Later this shop became the Abbott-Downing Company, which produced many coaches of historic interest, including thirty coaches for the Wells-Fargo Company of Omaha, Nebraska, and Buffalo Bill's Deadwood Coach.

John Burgum was a fine ornamental painter; he also painted portraits and made excellent drawings. For over fifty years he decorated coaches and wagons for the Concord company. Varied color combinations were used on them. English vermilion for the body and straw color for the gears were usually applied to the Overland Stages. In 1878 four coaches, bright canary yellow in color, were made especially for the Potter Palmer House in Chicago. On each of the doors Mr. Burgum painted a picture of the famous old hotel.

Other hotel coaches were painted with carmine bodies and red running parts. Frequently the likeness of a prominent actress, such as Lucca, Neilson, Mary Anderson, or Fanny Davenport, was painted on the dashboard. Although John Burgum was chief ornamental painter for the Concord firm, other painters like Thomas Yates, James E. Larken, Edward Pierce, Pliny Fiske, and Charles T. B. Knowlton, all of them fine craftsmen, worked for the company. John H. Caswell, James H. Sanders, Benjamin S. Rolfe, and George B. Davis were noted for their dexterity in lettering and scrollwork.

The coach decorator's son, Edwin Gannell Burgum, who was

born in 1858, learned his father's trade while working with him in the ornamenters' room of the Abbott-Downing Company's painting department. He says he began his apprenticeship by tracing scroll patterns and painting bits of the designs. Eventually, the son became as proficient as the father in this line of decorative work.

When the transcontinental railroads pushed Westward, the stagecoach days gradually came to an end; the man holding the lever supplanted the man grasping the reins. Edwin Burgum gave up his work in stagecoach ornamentation and for many years was employed in the painting department of the railroad repair shops in Concord. At the present time he uses his knowledge of ornamental painting to decorate antique furniture and trays, but he has never forgotten the technique of coach painting which he learned from his father. He says that his memory has enabled him to ornament three coaches with John Burgum's own designs and the colors in fashion at the time the coaches were made.

When Harold Jefferson Coolidge gave a Concord Coach to the Boston and Maine Railroad for exhibition purposes, Mr. Burgum was asked to redecorate it. This same coach was loaned to the New York World's Fair, 1939-1940, and appeared in "Railroads on Parade" in the big show. When "at home" it is on display in the large waiting room of the Boston and Maine Railway Station at Concord.

Another Abbott-Downing coach at the New York World's Fair, in the showroom of the Transportation Exhibit, was one of the first used in the service of the United States Post Office Department. It is owned now by Robert P. Peckett of Sugar Hill. In 1937 Mr. Burgum redecorated the vehicle, painting the picture of the Old Man of the Mountain on one door and that of Mt. Washington on the other. Another coach which he ornamented was once owned by the MacDowell Colony, but is now the property of Major A. Erland Goyette of Peterborough. On one side of this coach is painted a picture of President Pierce's birthplace in Hillsborough, and on the other, a view of Mt. Monadnock and Dublin Lake.

Frequently, ornamental painters made use of the craft of stenciling, the process of painting a design by using a cutout shield of cardboard or wood. Home owners found it an inexpensive method of decoration and often had stenciled designs applied on the walls of their homes. A type of stenciling common in New Hampshire was the allover patterned wall that is exemplified in the work of Moses Eaton and his less famous son, Moses Eaton, Junior. Eaton, born in 1753, worked in Hancock, and his son settled in Dublin. But the younger Eaton never quite mastered his restless blood. Tradition relates that the freedom of the road tempted him to an excursion Westward. Young Moses' kit, found in the attic of his home, contained eight brushes and seventy-five stencils which had also been used by Moses Eaton, the elder. Another man who did the same type of work in the neighborhood of Hancock and Dublin in the early part of the nineteenth century was Emery Rice, whose work kit was also found.

It is fairly certain that many of the stenciled walls were the work of traveling artists, for similar designs are often found in houses a hundred miles or more apart. The walls of the Wilson Tavern in Peterborough, built in 1797, were stenciled when the house was erected. This stenciling has since been covered by several layers of paper, and knowledge of what lies behind is dependent upon the memories of those who remember the patterns. The Bleak House, also in Peterborough and built in the same year, has been restored in part by following the fragmentary original designs and by retouching where the stencils were well preserved. The work in the hallway of this house was restored about twenty-five years ago by an old painter, Washington Greenwood, who was eighty years old at the time. Some of the patterns found here reappear in the Salmon Wood House in Hancock. The Peter Farnum House in Francestown is a fine example of this early art, and is thought to have been done by the same painter who decorated the Bleak and Wood houses, as well as others in the section.

There is a noticeable resemblance between the wall decorations in these houses and the ones in the Benjamin Pierce House in Hillsborough. This house was built in 1804, and it is thought that the stenciling was done soon afterward. Governor Pierce, a former Revolutionary soldier and General in the militia, chose Christmas holly and candles as the motif for the design on the ballroom wall, because he was born on December 25.

In 1824 Governor Pierce put an expensive French hand-blocked paper, called the "Bay of Naples", on the walls of the north parlor of his mansion. Comparatively few New Hampshire people, however, could afford to adorn their homes with such costly imported paper. Usually when home owners were affluent enough to decorate the walls of their parlors, bedchambers, and halls, they hired itinerant artists to paint pictures on them. These pictures were varied in design, but landscapes predominated. The wall decorations of three houses in Lyme, built in the early nineteenth century, are so similar in type that it is evident they were painted by this one man. The same hand probably executed the walls of the Prescott Tavern in East Jaffrey, for these pictures are replicas of those in the Lyme houses. The frescoes in the Culver House, built around 1809 in Lyme, are typical of the style found in the other houses of the neighborhood. The artist used a limited palette, principally yellow, green, brown, and gray to portray the tall elm trees, Lombardy poplars, white pines, apple trees, the frigate, the island, the houses, and the bare rocky peaks which make up the units of the composition of these unusual wall pictures.

A fresco which adapts a view in South Keene is painted over the mantel in the living room of the Nathan Fay House in East Alstead. A wall decoration in the Peavey House in Bennington is quite different, for it shows a dog chasing a fox, while a squirrel unconcernedly eating nuts perches on a bough above them. Some of the most unusual wall paintings in New Hampshire are in the parlor of the Central House in Stoddard. American eagles adorn the ceiling, and above the mantel a ship tossing on the sea has been portrayed in many colors. These decorations bear the signature "C. H. Tern. D.", the "singing tramp", who paid for his food and lodging at the inn by painting the walls for his host. Tern is one of the few of these itinerant artists whose names are known today. Another was Stephen Badger, who came to Candia in 1825. Badger painted frescoes on the walls of the Wheat and the Samuel Fitts Houses. The pictures in the Wheat House were landscapes, but they included also figures of men, women, and children. On one of the walls in the Fitts House the artist gave free rein to his imagination by painting a ship in full sail with a sea serpent near it.

A present-day artist who has decorated her own home with wall paintings is Edith Wyckoff Kuchler of Lyme. Her palette is much more extensive than those used by the nineteenth century wall painters, and her frescoes are developed in bold, natural colors. Mrs. Kuchler has also worked out a type of "folk art" in which she uses newspaper pulp for a material and glue for a binder. From the resultant mixture she models her favorite subjects—horses and other animals, and groups of people typical of both past and present-day life in the community in which she lives.

Nearly a hundred years before Edith Kuchler began making her little figures, another artist started a career by modeling in miniature groups of people engaged in their everyday occupations and amusements. Probably no artist or sculptor in America has enjoyed such popularity during his lifetime as did John Rogers. From 1860 to 1890, no well-furnished home was complete without at least one of his famous groups to ornament the family parlor.

Rogers' story is the familiar one of the youth whose parents, for economic reasons, objected to his following the arts as a vocation. He first served an apprenticeship as a machinist, a trade which brought him to New Hampshire, where, between 1849 and 1856, he was employed at the Amoskeag Machine Shop in Manchester. During his stay in Manchester he began to model the figurines that brought him fame.

The would-be sculptor took his clay from the banks of the Merrimack at Hooksett, and experimented with it in the kitchen of Charles Richardson's house on Middle Street in Manchester, where he was staying at the time. The first public exhibition of his work was at the New Hampshire Agricultural Society Fair, in Manchester, 1851. He showed two groups: a boy playing marbles, done in ordinary clay, and an old friar, done in a red substance, which some people believe to be the red clay of Hooksett.* He liked this material as a medium for his work, and, later in his life, said he had never found a clay so well adapted to his needs as that which he took from the brickyards on the Merrimack River above Manchester.†

An example of the artist's extraordinary patience and good nature is given in a letter to Mr. Fred W. Lamb of Manchester from Guy Hubbard, whose father, George Hubbard of Windsor, Vermont, lived with Rogers for a time at 56 Bridge Street in Manchester and became his closest friend. Speaking of the time when his father and Rogers were rooming together, Mr. Hubbard wrote in 1927: "One evening Mr. Rogers had practically finished a complicated group, which was, I believe, called 'The Checker Players'. Just as he was putting the finishing touches upon this, the board upon which the group was mounted slipped off the table, and the group lay in a shattered mass of clay upon the floor. Without saying a word, John Rogers got a broom and dustpan, swept up the litter, and began at once to reproduce the group, without showing the slightest petulance or disappointment. He worked all night upon it, and when my father arose in the morning Mr. Rogers had the group practically finished again."

Rogers established a studio in New York City in 1860, and spent much of his time there. He also lived for a time in New Canaan, Connecticut, where he died on July 26, 1904. He completed his last group, *The Watch on the Santa Maria,* in 1892. The largest collection of Rogers groups extant consists of fifty-five items owned by the New York Historical Society. The Essex Institute in Salem, Massachusetts, also has a number of the appealing little figures. But of the ninety-odd groups brought out by John Rogers, twenty-one pieces are in the possession of the Historic Association in Manchester, New Hampshire, where the sculptor spent the seven years which he called the gayest and happiest of his life.

* *Amoskeag Bulletin. April 15, 1916.*
† *Rogers Groups. Mr. and Mrs. Chetwood Smith. Boston. Charles E. Goodspeed and Company, 1934. p. 18.*

XVII

SHAKER CRAFTS

Their official name is *The United Society of Believers in Christ's Second Coming,* but they have never disdained the name Shakers, which was originally applied to them in ridicule and contempt by the "people of the world". Since they think of themselves as the "children of truth", they can afford to accept, with true Shaker humor and humility, this popular name. The work of their hands is done in the same humble spirit, but also in the proud and secret belief that they are God's chosen people. They are important in the story of New Hampshire arts and crafts, because theirs is the only truly folk tradition of workmanship which ever developed in the State.

On a hill at the end of a winding road in Canterbury, the last of the New Hampshire Shakers cling to the community that was started a century and a half ago by the donation of the rich, five-hundred acre farm of Benjamin Whitcher and his wife, Mary Shepherd. The Whitchers, as well as several other families, including the Cloughs and the Parkers, were impelled into Shakerism by a wave of emotional rapture during a period of revivalism. The remnant that is left today still maintains the dignity and industrious habits of the founders.

Formerly there were two Shaker societies in New Hampshire; both started in 1792—one at Canterbury, and one in a narrow valley on the shore of Lake Mascoma in Enfield. In Enfield the barns and dwellings, the shops and churches, built after the sturdy

Shaker way, are today topped with the gold crosses of a Roman Catholic seminary for boys. In the hills they planted apple orchards and grape vines; and they built an aqueduct system and camps for maple sugaring. Today the orchards and the pastures they cleared are snarled with new growth, and the stone walls which divided the fields are collapsing into heaps of rock. . . .

The Shakers in New Hampshire were converted by missionaries sent out by the mother societies in New York State, Watervliet and Mt. Lebanon. The Shaker societies carried on the most successful communistic experiment ever practiced in this country. Its motivating power was religion of an intensely eager and mystical kind. Yet it had only one well-defined theological doctrine: the bisexuality of God, a radical departure from the Trinity of the Calvinist religion, against which Shakerism rebelled. The Shakers, like the Essenes of old, were bound to their social system by the intangible force of their faith. The "Shaker way", like the "Shaker look", was the outward evidence of an habitual self-denial and of a passive way of meeting life.

Economically, they adjusted themselves easily to the outside world of the early nineteenth century. Spiritual separatism from the world was one of their cardinal laws; for they claimed to be a chosen people to whom God had vouchsafed a glimpse of the Second Creation. Practically, they were so successful in maintaining a rigidly self-supporting economy that they were able to sell their surplus products with profit. The Shaker brethren were shrewd and realistic traders, and until after 1850 they prospered in things material. But when manufacturing reached the mass production stage, it became a competitive force beyond their power to combat. Squeezed by such a pressure from the alien world, the Shakers began to retreat.

The arts and industries of the Shaker people are significant because they made nearly everything they needed for their own living, and because they displayed a strain of remarkable inventive ability. Moreover, everything they formed or built had about it a characteristic quality, a quality not encompassed within any description of the "Shaker type of thing". To say that a Shaker house was constructed on hard, square lines, with a high foundation, a fairly conservative roof angle, and low-ceilinged rooms, does not quite define the atmosphere of Shakerism by which it is marked.

The Shakers put into their lathe turning, their joining, and their finishing something decidedly peculiar to themselves. That they were apart from the world in spirit, is seen in the physical arrangement of their lives, in the way they laid out their communities, placed the furnishings in their dwellings, and put away the dead in their cemeteries. Certain characteristics marked everything they wrought; severity of line, honesty of construction, uniformity of style. No appreciation of the productions of their daily lives is possible without an understanding of the way of spiritual life that lay behind this workmanship.

The Shaker faith had its origin in the psychology of a persecuted people, the Camisards, French Protestants, who, in the troubled days of religious conflict in seventeenth-century France, rebelled with intense fury against the edicts of Louis XIV and were exiled to England. There, they settled in Manchester, and among those converted to their group were some Quakers, who became known to their persecutors as the "shaking Quakers", soon shortened to "Shakers". A woman by the name of Ann Lee, who began to manifest unusual capacities for seeing visions, was regarded by this Manchester group as the promised woman leader who they believed would fulfill their hopes.

In 1774 Mother Ann, as she was called by her followers, obeyed a vision and sailed for America to found her church. She died in 1785, but the expansion of her sect had begun. The official organizing of the church into a "body religious" was the work of a master of organization, Elder Joseph Meacham. The government was theocratic or mildly patriarchal, and in the monastic regime of each community the members shared alike in the labor and in the common goods.

The two New Hampshire societies, Canterbury and Enfield, formed a bishopric or unit of government by themselves. They were founded in an interesting way. An itinerant pedler, named Thompson, had brought wares from New York to Canterbury and with them news of the new religion, Shakerism. Certain members of the Freewill Baptist Church listened to him with speculative interest. Soon a delegation from Canterbury paid a visit to the nearest Shaker society, at Harvard, Massachusetts. In 1782 the elders at Mt. Lebanon, New York, sent two missionaries to New Hampshire, Ebenezer Cooley and Israel Chancy, who arrived at Enfield by way of Vermont.

James Jewett was working on a bridge in North Enfield when the strangers stopped in their travels to talk with him. Jewett invited them to spend the night with him at his farm on what is now called Shaker Hill. There they preached to Jewett's friends, several of whom formed a Shaker church soon after. For ten years the families comprising this group lived on land held in common near Jewett's house. Finally, they exchanged their land for a more desirable location across the lake, where they divided into three "families" and governed themselves in accordance with Father Meacham's plan. The first elder of the Enfield Society was Father Job Bishop, who welcomed a visiting President of the United States with the words: "I, Job Bishop, welcome James Monroe to our habitation."*

After Cooley and Chancy visited and preached at Canterbury, Benjamin Whitcher and his wife, who was an excellent business woman, built the little group of converts into a united body which also formed three families. Whitcher's farm was on the border of an uncultivated wilderness; the problem confronting the group was the development of the resources of this land into a means of support adequate for the needs of their co-operative venture in living. They built a reservoir north of the town of Canterbury, and cut a canal to carry the water to a pond near by; on the shores of the pond, a mill was built to grind their grain and saw their wood. They began to grow their own wheat as soon as the fields

---

* *Granite Monthly. Volume XVI (April 1894). "The Followers of Ann Lee."* Lloyd H. Chandler. *p. 259.*

were sufficiently cleared of stones and stumps. To make shoes for themselves and harnesses for their oxen and horses, they began at a very early date to tan and curry their own leather. They set up simple hand looms on which to do their first weaving. Upon the fashion of their clothes, as upon their furniture and architecture, they stamped the Shaker personality, manifested in a sombre quietness of color and a sharp-angled severity of line. From the time their first communities were formed, the brothers' plain broad-brimmed hat and the sisters' unornamented poke bonnet were an expression of the practicality, the directness, and the reserve of the Shaker mind.

The secular and religious lives of the Shakers were one and the same. Father Meacham expounded some cardinal rules by which the theories of Mother Ann Lee were to be practiced in active life. First was purity, or the virgin life; then honesty and humanity; next, the most quoted one concerning diligence in business: "Diligence in business, thus serving the Lord. Labor for all, according to strength and ability, genius and circumstance. Industrious, yet not slavish; that all may be busy, peaceable, and happy."*

Mother Ann's own precept, taught to the children who were taken into the society, was this: "Do all your work as though you had a thousand years to live, and as though you were going to die to-morrow."† In return for labor and self-denial, the Shakers found a calm though passive spiritual elevation. All their industry, thrift, temperance, and careful management were by-products of their religion. All their labor was "to make the way of God their own".

The motive behind Shaker craftsmanship was functionalism; an object was beautiful to them when it served the purpose for which it was designed. Mastery of design became of more importance than artistry in adornment, and simplicity was the mark of victory

---

* *Concise History of United Society of Believers Called Shakers.* Charles Evans Robinson. East Canterbury, *1893. p. 32.*

† *Shakers.* Frederick W. Evans. New York. D. Appleton and Co., *1859. p. 149.*

over the fleshly life. Yet the crude and awkward stage of Shaker workmanship did not last long. Anything they produced may have been severe in line, but the proportions were exceptionally well-balanced. A typical piece of Shaker furniture, for instance, was a combination cabinet containing both drawers and cupboards, with space under a hinged top for storing linen. The effect, from an artistic point of view, is neither top-heavy nor ill-proportioned. Its maker did not even pretend to be an artist; had he been one, he would not have become a Shaker. But he knew that an unsymmetrical piece of furniture was as much a sign of poor workmanship as one so carelessly joined that it fell apart in a short time.

Products of Shaker industry are also influenced by another feature: their construction to meet the needs of a group rather than an individual.

Visitors to a Shaker community were always welcome. The best time to visit was in the summer, when the crops were growing in long, sunlit rows down the fields, and the brothers were out early in the morning cutting a whole meadow of hay, working to the rhythm of a low, humming chorus.

The visitor saw a group of buildings set in neat rows, with herb gardens laid out between them, and the outlying fields divided by stone walls with oblong, granite gate posts. Of all the buildings, the barns were the largest and often the best built. An example of Shaker cleverness was the position of a barn behind a slope so that huge loads of newly cut hay could be driven directly into the loft of the barn; often this slope was built up artificially, with room underneath through which the cattle could be driven into the lower part.

Shaker dwelling houses were usually set very high on their foundations, were rectangular in shape, and had ordinary gable roofs. The earliest roofs of Shaker buildings were frequently flat with a covering of gravel, but painted tin was soon substituted when gravel proved impractical. The church at Canterbury, built in 1792, has a gambrel roof, which was reshingled only after a hundred years of service. Barrel roofs occur occasionally, usually on buildings used as laundries or barns. The floor of the church at Canterbury, incidentally, has pine boards fully eighteen inches wide, not unusual in Shaker buildings, and the woodwork is joined by hand-wrought nails with heads three-fourths of an inch in diameter.

Between the rows of buildings, well-matched and smooth-surfaced stone flags were used for walks. At Canterbury the walks were laid by Micaijah Tucker, a carpenter by trade, who split and hewed the granite singlehanded and dragged the blocks with ox-teams. He laid the stones in such a way that frost or thaw did not budge them from the ground. Near the office of each family was a landing stage, a raised stone platform from which the sisters could enter a carriage without assistance, since it was strictly contrary to the rules of the society for a man to touch a woman.

Another use of stone was in the making of steps, which consisted of single, oblong blocks of granite. A few important buildings in each society were erected entirely of granite. All the stone used by the Enfield Shakers was brought from the quarries which they owned in Canaan. The most costly Shaker building was the stone house at the Church family in Enfield; it was built in 1837, when the society was at the peak of prosperity, and next to the capitol at Concord, was proudly considered the finest piece of architecture in the State of New Hampshire. The blocks of granite were firmly joined with iron dowels, made in the Shaker foundries.

Most of the dwelling houses and workshops were covered with wooden clapboards, painted white. There were two doorways to the living quarters—one for the brothers and one for the sisters. Inside the house, the rooms were large, with low-studded ceilings. Plenty of light streamed in through the multipaned windows. Walls and woodwork were painted white, or a pale shade of blue, or yellow; but they were never papered. The broad-planked pine floors were never entirely covered but, shining with cleanliness, they were sprinkled with scatter rugs, woven or braided in the conservative Shaker design. A profusion of built-in cupboards, drawers, and closets typified a native love of order and efficiency; along wallboards near the ceilings, wooden pegs were placed, on which clothes, hats, unused chairs, and household equipment could be hung. Throughout the house there was a clean bareness, with just enough furniture to fit the needs of the occupants.

One example of their work was a sewing desk at which two sisters could simultaneously do mending or dressmaking. Another was a tailoring counter which combined the functions of a work table and a storage chest. And there are still in existence secretaries which were built so that two deacons or trustees could keep their accounts together; they are equipped with two sets of pigeonholes, numerous tiny drawers, and deep cupboards for books. One of the Shakers' favorite pieces of furniture was the drop-leaf table with two long, shallow drawers beneath the top, which expressed their instinct for utilizing all available space.

The most productive period of Shaker furniture making was during the first half of the nineteenth century. Candlestands, which went through a series of variations in design, were among the earliest of their furniture forms. The first of these little tables were square-topped and straight-legged; later examples show a more experienced use of the turning lathe, with round tops and graceful, refined lines, especially in the curved legs.

The rocking chair was adopted by the Shakers about 1825, long before it was manufactured in wholesale quantities in the rest of the country. It was the nearest approach to the forbidden luxury of an easy chair that they permitted themselves. The earliest chairs were characterized by broad, very short rockers, and by seats made of interwoven worsted tape. Shaker chairs all show Colonial derivation, especially in the slat backs and the finials—just as the best-turned table legs show the influence of the Sheraton furniture designs. The legs of their chairs and tables, however, were invariably footless, and a Shaker innovation was the mushroom knob which neatly finished off the ends of chair arms.

An early piece of furniture which the Shakers favored was the trestle type of dining-room table, with urn-shaped uprights, square or rectangular posts, and arched shoes. For a long time, benches were used instead of chairs in the dining rooms and also in the meetinghouses. The legs of these benches were usually cut in a typical Shaker motif, a Gothic arch, the same motif that appears on their doorways.

Paint was rarely applied to their furniture. But experimenting with methods of finishing, they had at one time treated wood with *aqua vitae*. Next, they tried shellac, mixed with chrome yellow. Finally, they adopted the process of dipping chairs in vats of dye made from butternut bark and sumac, a process which gives Shaker chairs their characteristic light cherry color.

Wood was the material in which they worked best. To take the simplest and most abundant material and use it in the fulfillment of their principles, was the sort of activity into which Shaker energy was instinctively directed. They were skillful at combining two or more kinds of wood in a single piece of furniture. In a table, for instance, they might make the legs of an enduring wood; and the top from a wood which would take a good polish, since cloths were never permitted on the tables from which they ate. The cabinetwork on casings, built-in cupboards, and drawers was never elaborate, but was patiently and neatly carved. Even drawer pulls were cunningly wrought of wood.

In the early part of the nineteenth century, woodenware was made in the communities for table use and for kitchen utensils. At Canterbury wooden plates of a shallow-rimmed, flat-bottomed design were used until after 1800; and pewter, shaped in the same design, was used until 1847. The orderly habit of putting everything away in a place of its own was an incentive for the manufacture of oval boxes with fitted covers. The boxes were made by wrapping a thin band of maple around an oval mold, with discs of pine fitted into the bottom. Dippers were made from ash and maple, in nests of three. Like the famous Shaker ash and hickory baskets, vended by the bonneted sisters at the country fairs in the autumn, these were products which sold readily.

The industries in which the two New Hampshire Shaker colonies specialized varied in accordance with the physical conditions

ENTRANCE TO SHAKER COLONY BUILDING *at Canterbury*.

HAND-WROUGHT SHAKER LATCH AND LOCK *at Shaker Colony in Canterbury*.

WEAVING *at the Shaker Colony in Canterbury.*

of each colony. Dairy and garden products were the most successful means of maintaining a living for the Enfield Shakers. The soil of their farm lands was exceptionally rich and fertile, and there was an abundance of water flowing down from pure springs in the hills. This supply of available waterpower was a determining factor in the mechanical industries which the Shakers developed. In 1841 they established knitting mills on the Mascoma River at the point where it enters Enfield. For several years flannel was manufactured in these mills and then made into underwear at the Shaker village. During this industrial period, Elder Caleb Dyer made regular trips to New York to negotiate for the sale of the underwear, and the heavy Shaker sweaters. By 1855 it was more profitable to sell the flannel in whole pieces, and soon the mills were sold under stress of competition from outside manufacturers. They then turned to industries that were better suited to the limitations of their system: on machines set up in small shops at the village they knit hosiery and sweaters, and in a great gristmill, finished under Elder Dyer's supervision prior to 1860, they ground grain and flour.

Caleb Dyer was a business genius; he was more responsible than any other man for the state of affluence attained by the Enfield Shakers in the middle of the century. The secret of his success was his insistence that they make the most of the resources at hand, and the efficiency with which he immediately introduced new industries to replace those which failed. Besides the gristmill, he established a lumber mill and a bedstead factory. After 1860 a small amount of business in furniture was done, confined mostly to chairs and low-posted Shaker beds. Pails, buckets, and butter tubs were made as fast as they could be profitably sold.

It was Dyer who conceived the idea of building across the narrowest part of Lake Mascoma, a structure long known as "the only Shaker bridge in the world", which endured until the hurricane of September, 1938, swept it away. The bridge was begun in the fall of 1848 so that the ice would hold the first spiles imbedded in the mud bottom of the lake. The Shaker virtues of patience and persistence were never more clearly shown than in the performance of this work. Long yokes of oxen hauled hundreds of sixty-foot logs and tons of stone to the shore of the lake. A log platform was sunk between the spiles, before spring melted the supporting ice. A layer of stone was placed upon the platform, and another log platform constructed on top of the stone. In less than a year the engineering feat, remarkable for its time, was completed.

A few people are still living who can remember when this Shaker bridge was in the making. One is Sister Myra Green, who, at the age of one hundred and four years, is lovingly cared for by the sisters at Canterbury. Another is Uncle Oscar Collins, Enfield's oldest citizen and a G. A. R. veteran. Interviewed regarding his recollections of the Shakers, Uncle Oscar remarked: "I can 'member taking my father's hot dinner down to him when he was workin' for the Shakers on the bridge—they had a tur'ble time gettin' that bridge done to suit 'em, but they finished it; Caleb Dyer saw to that. He got shot, you know—a fellow got to arguin' with him when he came for the two daughters he'd left with the Shakers when he went away to war. Caleb had a couple of brothers who carried on for him, tho'—Orville became elder and then there was Jerub—he was a doctor and used to see to the farm work, too. The Shakers were good people for all I knew of them— very honest—if you asked for a bushel of apples from them, you got a bushel and no rotten 'uns at the bottom either. . . ."

The most practical industry at the community in Canterbury was cloth manufacture, for it required a minimum of water power. In the high, sunny fields surrounding the colony, the Shakers planted flax seeds, and from the flax spun linen thread that was woven into fine hand towels, white and colored kerchiefs, and other linen goods. The pastures on the sloping hillsides were ideal for raising sheep, from whose wool they wove the flannel for soft, fine blankets and warm hose and underwear. Until 1812 the wool was carded by hand, and handlooms were used until 1824, when the spinning jenny was introduced. As early as 1796, and for many years after, there was more weaving done among the Canterbury

Shakers than any other handicraft. Cotton and wool were spun on "great wheels"; flax, on "little foot-wheels". For worsted, a machine called the "pleasant spinner" was used.

Housewives living near the Shaker village brought their rug wool to the community, where the women wove it into oval rugs with floral designs and dark borders. A typical design used a repetition of the main color in a deeper tone around the border. Mottled designs were often woven for carriage robes or chair backs, and a popular color combination was a neutral shade, such as gray, with a red, black, and gray striped border. The dress goods woven by the Shakers was famous for its durability. The material in the sisters' dresses was commonly homespun worsted, made from long wool merino with a cotton warp. The finished garment was designed with many plaits in the skirt, which was always long and full.

Leather was patiently curried in cold water vats, until near the middle of the century, when a much quicker steam process was introduced. The bark used in leathermaking was ground by horsepower in a stone grinder, until an improved water system was installed to provide hydraulic power.

Eight artificial ponds, covering from five to thirty acres each, were made by damming up meadows where melted snow had been allowed to collect. They rose one above the other in terraced fashion; from each one, water could be let down to a single factory or mill. At the foot of one stream there was a building for carding wool; at the foot of another, a woodsawing building. There was a gristmill with a "great wheel", thirty-four feet in diameter, and the space in which it turned had been drilled from solid rock. Through this wheel, power was obtained for sawing boards and pail staves, for grinding malt, and for other manufacturing processes. On the top floor of this same building, there was machinery for turning and finishing iron. Another plant was the domain of the community smith, who in sixty years manufactured some 1200 iron candlesticks.

Bark and roots were pulverized by a cannon ball which turned in a mortar, and there was also equipment for polishing metals. There was a separate clothing works, where woolen cloth and flannels were fulled and dressed; the teazels, used to raise the nap on cloth, were also grown by the Shakers. The tannery was combined with a shinglemaking mill and threshing room.

By 1840 this industrial system was running so smoothly that cultivation of the land had become a secondary business at Canterbury. The leading manager of the financial affairs of this colony was David Parker, who died in 1867. Throughout his lifetime, he was engaged in promoting many activities for the good of the community. One of them which brought a great source of income to the society was the assistance he gave Dr. Thomas Corbett in working out a formula for "Corbett's compound, concentrated Sarsaparilla".

Dr. Corbett, a brilliant self-taught botanist, did his laboratory work at Canterbury, in the little house next to the laundry. His sarsaparilla extract was composed of judicious proportions of the following ingredients: ". . . roots of sarsaparilla, dandelion, yellow-dock, mandrake, black cohash, garget, Indian hemp, and the berries of juniper and cubeb, united with iodide of potassium."*
This extract was used as a tonic for "debility and wasting diseases" and was sold to the public through a Boston drug firm for many years. The only recognition he ever received for his work was a diploma presented him by the Mechanics Fair of Boston, Massachusetts, in 1847.

The Shakers usually did much experimenting with the medicinal properties of the common roots and herbs of fields and woods. In 1820 the herbs cured by the Shakers were first sold to outsiders; by 1835 cultivated plants were grown in special gardens, and by 1850 they found it profitable to invest in machinery for pressing the juices of the plants. From constant experimental blending of formulas, valuable remedies were concocted.

Numerous other medical preparations came from the herbarium at Canterbury. Witch hazel or Hamelia was made into a soothing

* *Granite Monthly. Volume VIII (September-October, 1885). p. 310.*

SHAKER CRAFTS 233

lotion. Valerian was prescribed as a sedative; an extract of rhubarb as a laxative. "Shaker anodyne" was made from lovage root. An especially rare syrup was distilled from Jamaica ginger, but the Shakers did not intend it to be used as a beverage. Among the sweet-smelling products of their laboratories were slippery elm, sage, and summer savory, all of which were packaged in pulverized form. For their own table use, they even made a beverage called "Liberty tea" from wild plants, and a coffee substitute from Avans root. Their skill in botany was particularly profitable in the production of garden seeds which were shipped all over the world. It was proverbial that Shaker seeds never failed to sprout.

Their principal means of protection against ill health was their diet, which stressed vegetables, fruit, especially apples, cereals and meals, and fresh-water fish. Boiled cider applesauce was a concoction for which they were especially famous; it was very rich because it was made by cooking whole quarters of apples in a thick syrup of boiled cider. The sisters were expert at canning and made delicious maple confections.

Music was the Shakers' main source of pleasure. Most of their hymns, the emotional impetus for their early religious dances which are no longer used, were composed within their ranks. After the rule against musical accompaniment at meeting had been relaxed, a brother at Enfield made by hand the first organ used in the community. The best-known musician among the New Hampshire Shakers was Sister Dorothy Durgin of Canterbury. She composed and taught music all her life, and formed a famous group of singers who visited the other societies giving concerts. The popular Dorothy opera cloaks, made at Canterbury, were named after this talented sister whose gracious personality was representative of the Shaker woman.

The official journal of the Shaker world was a monthly magazine, called *The Manifesto.* In 1882 Henry Blinn, the beloved Canterbury elder, became its editor and held the office with distinction until the last issue was published in 1899. The Shaker religion was vigorously defended in its pages and an exchange department was maintained for letters from all the Shaker communities in the country. The actual news in this department was prosaic: the crops had been sown or harvested with profit or loss, so much ice had been cut on the lake, so many cords of wood chopped and sawed; the dun-clad sisters had canned jellies and fruit, had sold fancywork and butter, had woven straw mats, baskets, and bonnets.

The Enfield society declined more rapidly than did the Canterbury society. Toward the end of its existence, the work done by the sisters at Enfield became increasingly essential to the support of the members. On knitting machines that were installed on the top floor of the great stone house at the Church family, they made heavy shirts and sweaters; on sewing machines they stitched together custom shirts with linen bosoms for men. From the sale of these goods as well as their fancywork and handmade rugs, they paid for keeping the buildings painted and repaired, and purchased new equipment for the shops.

The lumber mill at Enfield was operated long after the gristmill of Caleb Dyer was sold in 1894. In the same year the South family closed its farm and the land and buildings were auctioned off. After 1885 a chief means of income was from the sale of the Eclipse Corn-Planter, a Shaker invention. In 1898 the patent was sold to a competing company. Small hand industries were continued until the last members of the community moved to Canterbury in 1922. Brooms and bonnets were handicraft articles made until the end. The bonnets, which are distinguishing features of Shaker feminine attire, were originally copied from fashionable "chip-bonnets" of the post-Revolutionary period. The brims of the first bonnets were pasteboard covered with silk, the cloth crown fitted to the head by plaiting. Later they were made largely of palm leaf; those made today are formed of oat or rye straw, prepared for weaving by alternate scalding and bleaching in the sun. The bonnet is woven on a flat loom of special size, and the narrow banding which binds it is woven on a still smaller one.

The sister society at Canterbury developed and maintained a dairy herd of fine Guernseys and Holsteins, from which they raised valuable young stock. Until after 1900 they were able to continue making household articles such as brass clocks, skimmers, copper teakettles, hair sieves, and hats, as well as their famous washing machines. This washing machine, invented at Canterbury, was patented in 1858 by David Parker, and won first prize at the Centennial Exposition of Philadelphia, 1875.

The only surviving Shaker community in New Hampshire is a symbol of peace in the midst of a confused and harried world. The white fences and the granite walls stand in straight lines down the roads and fields. Neatness and comfort prevail within the houses. Over the Shaker village there is the quiet of a people who have grown gracefully old.

XVIII

THE COUNTRY FAIR

For the past century and a quarter, peddlers of patent medicines and cheap luxuries, promoters of freak shows and gambling games, have brought their color to New Hampshire towns each fall at fair time. It is, however, only in this traditional element of carnival that the modern Country Fair resembles its predecessor, the Medieval Market. The Yankee version of this ancient institution emphasizes the interests of rural people.

During the eighteenth century, a special clause was inserted in the Royal Charters of many towns, sanctioning the holding of an annual or semiannual market after the English custom. The Charter of New Castle, the oldest preserved in New England, provided that the men of the town "shall have and enjoy and use the Ferry the days of the Fairs of New Castle. . . ."* The Charter of the Town of Londonderry, incorporated in June, 1722, provided for a fair to be held twice a year, as well as for a weekly market day. The fairs held in this town were patterned after the famous ones of Londonderry, Ireland, and were popular for many years. It is said to have been "conducted with order and propriety . . . every variety of home manufacture was here collected. The common was usually surrounded with tents containing merchandise, and with pens of cattle, sheep, and swine, for sale or exchange".†

---

* *New Castle, Historic and Picturesque.* John Albee. Boston. Cupples, Upham, and Company, 1884. p. 131.
† *History of Londonderry.* Edward L. Parker. Boston. Perkins and Whipple, 1851. p. 62.

THE COUNTRY FAIR

After the Revolutionary War, the original interest of New Hampshire men in fishing, lumbering, and shipbuilding gave way to a new interest in agriculture. The first county agricultural society was formed in Rockingham County in 1814. Within the next few years, several of these organizations were set up all over the State. They were the agencies for the establishment of the annual "cattle shows", where premiums or prizes were paid for the best oxen, milch cows, wheat crops, and "women's work". A Legislative Act gave one hundred dollars each to the Rockingham and Cheshire Agricultural Societies. The Act recommended that other societies be established for the promotion of agriculture and domestic manufactures "and that said society (Cheshire) be requested to include the subject of domestic manufactures with the objects of their association".* The ideal of all these organizations, in maintaining yearly fairs, was to demonstrate and keep alive the cooperative relationship between agriculture and the mechanical arts.

Fair time in the 1820's was popularly known as the "farmers' holiday", and usually came late in October, during the lull between harvesting and winter chores. Some fairs were confined to a single day of exhibition, but a really important one lasted from two to four days. The social life of the fairs was anticipated eagerly all year long. The farmers showed off their prize cattle, their woolladen sheep, and their sleekly curried horses; they held ploughing contests, and exchanged information on improved ensilage and increased milk production. And on the exhibition tables in the town hall or in tents, their wives and daughters laid out their handiwork of the past year: yards of kersey and flannel, figured table linen, stockings and mittens knit from merino wool, hearth rugs and rag carpeting, as well as samples of butter, cheese, bread, and wines of their own vintage.

These fairs were similar to the great national or international expositions in one respect: they were a means of measuring progress. To the Yankee farmers, progress meant the increased com-

* *Transactions of the New Hampshire State Agricultural Society, 1850-51-52.* Concord, N. H. Published by the State of New Hampshire. p. 15.

forts and conveniences that they were able to wrest from their rocky environment. Therefore, these annual events encouraged amateur as well as professional craftsmanship. An advertisement of the Hillsborough Agricultural Society for their 1854 fair reads: "Mechanics . . . workers in wood, metals, leather etc., will you bring in specimens of artistic skill? It will be an excellent way to advertise your carriages, carts, plows, boots, shoes, harnesses, and your numerous labor saving machines. . . . Ladies—no Fair can be successful without your presence and assistance. . . . You are invited to bring . . . anything and everything that is the production of useful industry or of a refined and sentimental taste."*

Clothmaking was the first home manufacture actively encouraged by the sponsors of the fairs; improvement of quality of the cloth was the primary aim. As early as 1821, an editorial in the *New Hampshire Patriot* observed: "The premiums offered for fine cloths have already had a good effect: much fine and well-colored cloth has been exhibited where formerly coarse and inferior cloth was produced."† Proof had to be presented that the wool in flannel or kersey was sheared within the county and that both the spinning and weaving was done at home. A rule for entering flannel in the Hillsborough County Fair specified that the flannel "must not have been wove, or the yarn of which it is made, spun at a manufactory, except the cotton yarn in the flannel, which may be factory yarn".‡ In the transitional period between home weaving and wholesale production by textile factories, woolen cloth was commonly sent to a fulling mill for finishing; if such was the case the product had to be designated as "fulled cloth".

Woolen fabrics were, as a rule, entered by men, and women more often competed for the premiums for linen and cotton goods. The fabrics entered by Seth King of Mason at the Hillsborough Fair in 1819 were praised by the judging committee with the comment: "His cloths for fabric, color and dressing shew that very

* *Granite Farmer. Concord, N. H. September 16, 1854. p. 2.*
† *New Hampshire Patriot and State Gazette. Concord, N. H. Tuesday, October 29, 1821. p. 2.*
‡ *Ibid. Tuesday, September 28, 1819. p. 1.*

little more is wanting to make them equal to the best English cloths."* And the same committee declared that an especially fine sample of homespun flannel submitted by Dr. Eaton "shews most clearly what every good farmer may do, provided they will only be convinced of the utility and importance of improving . . . their domestic industry".†

The work done by the farmers' wives was encouraged with cash premiums, which increased in number and amount as the agricultural societies became more prosperous. The highest award made at an early Pittsfield Cattle Show went to a farmer's wife for the greatest quantity and best quality of manufactured articles produced in a single family within a year. A visitor to one of the early Hillsborough County Fairs observes: "The specimens also of Rose Blankets would convince one, that for this article we need not be dependent on a foreign market. . . . The Broadcloths and Cassimeres . . . appeared to me to be superior, and I cannot imagine, who would not take peculiar satisfaction in wearing some of them, especially when it is considered that they were wrought by our fair country-women." Concerning a piece of table linen: "I have seen . . . no imported linens superior, if equal, to it. The figure . . . was simple and common and less handsome than that of the imported linen Damasks; but the fineness of the thread, the firmness of the texture, and the smoothness of the cloth were almost inimitable."‡

The policy that American industries should be as independent of foreign markets as possible, was a familiar doctrine in the political economy of the times. One of the first home industries in New Hampshire to show the effects of this doctrine was the making of straw and grass bonnets in imitation of imported leghorns. At a Cheshire County Fair, Mrs. Betsey Lawrence of Walpole exhibited straw bonnets, "so well manufactured they would replace Leghorns".

* *Ibid. Tuesday, October 26, 1819. p. 2.*
† *Ibid. Tuesday, October 26, 1819. p. 2.*
‡ *New Hampshire Patriot and State Gazette. Concord, N. H. Tuesday, October 22, 1821. p. 3.*

Inventors of new types of handwrought articles or of improvements in the making of old ones, were sure of recognition at the fairs. In 1821 a new handicraft appeared, the spinning of milkweed into useful articles of apparel. A lady's cape "singularly beautiful", a "richly-wrought scarf", a bonnet, all woven from the silk-like thread of the common milkweed, were presented for public approval at various fairs. By 1829 an improvement in this novelty was shown in a bonnet made from the down of the plant, woven upon a foundation of linen cloth.

In the 1820's New Englanders became very much interested in the ornamentation of their clothing and their homes; this trend was reflected in the premium lists of the fairs. At a Strafford County Fair, a large premium was given for "one gross of elegantly wrought silk buttons". At a Coös County Fair, awards were made for the best specimens of well-dressed calf skins and also for the "best and most elegant piece of cabinet work". Although craftsmen in cabinetwork, furniture making, and wood carving were encouraged to present their products at the fairs, they were slow in taking advantage of the opportunity. The establishment of the more cosmopolitan State Fair seemed necessary to attract the crafts that were more usually carried on in the larger towns and cities.

Leather tanning was a branch of the industrial arts which came within the jurisdiction of the agricultural societies. The making of boots and shoes was still a handicraft in the first quarter of the nineteenth century, and good premiums were offered at the fairs for specimens of finished leather and fine footwear. At the Rockingham County Fair one year, a pair of morocco shoes was shown, "well and skillfully" made by an Exeter man from the skin of a sheep which had been alive ten hours and thirteen minutes before the exhibition opened.

Accounts of these early fairs reveal that the judges' criticisms became more and more discriminating. No article of an inferior quality was ever given a premium merely because it was the only contribution in its line. On the other hand, additions to the comforts of the home were rewarded even when no provision had

THE COUNTRY FAIR 241

been made for them on the published list. To take care of unexpected novelties and inventions, a category called "special articles of improvement" was often added to the list, with a committee to have charge of it. Yankee moderation usually guided the decisions of the judges and prevented them from approving contributions of a bizarre nature, such as brilliantly colored tablecovers of an oriental trend.

The Merrimack County Agricultural Society was an especially prosperous and progressive organization. Its second "cattle show and fair", held in 1825 at the Court House in Concord, was somewhat more urban in its atmosphere than most county fairs. The first evidence of an interest in native silk culture appears in the report of this fair; while miscellaneous articles in the domestic department included wool hats, a lace veil, knitted and crocheted lace, a cambric muslin dress, a grass broom, and two ornamental vases.

The Merrimack Society carried on its fair with unabated enthusiasm long after the other societies had fallen into inertia, about 1830. It had been the first society to offer awards in the fields of dainty needlework, painting, and drawing. During the 1830's it still sponsored bookbinding, beadwork, and hooked rugs. At one of its fairs the judges recognized the excellence of a machine for rolling silver or copper, made by a blacksmith, as a specimen of good turning and filing. They suggested, however, that more forged work should be shown.

In 1827 the Merrimack Fair was held at Boscawen; two of that town's most famous citizens submitted articles they had made. One was Benjamin Morrill, the clockmaker, who showed for the first time an improved timepiece he had invented. The other was Dr. Samuel Wood of Boscawen, an educator and a preacher, and well-known for his hobby—the production of silk worms which fed on the leaves of the mulberry trees that grew in his back yard. At this fair, Dr. Wood was acknowledged the first person to plant the mulberry tree and to make silk in New Hampshire, and he received five dollars for a piece of finished material. Of the industries that might be of economic benefit to the community as a whole, none was publicized at country fairs more hopefully than silkmaking.

The 1840's saw the spirit of Victorianism reflected in the handicraft exhibits at fairs. The period of ottoman covers and embroidered lamp mats, patchwork quilts and "worsted wrought work", "Grecian" painting and seraphines, hair wreaths and hair jewelry, pellis work and carved whatnots had begun. Purely utilitarian crafts were giving way to those which were mediums for artistic expression.

The fabrics displayed were mostly of the smooth, shiny type: cassimere, satinet, doeskin, and *mouslin de laine*. Ladies of the period spent their leisure time doing embroidery work on upholstery for chairs, sofas, and tabourets. They made many artificial flowers with which they decorated their homes in winter. The more venturesome painted in oils and water colors, while others confined their efforts to "pictures in embroidery". "Specimens of needlework in crewel, one representing the last hours of Ann Boleyn, the other The Wandering Jew" were typical items on the premium lists. But many people still thought of handiwork as useful rather than creative, and were content to submit rugs lined with bed ticking, traveling bags made of needle-point, and miscellaneous articles that were knit, crocheted, or tatted.

In 1841 visitors to the Merrimack County Fair were thrilled by the "remarkable correctness" with which the human face was reproduced by a new art, born in France, called daguerreotyping. Photography developed during the last half of the century, and as fast as the photolithographic and actinic processes came out, they were exhibited and demonstrated at the fairs.

Active interest in fairs was climaxed in 1849 by the legislative chartering of the New Hampshire State Agricultural Society. The Society's annual fair was intended to be "an instructive museum to the farmer", to show the relationships between agriculture, manufacturing, and mechanical interests. In the next few years many regional societies were reorganized, the most prominent of which were those in Hillsborough and Belknap Counties, and in the Connecticut River Valley.

THE COUNTRY FAIR 243

The first State Fair was held in Concord in the fall of 1850. The premium lists were conservative rather than spectacular. Bookbinding, coopers' work, and woodenware were the outstanding craft products exhibited. In the section for domestic manufactures there were some fine quilts and bedspreads, woolen goods, carpeting, tufted and braided rugs, silk, woolen, and worsted knit hose, and raised worsted work. Several daguerreotypes and oil paintings were also displayed.

The State Fair which was held the following year in Manchester was much more colorful. Daniel Webster, New Hampshire's native son, of brilliant personality and fluent tongue, was the distinguished speaker of the day. The list of premiums was unusually long, and the competition for them was keen. "Fancy and ornamental needle work in great variety"* was entered. Many firms and individual workers sent in silverware and cutlery, woodenware and tinwork. A Boscawen man displayed the violins he had made, and a Manchester man exhibited his shell vases. Baskets and brooms, ivory swifts and patent reed pianofortes were on exhibition, along with gravestones, crayon portraits, a Gothic bird cage, an embroidered cloak, earthenware, *papier-mâché* articles, paintings, India ink and water color work, a grass tree, a shell harp, a pressed flower ornament, a miniature marble monument, and "specimens of furniture, imported in 1670". Special committees were appointed for the judging at future fairs of cabinetwork and furniture, tailoring and millinery.

At the next fair, held in Meredith Bridge (the old name for Laconia), some "finely-wrought articles of furniture" were shown. A local woman embroidered the upholstery for an entire set of parlor furniture for exhibition. The amount of richly decorative needlework was so large that a unique request was made by the judges, that competition be started for the coarser but more practical kinds of needlework, specifically darning and mending. Samples of neatly mended shirts and hose occupied dignified positions

---

* *New Hampshire Patriot and State Gazette. Concord, N. H. Wednesday, October 15, 1851. p. 2.*

in the premium lists of succeeding State Fairs. A Manchester man was given a diploma for his ability to engrave silver and to manufacture gold bosom pins. Handmade jewelry appeared frequently thereafter. This fair displayed rifles of home manufacture, paper work, fancy baskets and bags, and "fancy swifts, of bone of ingenious construction". A set of newly invented false teeth "chewed" mechanically for the duration of the fair.

The judges on the furniture committee at the 1854 State Fair, held at Keene, were disappointed at the meagreness of the exhibition. A Mr. S. D. Osborne was almost the sole exhibitor of original cabinetwork. This caused the judges to exhort, "Where were our furniture men of the western part of the State. . . . Do they think because they are not sure of the best they will not present anything? . . . Let us all carry in some of our productions . . . and see if we cannot learn something, and thereby be enabled to do as well as our neighbors. . . ."*

A trend towards delicacy in creation is apparent from the list of contributions to this fair: silverware, a sculptured bust of Psyche cut from Carrara marble, hair jewelry, lace scarfs, wrought Tibet shawls (made from goat's hair cloth), and specimens of Yankee whittling. Even paper was used imaginatively, for there was an exhibit of likenesses, "delicately cut from paper into minute yet very distinguishable figures and other representations."†

To judge from the Grecian chairs and Grecian paintings shown at the county fairs, the influence of the pseudoclassical movement penetrated the country homesteads of New Hampshire. There was a great deal of filigree and pellis woodwork, as well as decorative parlor pieces in the Victorian style, such as *papier-mâché* inlaid with pearl, pine cone frames, marine moses, shellwork, miniature carved ships, and Chinese shawls and lanterns.

At one of the State Fairs, an improved hand turning lathe was exhibited. Other new inventions shown in the same place were a

* *Transactions of the New Hampshire State Agricultural Society, 1857.* Concord, N. H. Published by the State of New Hampshire. p. 728.

† *Transactions of the New Hampshire State Agricultural Society, 1857.* Concord, N. H. Published by the State of New Hampshire, p. 271.

SHAKER SISTER *canning at a built-in brick stove.*

WOODEN BUCKETS *made by the Shakers.*

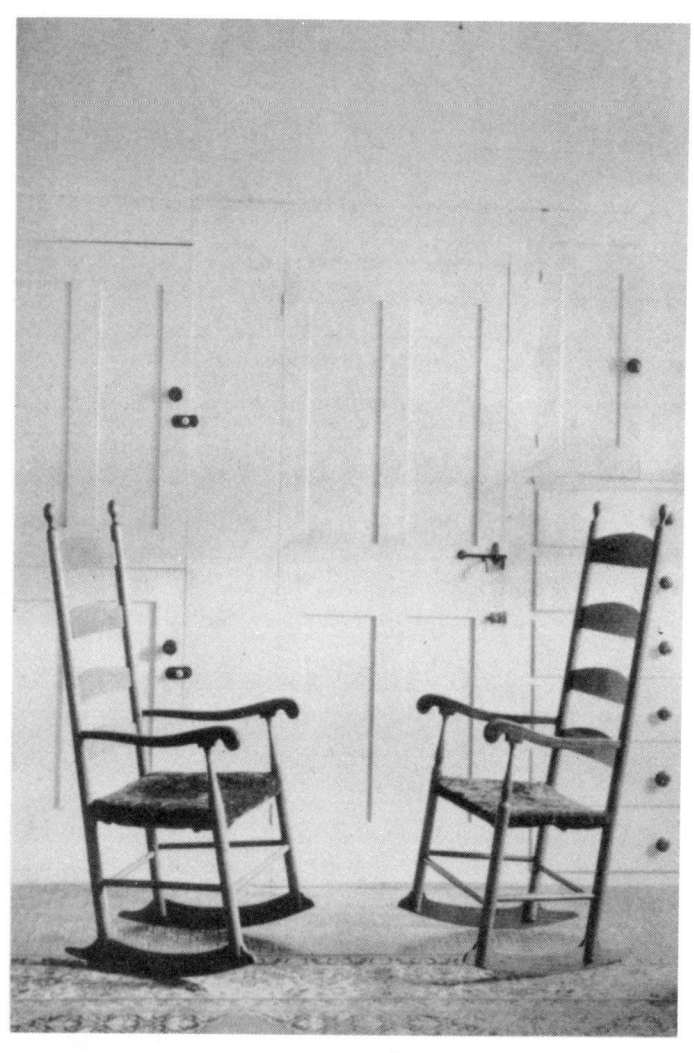

SHAKER ROCKERS *and* CUPBOARDS.

space-conserving arrangement of school desks and seats, made by Virgil Woodcock, a clock with an improved rotary pendulum, a soapstone parlor stove, and a model of a combination water wheel. The hope expressed by the judges, that the "home manufacture of nice summer hats will be encouraged", was fulfilled the following year by the appearance of a palm leaf hat made by a Manchester man.

Clothmaking equipment and homespun fabrics preserved from the eighteenth century were shown as antiquities by the middle of the nineteenth century. The hand loom weaving of cloth was no longer a matter of desperate necessity, but had become a recreational activity. The rural fairs, in particular, tried very hard to keep home weaving alive; year after year substantial awards were given for samples of the stocking yarn, flannel, fulled cloth, hand-loom gingham, and linen. At the age of eighty-three, Mrs. Hannah Adams of Dublin was still making the linen strainers for which she was famous, continuing "the good old practice of manufacturing with her own hands, the annual crop of flax, into various articles of domestic use."*

The Hillsborough Agricultural Society maintained the largest and most important County Fair during the latter part of the nineteenth century, just as the Merrimack Society had during the first half. In 1865 the Hillsborough Society offered premiums of from one to three dollars for the most successful experiment in the growth of Chinese sugar cane. The same year an Amherst man, Calvin Prince, caused a sensation with a fabric made from Indian hemp, "woody material that grows abundantly in that section, and the result resembles flax".† The presence of several articles made from the silk of milkweed pods, indicated that this material had continued to be used in spite of its fragility.

Fairs of the post-Civil War era were distinguished by an intense interest in scientific developments, though they continued to pay

* *Transactions of New Hampshire State Agricultural Society, Concord, N. H. Published by the State of New Hampshire, 1855. p. 273.*
† *New Hampshire Mirror and Farmer. Concord, N. H. Saturday, October 14, 1865. p. 1.*

tribute to the artistic. The State Fair of 1874, which was held in co-operation with the Manchester Art Association, sponsored an exhibition of water colors after the English school. There were specimens of graining in wood and marble, modeling in clay, pen and ink drawings, and a demonstration of "Tilghman's sand-blast engraving". This latter was a process which produced "upon glass, metals and stones the most beautiful examples of engraving and lettering" by means of sand being blown upon an object with a steam pressure of one hundred and forty pounds.*

But the exhibit which most excited the curiosity of the throngs was described as "a machine by which one prints by playing keys like a piano-forte. It is a simple machine, and it is claimed sixty words a minute can be written with it".† The typewriter had just been added to the list of the world's inventions.

The degeneration of the average County Fair into an excuse for horse racing was foretold by such tendencies as the belittling of the craft exhibits. One report of a Fair in 1874 refers contemptuously to "the patchwork and knitting of maidens in first or second childhood, admired only by grandparents on one hand or nieces on the other".‡ A comment on the last fair of the Merrimack County Agricultural Society, held the same year, runs: "A worsted bird of paradise poised on a silk tombstone and reading an excerpt from the fly-leaf of a family bible exhausts the supply of fancy articles."§

After 1875, Town Fairs became again alive and progressive events, manifesting the industry of the rural people. Town Fairs were usually jolly, informal meetings, devoid of horse racing or gambling games. They were held in the town hall, on the common, or on the grounds behind the church; there was no admission charge and cash premiums were rarely given. A spirit of friendly competition prevailed to see who brought in the biggest golden pumpkin, the most intricate quilt design, or the neatest hooked rug. The

---

* *New Hampshire Mirror and Farmer. Concord, N. H. Saturday, October 10, 1874. p. 1.*
† *Ibid. Saturday, October 10, 1874. p. 1.*
‡ *Ibid. Saturday, September 26, 1874. p. 2.*
§ *New Hampshire Mirror and Farmer. Saturday, October 3, 1874. p. 4.*

women served a big dinner in the church vestry, and sold the surplus products of a year's sewing and knitting; and there were always plenty of "rich cheeses, nice jars of jellies and preserves, and numerous brown loaves of bread. . . ."

Some of the famous annual Town Fairs were held in Derry, Chester, Acworth, Washington, Bradford-Newbury, Rochester, and Candia. An association of four towns in the Lebanon region at one time established a co-operative fair. The most active Town Fair in the State at the present time is that maintained since 1910 by the town of Sandwich and neighboring settlements. Every Columbus day, the Sandwich Town Hall holds an exhibition of the arts and crafts work that has been produced in the region during the preceding year. A traditional part of the fair is the grand parade, featuring a number of yokes of the finest oxen that can be found. The Pittsfield and Deerfield Fairs share equal honors in bringing together in a similar way the resources of the eastern Merrimack region. And the Canaan, or Mascoma Valley Fair now serves western New Hampshire as the old Connecticut Valley and Grafton County Fairs used to do.

The last State Fair was held in 1885. Its place was taken by the first of the State-wide fairs held under the direction of the Grange Fair Association, at the Franklin and Tilton Driving Park in 1886. The Grange, or Patrons of Husbandry, had assumed the leadership in agricultural activities. The first local Grange Fair had been held in 1874 by the Amoskeag Grange of Manchester. The State-wide event which was held for several years at Tilton was noted for its efficiency and its atmosphere of wholesomeness. Liquor was forbidden from the beginning. The racing stables were overcrowded with fine horses, and the finest cattle in the State were shown within the enclosures.

Concerning the craftwork which was entered for competition at these fairs, the chief requirement of the judges seems to have been common sense. The brief comment in the *Farmer and Mirror* on the ladies' department at one of the earlier fairs, shows very little enthusiasm for such objects of wasted industry as "**ornamental toad-**

stools politely called fungus-work". Yet eccentric works of art occasionally crept into the exhibits of even this dignified and conservative farmers' gathering; there was, for instance, the "conglomeration picture". This was a picture and frame made entirely from corn, grain, shells, nuts, and seeds, including nineteen kinds of corn and over forty kinds of seeds and cones.

Several localized Grange Fair Associations were formed between 1890 and 1910. In 1895 Colonel George L. Ordway of Warner proposed that a Merrimack County Grange Fair Association should be organized to direct an annual fair at River Bow Park; the success of this plan proved the efficiency of leaving the management of fairs to a society formed specifically for that purpose. In 1910, however, the only typical agricultural fair in the southern part of the State was the Londonderry Grange Fair. But in that same year the Union Grange Fair Association was formed by sixteen Granges in central New Hampshire. It has held notable fairs ever since; at present they are famous for exhibits of needlework, rugs, and quilts, which are proof that modern women still know how to use a needle. The Rochester Fair, another modern descendant of the Yankee Cattle Show, encourages contributions of handmade novelties, such as knitted and crocheted bedspreads, and unusual needlepoint handbags, with Spanish or Italian designs in rich colors. This Fair is maintained by a share-holding organization, the Rochester Agricultural and Mechanical Association, organized in 1874 by fifty-two men who contributed one dollar apiece towards its capital fund.

The League of New Hampshire Arts and Crafts has assembled an exhibition of its work in a six-day fair which has been held every summer for the past six years. The first Craftsman's Fair was held in 1934 at the Crawford House, Crawford Notch, where a large barn housed the exhibits. In 1935 Hancock was the scene of the Fair, in 1936 Little Boar's Head, Rye Beach, in 1937 Laconia, in 1938 Whitefield, and in 1939 Durham. The Durham meeting was held in the new Field House of the State University. The 1940 Fair was held at Plymouth. The advantages of League membership are presented to the public not only by the exhibition of the articles made by the League's members, but by demonstrations of the actual processes of creation, something which the promoters of the old agricultural fairs never thought of doing. The significance of work done by hand is more apparent to the observer when he sees pewter and bronze being beaten into meaningful shapes, and when he watches the woven cloth fall from the loom under the skilled fingers of a modern Penelope.

Country Fairs have not gone out of date. The original reason for holding fairs, the gratification of curiosity, is as true today as when they were "cattle shows". Each frosty autumn the fairgrounds all over the State are opened to a vast concourse of eager visitors. For there is something about a fair that has a perennial charm; it seems to satisfy the human need for an occasional touch of the carnival spirit. In fact, an anonymous versifier has put it this way:

> Fakers and hawkers,
> Children and gawkers,
> Dust everywhere!
>
> Sore feet and bunions,
> Hamburg 'n' onions,
> Waft thru the air.
>
> Horses and races,
> Young and old faces,
> All without care.
>
> Popcorn and barkers,
> Peanuts and sharkers—
> All should beware!

XIX

TRENDS IN ORGANIZED HANDICRAFTS

Surviving a rumor that it inspired the beginning of the League of New Hampshire Arts and Crafts, a flock of sheep grazing on a hillside in Sandwich has become a symbol of the contribution that New Hampshire people have given to the revival of handicrafts.

Whether the sheep literally deserve all the credit bestowed upon them is a debatable point and an unimportant one. Figuratively, nothing could be more fitting. Spinning native wool into yarn, weaving it into warm blankets to make living in the cold New Hampshire winters more comfortable, selecting colors to make the blankets serve more than a physical need, creating and perfecting designs until they are a means of individual self-expression, this was the spirit of the handicrafts of our forebears and has become the spirit of craftsmanship today.

People from all over the country are asking constantly, either by letter or by personal call, how the League of New Hampshire Arts and Crafts is run, whom it helps, and how it is supported. Frequently the men and women who make these inquiries are sent by the Governors of their own States to discover the methods by which similar agencies can be organized and promoted for the good of their citizens.

The idea from which this pioneer State-wide handicraft movement came, the first to be sponsored by any legislative body in the United States, was tested originally in the mountain encircled village of Center Sandwich. In 1925, a committee from the Sandwich Historical Society, with Mrs. J. Randolph Coolidge as chairman, interested a number of the townspeople in offering handmade articles for sale on a co-operative basis. For five summers, under Mrs. Coolidge's guidance, the members of the Sandwich Home Industries, as the town's craftworkers called themselves, maintained a salesroom and a tearoom near the center of the village. Small committees, working through a chairman and council, managed the shop and the craft classes held during the winter months; volunteer workers carried on the tearoom.

The tangible results of their first season's activities in spinning, weaving, and rugmaking were so gratifying that the Sandwich craftworkers added baskets, furniture, and wrought-iron utensils to their original list of salable articles.

By 1931 the local venture had attracted considerable interest throughout the State. The report of clicking looms, whirling wheels, and ringing hammers, embellished with human interest stories of the widow who paid her taxes with "rug-money"' and of the man who was earning a real livelihood by selling handmade baskets, eventually reached the ears of New Hampshire's Governor.

Governor John G. Winant was convinced that here was a great opportunity for the people of the State, especially those living in small villages and rural sections, to bring their handiwork to the attention of the outside world. As the first step in putting his convictions into practical form, the Governor appointed an Arts and Crafts Commission composed of prominent men and women to consider the educational and economic possibilities of a State-wide organization to promote handicrafts. From this commission's investigations and reports developed the League of New Hampshire Arts and Crafts. According to its own records, the League was to apply a State appropriation to "instruction, standards, and production in arts and crafts, including administration for the economic and educational advantages of all citizens of the State".

The organization functions through an unpaid governing council and a paid, full-time director with offices at the League headquarters in Concord. Mrs. Coolidge, who has from the very beginning been an outstanding figure in the League's development, serves as its president.

At present there are approximately thirty Home Industries groups, each with its own chairman and committees who are familiar with local conditions. These men and women know exactly what their neighbors can produce in the way of handwork. About eighteen of the groups maintain self-supporting shops, located at strategic points throughout the State, where League products are sold. There is an interchange of goods made by all the groups. Marketing control is centralized so that certain wares will be found in neighborhoods where the demand for them is greatest. One of the important duties of the main office in Concord is to direct a proper distribution of all commodities, so that there will not be an overproduction of any one article or a shortage of something which patrons confidently expect to buy in a certain locality.

Every article that is sold in the shops bears a distinctive label, on which is an outlined map of the State. This label tells the public that the piece of furniture, basket, sampler, woven luncheon set, or pewter bowl has been inspected by the League's jury and has met the rigid standards of design, workmanship, and right use of materials which are required before the articles are accepted by the main office for distribution through the League's shops. The jury has another and equally important function: that of encouraging and educating League craftsmen in the future production of wares that will meet increasingly rigid tests. This is accomplished by teachers.

Under the Smith-Hughes Act, the League receives substantial Federal aid for teaching crafts. This source of income, administered through the State Board of Education, is used to pay instructors of superior training and ability, who are selected by the Director. They travel about the State, spending a few days with one group and then going on to other classes where instruction is wanted.

Craftsmen who do outstanding work earn the title "Master Craftsman". A system of patents protects their original designs from imitation. They are further protected by a "gentlemen's agreement" not to copy one another's work.

A close contact is maintained between the various groups and with the main office. The Director visits each unit frequently, but an important interchange of ideas comes from the Craftsmen's Advisory Board, composed of members elected by each group. The Board is an open forum where the individual and group problems are discussed and constructive suggestions made. The findings of the Board are then reported to the League Governing Council for consideration.

A few of the League shops, like the one in Meredith, are attractive small houses, built through the efforts of the local group. Usually they have started very modestly. The shop of the Sandwich Home Industries was originally located in a building which had been unoccupied for years; when it burned in a fire that swept through a section of the village, a new shop designed to hold more salesrooms and a larger tearoom was erected at a spot where visitors to Center Sandwich will see it immediately. Wherever you find a League shop, whether housed in a rented room or a building of its own, you will see swinging over the door the League sign representing a traditional white New England cottage with a red chimney.

The revival of old-time New Hampshire crafts is an essential part of the League's program. For instance, Sandwich weavers color fabrics with old-fashioned vegetable dyes made by the same formulas their grandmothers used. In Andover, pieces from an antique pewter communion set, formerly used in the old church, furnish the designs for vases made by the town's metalworkers. In Hancock, needleworkers piece up and appliqué quilt covers patterned on their treasured family heirlooms.

Occasionally an old-time craft is revived to meet a sudden demand for work that is practically unknown today. An unsolicited order for a length of netting which came to the Concord office was instrumental in bringing to light again an almost forgotten art.

Gradually, different localities have come to specialize in their own particular crafts, a specialization that is somewhat determined by what materials are available and, more important, by the skills and interests of the craftsmen in that region. Thus, Sandwich is noted for its weaving, Wolfeboro for metalwork, Winchester for needlework, and Dover for wood carving. Toys are made in Peterborough, hooked rugs in Hampton Falls, mittens in South Acworth. In Meredith, women embroider the linen which is manufactured in the local mills. In Nashua, dolls are dressed in the traditional costumes of the city's different nationality groups.

Whenever possible the handicrafts of these peoples have been fostered and have greatly enriched those native to New Hampshire. Intricate weaving designs known to generations of Finnish and Swedish women, the delicate embroidery patterns originally developed in Switzerland and Italy, sturdy knitting stitches from the heaths of Scotland, all have been encouraged and have made an invaluable contribution to the variety and the beauty of New Hampshire craftwork.

Within the League organization, craftsmen who are interested in the same types of work have formed small groups who meet to discuss plans and to study the history and the technique of their chosen arts. The needleworkers make up the Saffron and Indigo Society; the rugmakers are known as the State Rug Group; and, as the name indicates, the Weaving Guild is a clearinghouse for the ideas of men and women who use hand looms.

The League is also engaged in a vigorous campaign to educate the public in the appreciation of well-designed, finely made articles of genuine artistic quality. The potential buyer who recognizes the beauty in a hooked rug design and understands something of the technique involved in rugmaking, and the customer who sees a lump of clay in the potter's hand turn into a graceful bowl are more valuable to the real progress of the League than are people who unknowingly give their money for shoddy "handmade" goods.

Sometimes, in furthering this educational campaign, exhibitions like a display of the detailed colored drawings of crewel embroideries painted by artists on the WPA Art Program for the Index of American Design, are sponsored by the League. In 1937 the Bristol and the Meredith Home Industries made a motion picture in color showing how rugmakers produce their wares. But the greatest contribution to this part of the program is at the annual Craftsmen's Fairs where thousands of people see the blacksmith at his forge, the woodworker at his bench, the potter at his wheel, and the weaver at his loom.

Long before Sandwich women brought their grandmothers' spinning wheels from the attic and Concord woodworkers first attempted to fashion old-time applewood knife and fork handles and wooden tableware, another agency was constructively promoting the arts and crafts movement in New Hampshire. About forty years ago the interests of two local societies, the Manchester Electric Club and the Manchester Art Association were merged to form the Manchester Institute of Arts and Sciences.

The first activities of the Institute were mostly along the lines of science and nature study. But the classes in modeling under William E. Burbank, wood carving under Mrs. Melusina Varick, and water color painting under Mrs. Maud Briggs Knowlton became increasingly popular and eventually formed the nucleus of a Fine Arts Department.

Ten years after the Institute was opened, Albert L. Clough, then, as now, president of the organization, reported that interest in nature study was being gradually supplanted by an interest in arts and crafts.[*] Under the leadership of Mrs. Jennie C. Young, chairman of the Fine Arts Department for over twenty years, the classes in handicrafts increased yearly in variety and in membership.

A juvenile department in arts and crafts instruction was launched in 1903 in which Mrs. W. Livesey Cass opened the first basketry classes for children. These classes were most successful and within a very few years ten assistants were needed to carry on the work. In 1906 the first basketry class for adults was held with Mrs. M. E. Gleason as teacher. Basketry was a popular craft for several years and instruction was given continuously in the art until 1934.

Until she was appointed Director of the Currier Gallery of Art in Manchester in 1929, Mrs. Maud Briggs Knowlton was an outstanding instructor in the Fine Arts Department of the Insti-

[*] *Daily Mirror and American. Manchester, N. H. Monday, January 4, 1909.*

tute. Her courses in the theory of design and color prepared students for advanced courses in applied design, in which stenciling, block printing, gesso, and hand-printed textile work were studied. Bookbinding and leatherwork were also added to her courses, and later she conducted classes in Colonial, Tapestry, Swedish Stick, and Embroidery weaving. Mrs. Knowlton made a special contribution to the Institute's crafts program by introducing metalwork and by starting jewelry classes which have been a permanent part of the Fine Arts Department since 1908.

The courses in jewelry making were continued by Miss Helen Chandler, a pupil of Mrs. Knowlton and of Thorwolde Christianson of Boston. Miss Chandler has achieved considerable reputation for her designs and her work, especially for a ring of eighteen carat gold set with topaz. This ring was exhibited at the Philadelphia Art Alliance and from there was sent to the 1937 Paris Exhibition as a specimen of fine American craftsmanship. Later, the American Federation of Arts sent the exhibit of jewelry, in which Miss Chandler's work was included, about the United States.

For several years the late Miss Penelope W. Snow has acted as chairman of the Fine Arts Department of the Institute. With such instructors as Miss Helen Chandler in jewelry, Wilson F. Higgins in metalwork, Miss Kate Gooden in leatherwork, gesso, bookbinding, and applied design, Mrs. Louise Campbell Martin in weaving, Mrs. Martha Watson in rugmaking, Miss Elizabeth Christophe in embroidery, and Richard Moll in pottery, arts and crafts classes turn out work of exceptionally high quality.

At first all craftwork done at the Institute was of an entirely uncommercial nature. But in 1923, when some of the students wished to sell their work, an arts and crafts society, the forerunner of the present Craftworkers' Guild, was formed. All articles which members put on sale at local exhibits held in Manchester and at the summer shop sponsored by the Guild in Truro, Massachusetts, must pass rigid requirements set by a jury of artists and craftsmen.

The influences of the League and of the Institute are in no sense isolated or restricted in scope. An instructor at the Institute frequently teaches a group of craftsmen working under League guidance; a master craftsman in the League often advises arts and crafts workers who are affiliated with quite different agencies. Mrs. Fred Wilman of Tilton, chairman of the Fine Arts Department of the New Hampshire Federation of Women's Clubs, is a member of the Saffron and Indigo Society; Miss Helen Chandler teaches Wolfeboro clubwomen how to make jewelry; Leo Malm has carried on wood carving classes for both the League and the Institute; Mrs. Martha Watson shows girls in a National Youth Administration Center how to hook rugs.

Tracing back the story of organized handicrafts in New Hampshire we find that just prior to the time the Institute was organizing formal classes in craftwork, a Handicraft Society was organized in Peterborough. It was formed in 1904 by Miss Mary Adams and Miss Mary Morrison and had for its main objective the production of salable handiwork of genuine merit. Originally, the members of the society concentrated on embroidery and basketry. But it really was Italian cutwork that made the Peterborough group famous. Reticella, as this type of needlework is called, was first taught in a class conducted by the society in 1905. Up until that time reticella was practically an unknown art in northern New England. Miss Morrison studied the technique in Italy and brought home samples of the work which the class used as models.

The society's basketry classes were so popular that two teachers were needed to instruct the applicants. Another venture of the Peterborough craftsmen was the weaving of linen and of rugs. By 1911 they were engaged in making tooled leather, cross-stitch embroidery, and crocheted woolen garments for children. The products of their industry, including homemade preserves and jellies, were sold in a shop carried on by the society. After the death of the leader in 1917, the organization disbanded, but many of the former members kept up their interest in handicrafts and now have an active affiliation with the League of New Hampshire Arts and Crafts.

New Hampshire has several social agencies, similar to those of other States, which not only promote work with the hands as an educational experience, but which also use arts and crafts as means of occupational therapy for rehabilitation purposes. Since 1930, the Home Industries for the Blind has established itself in a quiet, unassuming way, under the supervision of James T. Ribberhold, Director of the Services for the Blind. Miss Charlotte M. Newing, a trained craftworker, travels constantly about the State teaching handicrafts, like weaving, basketry, knitting, woven rugmaking, and leatherwork, to blind people. The New Hampshire Crippled Children's Society performs a similar service for handicapped people of all ages. Crafts are taught by Miss Minnie F. Witham of East Northwood who conducts classes in forty-six towns in nine counties of the State.

Craftwork plays an important part in the programs of the Boy Scouts, the Girl Scouts, the 4-H Clubs, and the National Youth Administration. In the NYA the boys and girls save up dimes and nickels to buy materials, and the work produced is somewhat restricted by the costs of production. However, Mrs. Inez Rich, who teaches and supervises craftwork at the Center in Manchester, has accomplished excellent results. Some leather tooling and a little copper work have been attempted and many interesting pieces of jewelry made by patiently chipping amberol. A few reproductions of Shaker furniture have been undertaken and, with some encouragement, might be turned into an independent industrial enterprise.

Since 1921 the Extension Service of the University of New Hampshire has brought instruction in craftwork to the people of rural communities. At first the resources of the Home Demonstration Department in this line were limited to helping farm women upholster furniture, reseat chairs, and brighten their homes with paint and paper. Gradually, classes were added in which the women could learn to make household articles, such as lamp shades, rugs, and baskets. Some experimenting was done in "tied-and-dyed" work and in stenciling and in making magazine racks and sewing screens. The three objectives of this work, according to Daisy Deane Williamson, State Home Demonstration Leader, are to make homes more attractive, to help people save money, and to increase domestic efficiency.

In 1934 the program of the Extension Service added classes in simple crafts. Rugmaking, frame weaving, and novelty amberol jewelry making are examples of the type of work done. Recently, work with silver and with gem stones has been attempted in one county. At present Coös and Cheshire Counties lead the rest of the State in craftwork sponsored by the Recreation Department. This program fulfills a need for creative tasks that is even more urgent in the country than in the larger towns. As M. L. Wilson, Under-Secretary of the U. S. Department of Agriculture, said in commenting on the Exhibition of Rural Arts held in Washington in 1938: "This is the people's art; it has nothing to do with queerisms or elaborate theories. It is born of utility. Art here means doing well something that needs to be done."*

When the Reverend James MacGregor preached the first sermon for the settlers of Londonderry, under the open sky on an April day in 1719, it is recorded that he took for his text a verse from the prophecy of Isaiah: "And a man shall be as a hiding place from the wind, . . . as the shadow of a great rock in a weary land." The men and women who listened to the pioneer preacher were a hardy and plain-thinking people, infused with a practical genius for solving with their hands the problems of everyday existence. This book has been largely concerned with the cavalcade of such men and women who have added, each his own measure, to the whole substance of life in a New England State. A man in a little northern town worked all his life making nothing but chairs. Another man came to a Cheshire town when he was young and spent the rest of his years fashioning good wooden clocks. And a widow in an obscure hamlet supported eighteen children by weaving into linen cloth the yarn spun by her daughters. They lived and died without fame; they were the common people, building against chaos and distress a refuge upon the land. . . .

The hands of the common people have left their mark on the ships that traded across the seas; they have raised buildings for the

* *American Home. Vol. XX (June 1938). "Know American Arts and Crafts First." Charlotte E. Conway. p. 15.*

beginnings of communities set along river valleys and in the mountain passes. To temper and refine the bare routine of living, they have fashioned violins and bright shapes of pottery, gracefully carved furniture, and fine silverware to be handed down as a symbol of unity in family life.

The hands of countless women like Molly Stark have given richness and warmth to a social life which, in one respect, has been basic to the industrial, political, and intellectual development of New Hampshire. This is not life in the languid South, the level Midwest, or fruitful California. This is life in a State where the winters are sharp with cold, emerging out of sultry, golden autumns and merging again into the purity and greenness of northern springs. The summit of nearly every hill in New Hampshire looks out upon the rocky slopes of other hills. Here the resources are neither poor nor rich, but represent the fundamental materials out of which the common people have always been able to build their daily life: out of wood and clay and a little metal, a handful of sand and stones, and a few wild herbs gathered in the fields. In this austere and rugged country, with the simplest of materials, the hands of craftsmen, past and present, have helped and are still helping to build the State that is New Hampshire.

BIBLIOGRAPHY
Published Works and Periodicals

CHAPTER I—*Basketmaking: A Legacy*

Bowles, Ella Shannon. *Homespun Handicrafts.* New York. J. B. Lippincott, 1931.
Carr, Lucien. *Dress and Ornaments of Certain Indians.* Worcester, Mass. American Antiquarian Society, 1898.
Chamberlain, Alexander F. *Contribution of the American Indian to Civilization.* Proceedings of the American Antiquarian Society, Vol. XVI.
Copeland, Jennie F. *Every Day But Sunday.* Brattleboro, Vt. Stephen Daye Press, 1936.
Eaton, Allen H. *Handicrafts of the Southern Highlands.* New York. Russell Sage Foundation, 1937.
Hodge, Frederick Webb. *Handbook of the American Indians.* Washington. Smithsonian Institution, 1907.
Krieger, Herbert W. *American Indian Costumes in the United States National Museum.* Washington. Annual Report of Board of Regents. Smithsonian Institution, 1928.
Little, William. *History of Weare, New Hampshire.* Published by the Town, 1888.
Mason, Otis Tufton. *Woman's Share in Primitive Culture.* New York. Appleton Co., 1897.
Moorehead, Warren K. *Prehistoric Implements.* Saranac Lake. Allen I. Vosburgh, 1900.
Proctor, Mary A. *Indians of the Winnipesaukee and Pemigewassett Valleys.* Franklin, N. H. Towns and Robie, 1921.
Scales, John. *History of Strafford County.* Chicago. Richmond-Arnold, 1914.
Seward, Josiah. *History of the Town of Sullivan.* Keene, N. H. Sentinel Co., 1921.
Schoolcraft, Henry. *Information Respecting the . . . Indian Tribes in the United States.* Bureau of Indian Affairs per Act of Congress, March 3, 1847.

* * *

Boston Evening Transcript. (February 19, 1907).
Willoughby, Charles C. *Houses and Gardens of the New England Indians.* American Anthropologist, Vol. VII (1906).

CHAPTER II—*Out of Seafaring Days*

Albee, John. *New Castle, Historic and Picturesque.* Boston. Cupples, Upham & Co., 1884.
Chapelle, Howard. *History of American Sailing Ships.* New York. W. W. Norton Co., 1935.
Clark, Arthur H. *The Clipper Ship Era.* New York. G. P. Putnam's Sons, 1916.
Davis, Charles G. *Ships of the Past.* Salem, Mass. Marine Research Society, 1929.
Howells, John Mead. *Architectural Heritage of the Piscataqua.* New York. Architectural Book Publishing Co., Inc., 1937.
Maclay, Edgar S. *History of American Privateers.* New York. D. Appleton Co., 1899.
Robinson, John. Dow, George F. *The Sailing Ships of New England, 1607-1907.* Salem, Mass. Marine Research Society, 1922.
Roux, Antoine. *Ships and Shipping.* Salem, Mass. Marine Research Society, 1922.
Taylor, D. F. *The Piscataqua River Gundalow. Historic American Marine Survey No. 171.* Works Progress Administration, Federal Writers' Project of Massachusetts. Sponsored by the Smithsonian Institution, 1936.

* * *

Davis, Charles G. *Clipper Ships—Ancient and Old.* Yachting. Vol. 51 (March 1932).
Keyes, Homer Eaton. *Bellamy's Style and Its Imitators.* Antiques. Vol. XXVII (March 1935).
Mather, Frank J. *A Clipper Ship and Her Commander.* Atlantic Monthly. Vol. XCIV (November 1904).
New Hampshire Patriot and State Gazette. (May 10, 1849).
Safford, Victor. *John Haley Bellamy, the Wood Carver of Kittery Point.* Antiques. Vol. XXVII (March 1935).
Scales, John. *Shipbuilding in Dover and Along the Piscataqua River.* Granite Monthly. Vol. 60 (October 1928).

CHAPTER III—*Men Who Made New Hampshire Buildings*

Adams, Nathaniel. *Annals of Portsmouth.* Portsmouth, N. H. Published by the Author, 1825.
Aldrich, George. *Walpole As It Was and As It Is.* Claremont, N. H. Claremont Manufacturing Co., 1880.
Annett, Albert and Lehtinen, Alice E. *History of Jaffrey.* Published by the Town, 1937.
Bouton, Nathaniel. *History of Concord.* Concord, N. H. Sanborn, 1856.
Brewster, Charles W. *Rambles About Portsmouth.* Portsmouth, N. H. Brewster, 1869.
Browne, George Waldo. *History of Hillsborough.* Published by the Town, 1921.
Burbank, Leonard F. *History of the First Unitarian Society in Dunstable, now Nashua.* Nashua, N. H. F. E. Cole & Co., 1926.
Chase, Frederick A. *History of Dartmouth College and the Town of Hanover.* Cambridge, Mass. John Wilson & Son, 1891.
Cochrane, W. R. and Wood, George K. *History of Francestown.* Published by the Town, 1895.
Coffin, Charles C. *History of Boscawen and Webster from 1733 to 1878.* Concord, N. H. Republican Press Association, 1878.
Cram, Ralph Adams. *Convictions and Controversies.* Boston. Marshall Jones Co., 1935.
Cram, Ralph Adams. *My Life in Architecture.* Boston. Little, Brown and Co., 1936.
Cutter, Daniel B. *History of the Town of Jaffrey.* Concord, N. H. Republican Press Association, 1881.
Hayley, Rev. John W. *History of Tuftonboro.* Concord, N. H. Rumford Press, 1923.
Howells, John Mead. *Architectural Heritage of the Piscataqua.* New York. Architectural Book Publishing Co., 1937.
Hurd, D. Hamilton (ed.). *History of Merrimack and Belknap Counties.* Philadelphia. J. W. Lewis and Co., 1885.
Jackson, James R. *History of Littleton.* Published by the Town, 1905.
Livermore, Abiel A. and Putnam, Sewall. *History of the Town of Wilton.* Lowell, Mass., Marden & Rowell, Printers, 1888.
Locke, Emma P. *Colonial Amherst.* Milford, N. H. W. B. & A. B. Rotch, 1916.
Lyford, James Otis. *History of Canterbury.* Vol. 2. Concord, N. H. Rumford Press, 1912.
May, Ralph. *Early Portsmouth History.* Boston. C. E. Goodspeed, 1926.
Moore, J. Bailey. *History of the Town of Candia.* Manchester, N. H. George W. Browne, 1893.
Norton, John F. *History of Fitzwilliam.* New York. Burr Printing House, 1888.
Parker, Benjamin F. *History of Wolfeborough.* Published by the Town, 1901.

BIBLIOGRAPHY

Parker, Edward E. *History of Brookline.* Published by the Town, 1914.
Parker, Edward E. (ed.). *History of the City of Nashua.* Nashua, N. H. Nashua Telegraph Publishing Co., 1897.
Parsons, Langdon B. *History of the Town of Rye.* Concord, N. H. Rumford Printing Co., 1905.
Plummer, George F. *History of the Town of Wentworth.* Concord, N. H. Rumford Press, 1930.
Robinson, Albert G. *Old New England Houses.* New York. Charles Scribner's Sons, 1920.
Runnels, M. T. *History of Sanbornton.* Boston. Alfred Mudge & Son, 1881.
Scales, John. *History of Dover.* Printed by the authority of the City Council, 1923.
Secomb, D. F. *History of Amherst.* Concord, N. H. Evan, Sleeper, and Woodbury, 1883.
Somers, Rev. A. N. *History of Lancaster.* Concord, N. H. Rumford Press, 1899.
Stackpole, Everett S. and Thompson, Lucien. *History of the Town of Durham.* Published by the Town, 1913.
Waite, Otis F. R. *History of the Town of Claremont.* Published by the authority of the Town, 1895.
Wallace, William A. *History of Canaan.* Concord. Rumford Press, 1910.
Wood, James A. *New Hampshire Homes.* Concord. James A. Wood, 1895.
Woodbury, B. P. Savage, Thomas and Patten, William. *History of Bedford.* Published by the Town, 1903.

CHAPTER IV—*Cabinet Makers Past and Present*

Bouton, Nathaniel. *History of Concord.* Concord, N. H. Sanborn, 1856.
Brewster, Charles W. *Rambles About Portsmouth, Second Series.* Portsmouth, N. H. Brewster, 1869.
Chandler, Charles H. and Lee, Sarah F. *History of New Ipswich.* Fitchburg, Mass. Sentinel Printing Co., 1914.
Chase, Benjamin. *History of Old Chester.* Auburn, N. H. Published by the Author, 1869.
Cochrane, W. R. *History of Antrim.* Manchester, N. H. Published by the Town, 1880.
Cogswell, Leander W. *History of Henniker.* Concord, N. H. Republican Press Association, 1880.
Moulton, Henry W. *Moulton Annals.* Chicago. Edward A. Claypool, 1906.
Secomb, Daniel F. *History of Amherst.* Concord. Evans, Sleeper, and Woodbury, 1883.

* * *

American Patriot.
Burroughs, Paul. *Furniture Widely Made in New Hampshire.* American Collector. Vol. VI (June 1937).
Decatur, Stephen. *John and George Gaines of Portsmouth, N. H.* American Collector. Vol. VII (November 1938).
Keyes, Homer Eaton. *The Editor's Attic.* Antiques. Vol. XXIX (April 1936).
Koch, William F. *Repairing and Refinishing Old Furniture.* Antiquarian. Vol. VIII (April 1927).
Lyon, Irving P. *The Oak Furniture of Ipswich, Massachusetts.* Antiques. Vol. XXXIII (April 1938).
New Hampshire Patriot and State Gazette. (July 14, 1823—Nov. 14, 1809—Oct. 24, 1825—Nov. 6, 1826).
Portsmouth Gazette. (August 4, 1798).

CHAPTER V—*Time and Music*

Annett, Albert and Lehtinen, Alice E. *History of Jaffrey.* Published by the Town, 1937.
Bouton, Nathaniel. *History of Concord.* Concord, N. H. Sanborn, 1856.
Chase, Benjamin. *History of Old Chester.* Auburn, N. H. Published by the Author, 1869.
Coffin, Charles Carleton. *History of Boscawen and Webster.* Concord. Republican Press Association, 1878.
Griffin, S. G. *History of the Town of Keene.* Keene, N. H. Sentinel Printing Co., 1904.
Hutchins, Levi. *Autobiography.* Cambridge, Mass. Riverside Press, 1865.
Lane, Samuel. *Journal.* Edited by Charles L. Hanson. Concord, N. H. New Hampshire Historical Society, 1937.
Little, William. *History of Weare.* Published by the Town, 1888.
Lyford, James O. (ed) *History of Concord.* Concord, N. H. Rumford Press, 1903.
McDuffie, Franklin. *History of the Town of Rochester.* Manchester, N. H. John D. Clarke and Co., 1892.
Miller, Edward C. *American Antique Furniture, Vol. II.* Baltimore. Lord Baltimore Press, 1937.
Moore, N. Hudson. *Old Clock Book.* New York. Frederick A. Stokes, 1911.
Nutting, Wallace. *The Clock Book.* Framingham, Mass. Old America Co., 1924.
Nutting, Wallace. *Furniture Treasury, Vol. II.* Framingham, Mass. Old America Co., 1928.
Nutting, Wallace. *Furniture Treasury, Vol. III.* Framingham, Mass. Old America Co., 1933.
Secomb, Daniel F. *History of the Town of Amherst.* Concord, N. H. Evans, Sleeper, and Woodbury, 1883.
Smith, Albert. *History of Peterborough.* Boston. George H. Ellis, 1876.
Smith, Charles J. *History of the Town of Mont Vernon.* Boston. Blanchard Printing Co., 1907.
Whitcher, William F. *History of the Town of Haverhill.* Concord, N. H. Rumford Press, 1919.

* * *

Boston Globe. (December 27, 1938).
Concord Daily Monitor. (January 6, 1868).
Manchester Union. (January 3, 1940).
New Hampshire Patriot and State Gazette. (December 13, 1797—May 26, 1852 —June 2, 1852).
Sunday Union Leader. (July 29, 1923).

CHAPTER VI—*Craft of the Woodworker*

Aldrich, George. *Walpole As It Was and As It Is.* Claremont, N. H. Claremont Manufacturing Company, 1880.
Annett, Albert and Lehtinen, Alice. *History of Jaffrey.* Published by the Town, 1937.
Bemis, Charles A. *History of the Town of Marlborough.* Boston. Ellis Press, 1881.
Caverley, A. M. *Historical Sketch of Troy and Her Industries, 1764-1855.* Keene, N. H. Sentinel Office, 1859.
Chase, Benjamin. *History of Old Chester.* Auburn, N. H. Published by the Author, 1869.
Coffin, Charles C. *History of Boscawen and Webster, 1733-1878.* Concord, N. H. Republican Press Association, 1878.
Cronk, C. P. *Forest Industries of New Hampshire and Their Trend of Development.* Concord, N. H. State of New Hampshire Forestry and Recreation Commission, 1936.

BIBLIOGRAPHY

Davis, Bailey K. *Traditions and Recollections of Berlin*. Published by the City, c. 1926.
Eastman, John R. *History of Andover*. Concord, N. H. Rumford Press, 1910.
Fogg, Alonzo J. *Statistics and Gazeteer of New Hampshire*. Concord, N. H. D. L. Guernsey Co., 1874.
Fassett, James H. *Colonial Life in New Hampshire*. Boston. Ginn and Co., 1899.
Griffin, S. G. *History of Keene from 1732 to 1874*. Keene, N. H. Sentinel Printing Co., 1904.
Harriman, Walter. *History of Warner*. Concord, N. H. Republican Press Association, 1879.
Hurd, D. Hamilton. *History of Cheshire and Sullivan Counties*. Philadelphia. J. W. Lewis Co., 1886.
Hurd, D. Hamilton. *History of Merrimack and Belknap Counties*. Philadelphia. J. W. Lewis Co., 1885.
Little, William. *History of Warren*. Manchester, N. H. Wm. E. Moore, 1870.
Little, William. *History of Weare*. Lowell, Mass. S. W. Huse & Co., 1888.
Lyford, James Otis. *History of Canterbury*. Concord, N. H. Rumford Press, 1912.
Merrill, J. L. *History of Acworth*. Published by the Town, 1869.
Parker, Edward E. *History of Brookline*. Published by the Town, 1914.
Powers, Grant. *Historical Sketches of The Coös Country*. Haverhill, N. H. J. F. C. Hayes, 1841.
Rawson, Marion Nicholl. *Little Old Mills*. New York. E. P. Dutton, Inc., 1935.
Read, Benjamin. *History of Swanzey*. Salem, Mass. Salem Press, 1892.
Robinson, Margaret C. *Hannah Davis, Pioneer Maker of Bandboxes*. Published by Jaffrey Village Improvement Society.
Stearns, Ezra S. *History of the Town of Rindge*. Boston. Ellis Press, 1875.
Stone, Melvin T. *History of Troy*. Keene, N. H. Sentinel Publishing Co., 1897.
Whittemore, Joel. *History of Fitzwilliam from 1752 to 1887*. New York. Burr Printing House, 1888.
Worthern, Augusta H. *History of Sutton*. Concord, N. H. Republican Press Association, 1890.

* * *

Cram, William Everett. *Jack of All Trades—Master of None*. The American Review. Vol. VIII (March 1937).
New Hampshire Patriot and State Gazette. (March 17, 1812).

CHAPTER VII—*Modern Ornamental Wood Carving*

Hasluck, Paul N. *Wood Carving*. Philadelphia. David McKay, 1909.
Wellman, Rita. *Victoria Royal*. New York. Charles Scribner and Son, 1939.

* * *

Atwood, Frederick S. (ed.). *Old Fiddler's Throne in Deerfield, N. H.* Antiques. Vol. 1 (June 1922).
Manchester Leader (files of 1902-1940).
Manchester Mirror and American (files of 1908-1912).
Manchester Union (files of 1902-1940).
New Hampshire League of Arts and Crafts. *Monthly Bulletin*. (June 1934, February 1936, March 1936, April 1936, July 1936, January 1937, June 1938, August 1938, September 1938, October 1938, May 1939). Edited by Mrs. Foster Stearns, Concord. Sponsored by the Commission of Arts and Crafts.

CHAPTER VIII—*Clay Kiln and Potter's Wheel*

Annett, Albert and Lehtinen, Alice. *History of Jaffrey*. Published by the Town, 1937.
Bell, Charles H. *History of the Town of Exeter*. Published by the Town, 1888.

Cochrane, W. R. and Wood, George K. *History of Francestown.* Published by the Town, 1895.
Coffin, Charles C. *History of Boscawen.* Concord, N. H. Republican Press Association, 1878.
Cox, George J. *Pottery.* New York. Macmillan Co., 1926.
McDuffee, Franklin. *History of Rochester Vol. II.* Manchester, N. H. John B. Clarke Co., 1892.
Merrill, Georgia Drew. *History of Carroll County.* Boston. W. A. Fergusson Co., 1889.
WPA New Hampshire Historical Records Survey. *Town Government of New Hampshire Vol. 3.* (Preliminary Edition. Based on Laws of New Hampshire).
Saunderson, Henry H. *History of Charlestown.* Claremont, N. H. Published by the Town, 1876.
Stearns, Ezra S. *Genealogical and Family History of the State of New Hampshire.* New York. Lewis Publishing Co., 1908.
Stone, Melvin T. *History of Troy.* Keene, N. H. Sentinel Publishing Co., 1897.
Weeden, William B. *Economic and Social History of New England Vol. I.* Boston. Houghton, Mifflin Co., 1891.

* * *

Burbank, Leonard. *Lyndeboro Pottery.* Antiques. Vol. XIII (February 1928).
New Hampshire Patriot and State Gazette. (March 9, 1819.
September and October 1827. March 1, 1833. February 13, 1837).
Norton, F. H. *Osborne Pottery at Gonic.* Antiques. Vol. XIX (February 1931).
Norton, F. H. *Crafts Pottery in Nashua.* Antiques. Vol. XIX (April 1931).
Norton, F. H. *Exeter Pottery Works.* Antiques. Vol. XXII (July 1932).
Ramsay, John. *Early American Pottery: a Resume.* Antiques. Vol. XX (October 1931).

CHAPTER IX—*Stonecutters*

Bell, Charles. *Facts Relating to the Early History of Chester.* Concord, N. H. G. Parker Lyons, 1863.
Cochrane, Rev. W. R. and Wood, George K. *History of Francestown.* Nashua, N. H. Published by the Town, 1895.
Forbes, Harriette M. *Gravestones of Early New England and the Men Who Made Them.* Boston. Houghton-Mifflin, 1927.
Hillsborough County. *Records of Probate Office.* Nashua, N. H.
Hitchcock, C. H. *The Geology of New Hampshire.* Concord, N. H. Published by the State, 1876.
Hurd, D. Hamilton. *History of Rockingham and Strafford Counties. New Hampshire.* Philadelphia. J. W. Lewis, 1882.
Jackson, Charles T. *Final Report of the Geology of the State of New Hampshire.* Concord, N. H. Carroll and Blake, 1844.

CHAPTER X—*New Hampshire Glass*

Barber, Edwin Atlee. *American Glassware.* Philadelphia. Patterson & White, 1900.
Blood, Henry Ames. *History of Temple.* Boston. Geo. C. Rand and Avery, 1860.
Bond, Harold Lewis. *An Encyclopedia of Antiques.* Boston. Hale, Cushman & Flint, 1937.
Bowles, Ella Shannon. *Let Me Show You New Hampshire.* New York. Alfred A. Knopf, 1938.
Carter, Rev. N. F., and Fowler, Hon. T. L. *History of Pembroke, N. H.* Vol. I. Concord, N. H. Republican Press Association, 1895.
Child, Hamilton. *Gazetteer of Cheshire County, N. H.* Syracuse, N. Y. Published by the Author, 1885.

BIBLIOGRAPHY

Clarke, E. Palmer. *Holiday Hearsay.* Center Ossipee, N. H. Independent Press, 1939.
Donovan, Rev. D., and Woodward, Jacob A. *The History of the Town of Lyndeborough, New Hampshire.* Lyndeborough, N. H. Published by the Town, 1906.
Gould, Isaiah. *History of Stoddard, Cheshire County, N. H.* Keene, N. H. Maria A. Gould Giffin, 1897.
Griffin, S. C. *History of the Town of Keene.* Keene, N. H. Sentinel Printing Co., 1904.
Guild, Lurelle Van Arsdale. *The Geography of American Antiques.* Garden City, N. Y. Doubleday & Co., 1935.
Knittle, Rhea Mansfield. *Early American Glass.* New York. Century, 1927.
Moore, N. Hudson. *Old Glass, European and American.* New York. Frederick A. Stokes Co., 1924.
New Hampshire Business Directory. (1868).
Rawson, Marion Nicholl. *Candleday Art.* New York. E. P. Dutton & Co., 1938.
Stackpole, Everett S. *History of New Hampshire.* Vol. I. New York. American Historical Society, 1916.
Van Rensselaer, Stephen. *Early American Bottles and Flasks.* Peterborough, N. H. Transcript Printing Co., 1926.
Weygandt, Cornelius. *The White Hills.* New York. Henry Holt & Co., 1934.

* * *

Antiques. Vol. XXXV. (February 1939).
Columbian Centinel. (July 21, 1830).
Concord Daily Monitor. (April 27, 1927).
Hayward, Mrs. Robert P. *Early American Glass.* Collections of the Historical Society of Cheshire County. No. 2. (July 1930).
Heald, Charles B. *First Glass Making in America.* Granite State Magazine. Vol. III (January 1907).
Irwin, Frederick T. *Glassmaking in New Hampshire.* Granite State Magazine. Vol. LX (January 1928).
Manchester Union-Leader. (April 8, 1923; May 5, 1927; December 2, 1935; December 6, 1936; March 29, 1938).
McKearin, George S. *Early American Glass.* Country Life. Vol. 46 (September 1924).
The Mentor. (January 1929).
Milford Cabinet. (Files of 1936).
New Hampshire Patriot and State Gazette. (July 27, 1840; August 27, 1851).
New Hampshire Sentinel. (November 25, 1815).
O'Connor, Johnson. *Keene Masonic Bottle.* Antiques. Vol. V (February 1924).
The Repertory. Vol. I. No. 2. (January 1925).
State Highway Department. *New Hampshire Highways.* (September 1932).
Watkins, Laura Woodside. *Stoddard Glass.* Antiques. Vol. XXIV (August 1933).

CHAPTER XI—*Workers in Metal*

Adams, Nathaniel. *Annals of Portsmouth.* Portsmouth, N. H. Published by the Author, 1825.
Avery, C. Louise. *Early American Silver.* New York. Century Co., 1930.
Bell, Charles H. *History of the Town of Exeter.* Published by the Town, 1888.
Bigelow, Francis H. *Historic Silver of the Colonies and Its Makers.* New York. Macmillan Co., 1917.
Blood, Henry Ames. *History of Temple.* Boston. Rand and Avery, 1860.
Boston Marriages, 30th Reports of Commissioners, Document 101.
Bouton, Nathaniel. (ed.) *New Hampshire Provincial and State Papers.* Vol. I. Concord, N. H. Published by the State, 1867.

Brewster, Charles W. *Rambles About Portsmouth.* Portsmouth, N. H. Brewster, 1859.
Chase, Benjamin. *History of Old Chester.* Auburn, N. H. Published by the Author, 1869.
Currier, Ernest M. *Marks of Early American Silver.* Edited by Kathryn C. Buhler. Portland, Maine. Southworth-Anthoesen Press, 1938.
Cutten, Dr. George Barton. *The Silversmiths, Watchmakers and Jewelers of the State of New York.* Hamilton, N. Y. Privately Printed, 1939.
Donovan, Rev. D. and Woodward, Jacob A. *The History of the Town of Lyndeborough.* Published by the Town, 1906.
Dow, George Francis. *The Arts and Crafts in New England, 1704-1735.* Topsfield, Mass. The Wayside Press, 1927.
Dow, George Francis. *Everday Life in Massachusetts Bay Colony.* Boston. Published for the Society for the Preservation of New England Antiquities, 1935.
Dow, Joseph. *History of the Town of Hampton.* Salem, Mass. Published by Lucy E. Dow, 1893.
Dyer, Walter A. *Creators of Decorative Styles.* New York. Doubleday Page & Co., 1917.
Eberlein, Harold D. *Practical Book of Early American Arts and Crafts.* Philadelphia. J. B. Lippincott, 1916.
Elwell, Newton W. *Colonial Silverware of the 17th and 18th Centuries.* Boston. George W. Polley & Co., 1899.
Ensko, Stephen. *American Silversmiths and Their Marks.* New York. Published by the Author, 1927-37.
WPA Federal Writers' Project of New Hampshire. *New Hampshire Guide.* Boston. Houghton, Mifflin Co., 1938.
Fitts, Rev. James Hill. *History of Newfields.* Concord, N. H. Rumford Press, 1912.
Foster, Sarah H. *Portsmouth Guide Book.* Portsmouth, N. H. Joseph H. Foster, 1876.
French, Hollis. *Early American Silversmiths and Their Marks.* Boston. Printed for the Walpole Society, 1917.
Gerrish, Ralph F. *Gerrish Genealogy.* 1919.
Griffin, S. G. *History of the Town of Keene.* Keene, N. H. Sentinel Printing Co., 1904.
Gooding, Rev. Alfred. *Records of South Church, Portsmouth, New Hampshire.*
Hackett, Frank W. *Portsmouth Records.* Portsmouth, N. H. Privately Printed, 1886.
Hayden, Arthur. *Chats on Old Silver.* New York. Stokes, 1916.
Hazlett, Charles A. *History of Rockingham County.* Chicago. Richmond-Arnold Publishing Co., 1915.
Hurd, D. Hamilton. *History of Essex County, Massachusetts.* Philadelphia. J. W. Lewis Co., 1888.
Indices, Registry of Deeds of Rockingham County, New Hampshire.
Langdon, William C. *Everyday Things in American Life, 1607-1776.* New York. Charles Scribner's Sons, 1937.
Lee, Arthur Gilman. *Genealogy of the Gilman Family.* Town of Exeter, 1869.
Little, William. *History of Weare, New Hampshire.* Published by the Town, 1888.
Locke, Arthur H. *Portsmouth and Newcastle, N. H. Cemetery Inscriptions.* Portsmouth, N. H. Privately Printed, 1907.
Lyford, James O. (ed.) *History of Concord.* Concord, N. H. Rumford Press, 1903.
Metcalf, Henry H. (ed.) *Laws of New Hampshire. First Constitutional Period, 1784-1794.* Published by the State, 1904-1920.
New Hampshire State Papers. Revolutionary Documents. Concord, 1911.
New Hampshire State Papers. Vol. XV.

BIBLIOGRAPHY

Parish Records. St. John's Church, Portsmouth, New Hampshire.
Peabody, Mrs. R. P. *History of Shelburne.* Gorham, N. H. Mountaineer Print, 1882.
Pearse, John B. *Concise History of the Iron Manufacture of the American Colonies up to the Revolution, and of Penn. to the Present Time.* Philadelphia. Allen, 1876.
Phillips, John Marshall. *Art in New England, Masterpieces of New England Silver.* (Catalog) Yale University, 1939.
Portsmouth Directory. (All years of publication).
Prime, Phoebe P. (ed.) *Three Centuries of Historic Silver.* Loan exhibitions under the auspices of the Pennsylvania Society of the Colonial Dames of America. Colonial Dames of America, 1938.
Probate Records of Rockingham County, New Hampshire.
Report on the Affairs of the New Hampshire Iron Factory Co. Salem, N. H. Printed by Thomas C. Cushing, 1810.
Rimes, Edward F. *Old Historic Churches of America.* New York. Macmillan Co., 1936.
Somers, Rev. A. N. *History of Lancaster.* Concord, N. H. Rumford Press, 1899.
Stackpole, Everett S. *Old Kittery and Her Families.* Lewiston, Maine. Press of Lewiston Journal Co., 1903.
Sweetser, M. F. *The White Mountains.* Cambridge, Mass. Houghton, Osgood & Co., 1879.
Vincent, John Martin. *Aids to Historical Research.* New York. D. Appleton-Century Co., 1934.
Waite, Otis F. R. *History of the Town of Claremont.* Published by the authority of the Town, 1895.
Weeden, William B. *Economic and Social History of New England.* New York. Houghton, Mifflin Co., 1891.
Wertenbaker, Thomas Jefferson. *The First Americans.* New York. Macmillan Co., 1927.
Weygandt, Cornelius. *The White Hills.* New York. Holt, 1934.
Wyler, Seymour B. *Book of Old Silver.* New York. Crown Publishers, 1937.

* * *

American Magazine of Art. Vol. 25 (July 1932-December 1932).
Antiques. Vol. XXXVI (October 1939).
Decatur, Stephen. *Early Church Silver of Kittery, Maine.* American Collector. Vol. V (November 1936).
New Hampshire Patriot and State Gazette. (September 30, 1839).
Proceedings of the New Hampshire Historical Society. Vol. IV (1899-1905.)
Robinson, J. W. *Captain Henry Lovejoy.* Granite Monthly. Volume XV (May 1893).
Smith, Helen Burr. *William Cario's Life History Less Vague.* New York Sun. (July 29, 1939).
Tibbitts, Charles W. (ed.) *New Hampshire Genealogical Record.* Official Organ of the New Hampshire Genealogical Society. (1907-1909).
Upham, George B. *Pre-Revolutionary Life and Thought in a Western New Hampshire Town.* Granite Monthly. Vol. LIV (April 1922).

CHAPTER XII—*Spinning Wheel and Hand Loom*

Bowles, Ella Shannon. *Homespun Handicrafts.* New York. J. B. Lippincott, 1931.
Browne, George Waldo. *History of Hillsborough.* Published by the Town, 1921.
Chase, Benjamin. *History of Old Chester.* Auburn, N. H. Published by the Author, 1869.
Earle, Alice M. *Home Life in Colonial Days.* New York. Macmillan Co., 1899.
Goodrich, F. *Mountain Homespun.* New Haven. Yale University Press, 1931.

Hayley, Rev. John W. *History of Tuftonboro.* Concord, N. H. Rumford Press, 1923.
Hoyt, Charles B. *Sheep Husbandry.* New Hampshire Agriculture. Report of the Board of Agriculture from Oct. 1, 1898 to Jan. 1, 1901. Manchester, N. H. Arthur E. Clarke, 1901.

* * *

New Hampshire Patriot and State Gazette. (June 2, 1818—November 2, 1835—October 31, 1836—October 23, 1837—October 21, 1841).
New Hampshire Recorder and Weekly Advertiser. (December 30, 1787).

CHAPTER XIII—*With Thread and Needle*

Christie, Grace. *Samplers and Stitches.* London. B. F. Batsford, 1929.
Day, Lewis F. and Buckle, Mary. *Art in Needlework.* New York. Charles Scribner's Sons. London. B. F. Batsford, 1908.
Drew, Joan H. *Embroidery and Design.* London. Isaac Pitman Sons, 1929.
Fitzwilliam, Ada Wentworth. *Jacobean Embroidery.* London. Kegan Paul, Trench, Trubner, 1928.
Harbison, Georgianna Brown. *American Needlework.* New York. Coward McCann, Inc., 1938.
Peabody, Mrs. R. P. *History of Shelburne.* Gorham, N. H. Mountaineer Print, 1882.
Sewell, Brice H. *New Mexico Colonial Embroidery.* State Capitol. Sante Fe, New Mexico. May, 1935 (Mimeographed).
Sharp, Mary. *Point and Pillow Lace.* New York. E. P. Dutton & Co., 1890.
Singleton, Esther. *The Collector of Antiques.* New York. McMillan & Co., 1926.
Wheeler, Mrs. Candace Thurber. *The Development of Embroidery* in America. New York. Harper Brothers, 1921.
Whiting, Gertrude. *A Lace Guide for Makers and Collectors.* New York. E. P. Dutton & Co., 1917.

* * *

Antiques. Vol. XII (November 1927).
Daily Mirror and American. (June 2, 1909).
League of New Hampshire Arts and Crafts. *Bulletin.* Issue No. 54 (Nov.-Dec. 1939).
Manchester Union-Leader (June 3, 1927).

CHAPTER XIV—*Samplers and Quilts*

Ashton, Leigh. *Samplers.* Plymouth, Mass. The Mayflower Press, 1926.
Bolton, Ethel Stanwood and Coe, Eva Johnston. *American Samplers.* Massachusetts Society of Colonial Dames of America, 1921.
Bowles, Ella Shannon. *About Antiques.* Philadelphia. J. B. Lippincott, 1929.
Bowles, Ella Shannon. *Homespun Handicrafts.* New York. J. B. Lippincott, 1931.
Christie, Grace. *Samplers and Stitches.* London. B. F. Batsford, 1929.
Peabody, Mrs. R. P. *History of Shelburne.* Gorham, N. H. Mountaineer Print, 1882.
Wheeler, Candace. *The Development of Embroidery in America.* New York. Harper's, 1921.

* * *

Antiques. Vol. II (December 1922), Vol. III (June 1923), Vol. V (January 1924), Vol. XIV (July 1928).

CHAPTER XV—*Home Rug Making*

Albee, Helen R. *Abnakee Rugs.* Cambridge, Mass. Riverside Press, 1903.
Albee, Helen R. *Mountain Playmates.* Boston. Houghton, Mifflin Company, 1900.

BIBLIOGRAPHY

Bowles, Ella Shannon. *Handmade Rugs.* Boston. Little, Brown and Company, 1927.
Chase, Persis F. *The Lancaster Sketchbook.* Brattleboro, Vt. Frank E. Housh and Company, 1887.
Cram, Ralph Adams. *Convictions and Controversies.* Boston. Marshall Jones, 1935.
Drage, Dorothy. *Rug Making.* London. Isaac Pitman and Sons, 1937.
McGown, Pearl. *The Dreams Beneath Design.* Boston. B. Humphries, Inc., 1939.
Kent, William Winthrop. *The Hooked Rug.* New York. Dodd & Co., 1930.
Transactions of the New Hampshire State Agricultural Society, for 1850, 1851, and 1852.

* * *

Christian Science Monitor. (November 4, 1938).
Keyes, Homer Eaton. *The Editor's Attic.* Antiques. Vol. XIII (April 1928).

CHAPTER XVI—*Art and Near Art*

Brewster, Charles. *Rambles About Portsmouth.* Portsmouth, N. H. Brewster, 1859.
Brown, C. A. *Manchester Business Directory.* Manchester, N. H. Brown, 1848.
Bouton, Nathaniel. *History of Concord.* Concord, N. H. Sanborn, 1856.
Carrick, Alice Van Leer. *Shades of Our Ancestors.* Boston. Little, Brown and Co., 1928.
Crawford, Mary. *Among Old New England Inns.* Boston. Page & Co., 1907.
Dow, Joseph. *History of Hampton.* Salem, Mass. Published by Lucy E. Dow, 1893.
Emery, J. P. *Manchester Directory.* Manchester, N. H. Emery, 1844.
Hawthorne, Nathaniel. *American Notebooks, 1804-1864.* New Haven. Yale University Press, 1932.
Kidder & Gould. *History of New Ipswich.* Boston. Gould-Lincoln, 1853.
Little, William. *History of Warren.* Manchester, N. H. Moore, 1870.
McClintock, John N. *History of New Hampshire.* Boston. Russell, 1889.
Moore, J. Bailey. *History of Candia.* Manchester, N. H. Brown, 1893.
Rawson, Marion Nicholl. *Candleday Art.* New York. E. P. Dutton and Co., Inc., 1938.
Singleton, Esther. *Furniture of Our Forefathers.* New York. Doubleday-Page, 1900.
Smith, Mr. and Mrs. Chetwood. *Rogers' Groups.* Boston. Charles E. Goodspeed and Co., 1934.
Waring, Janet. *Early American Stencils.* New York. William R. Scott, 1937.
Worthen, Augusta H. *History of Sutton.* Concord, N. H. Republican Press Association, 1890.

* * *

Abbott, Winifred. *Some Old College Silhouettes.* Antiques. Vol. VII (June 1925).
American Collector. Vol. VIII (August 1939).
Allen, Janet. *Scenic America.* Country Life. Vol. I (November 1912).
Amoskeag Bulletin. (April 15, 1916).
Dartmouth Gazette. (March 24, 1806).
Fraser, Esther. *Painted Furniture in America.* Antiques. Vol. VI (September 1924).
Godey's Lady's Book. (May 1855, March 1864).
Granite Monthly. Vol. 25 (October 1898).
Manchester Union. (May 31, 1910).
New Hampshire Patriot and State Gazette. (Aug. 14, 1837, Sept. 21, 1840, May 14, 1841, October 16, 1845, June 17, 1847, Sept. 2, 1847).
Northend, Mary H. *Wall Paper.* International Studio, Vol. LXXV, No. 299.

CHAPTER XVII—*Shaker Crafts*

Andrews, Edward D. and Faith. *Shaker Furniture*. New Haven. Yale University Press, 1937.
Andrews, Edward D. *The Community Industries of the Shakers*. Albany. University of the State of New York, 1932.
Blinn, Henry C. (ed.) *The Life and Gospel Experience of Mother Ann Lee*. Canterbury, N. H. Published by the Shakers, 1901.
Dyer, Caleb. *Biography of Life and Tragical Death of, Together with the Poem and Eulogies at His Funeral*. Manchester, N. H. Gage, Moore, & Co., 1863.
Elkins, Hervey. *Fifteen Years in the Senior Order of Shakers*. Hanover, N. H. Dartmouth Press, 1853.
Evans, Frederick W. *Shakers*. New York. D. Appleton and Co., 1859.
Lyford, James Otis. *History of Canterbury*. Vol. 1. Concord, N. H. Rumford Press, 1912.
Perkins, Elder Abraham. *Autobiography and in Memorium*. Concord, N. H. Rumford Press, 1901.
Robinson, Charles Evans. *Concise History of United Society of Believers called Shakers*. East Canterbury, N. H. Published by the Shakers, 1893.

* * *

Andrews, Edward D. *Communal Architecture of the Shakers*. Magazine of Art. Vol. 30 (December 1937).
Chandler, Lloyd H. *The Followers of Ann Lee*. Granite Monthly. Vol. 16 (April 1894).
Granite Monthly. Vol. 8 (September-October, 1885).
Manifesto. Vol. 1-29 (1871-1899). Published by the Shakers.

CHAPTER XVIII—*The Country Fair*

Albee, John. *New Castle, Historic and Picturesque*. Boston. Cupples, Upham & Co., 1884.
Manchester Historic Association Collections. Vol. 5 and 6. Manchester, 1909.
McDuffee, Franklin. *History of Rochester, N. H.* Manchester, N. H. John Clark Co., 1892.
Metcalf, Henry H. *New Hampshire Agriculture, Personal and Farm Sketches*. Concord, N. H. Republican Press Association, 1897.
Parker, Edward L. *History of Londonderry*. Boston. Perkins and Whipple, 1851.
Transactions of the New Hampshire State Agricultural Society. 1850-1860. Concord, N. H. Published by the State.
Weeden, William B. *Economic and Social History of New England. 1620-1789* Boston. Houghton, Mifflin Co., 1891.

* * *

Alexander, R. S. *Commercial Fairs and Exhibitions*. Harvard Business Review. Vol. 5. (July 1929).
Architectural Forum. Volume 65 (September 1936).
Farmer's Monthly Visitor. Manchester, N. H. (Files of 1840-1854).
Granite Farmer. Concord, N. H. (September 16, 1854).
Manchester Daily Mirror. (September 24, 1902. September 29, 1910. October 5, 18, 21, and November 9, 1911.
Manchester Sunday Union. (March 13, 1910).
Moses, George H. *The Grange Fair by Pen and Camera*. Granite Monthly. Vol. XVII (October 1894).
New Hampshire Agriculturist and Patrons' Journal. Vol. 1 (1895).
New Hampshire Patriot and State Gazette. (Files of 1819-1845).

BIBLIOGRAPHY

CHAPTER XIX—*Trends in Organized Handicrafts*

Code of the Laws of the United States of America (in force January 1935). Washington, D. C. U. S. Government Printing Office, 1935. Title 20, Chapter 2, Sections 12, 13, 14, concerned with the Smith-Hughes Vocational Guidance Act.

Institute Circulars. State Board of Education, 1928-29, 1929-30.

Laws of New Hampshire relating to the Public Schools, State Board of Education. Manchester, N. H. Granite State Press, 1937.

Program of Studies, recommended for the Elementary Schools of New Hampshire, State Board of Education. Concord, N. H. Evans Printing Co., 1919, 1930, 1932.

* * *

Boston Evening Transcript. (February 19, 1907).

Bulletins of New Hampshire League of Arts and Crafts. Mrs. Foster Stearns, Editor. Concord.

Conway, Charlotte E. *Know American Arts and Crafts First.* American Home. Vol. XX (June 1938).

Doe, Jessie. *The League of New Hampshire Arts and Crafts.* Yankee. Vol. 5 (July 1939).

Manchester Mirror and American.

Manchester Union Leader.

INDEX

Abbot, John, Jr., silversmith, 143.
Abbot, William, master builder, 26.
Abbott-Downing Company, 214-215.
Abbott, John W., silversmith, 141, 143.
Abnakee Rugs, 195-196.
Acworth Town Fair, 247.
Adams, Arad, clothespinmaker, 70.
Adams, Cass, 24.
Adams, Captain Edward H., gundalow maker, 22-24.
Adams, Charles E., glass collector, 130.
Adams, Mrs. Hannah, weaver, 245.
Adams, Miss Mary, craftswoman, 257.
Adams, Stephen, cabinetmaker, 42.
Adams, William, 109.
Adams Point, 22, 24.
Africa, Mrs. Walter M., present-day needleworker, 164.
Aked, Ruth, needleworker, 178.
Albee, Helen Rickey, rugmaker and author, 194-196.
Albee, John, historian, quoted, 21.
Alden, Luther, cabinetmaker, 44.
Aldrich, Ella, rugmaker and weaver, 158.
Alice, ship, 20.
All Saints Church, 35.
Alstead, N. H., 97.
America, 17, 25, 79, 84, 85.
America, ship, 21.
American Antiquarian Society, 210.
American architecture, 30.
American Federation of Arts, 159, 256.
American Indian, 2.
Ames, Mrs. Mabel F., present-day needleworker, 165, 187.
Amesbury, Massachusetts, 54.
Amherst, N. H., 57, 58, 106, 110, 245.
Ammonoosuc River, 3.
Amoskeag Grange, Manchester, 247.
Amoskeag Mills, 91.
Anderson, Mary, actress, 214.
Andover, N. H., 73, 154.
Annett, Thomas, woodworker, 69.
Annie F. Conlin, ship, 20.
Antiques, 203.
Antrim, N. H., 43, 100, 103, 125, 152, 156.
Applegate, Frank, potter, 99.
Appleton, Isaac, chairmaker, 44.
Appleton and Elliot, glass manufacturers, 122.
Architecture, 30, 33-38, 225.
Arts and Crafts Commission, 251.
Arts and Crafts Guild of Boston, 81.
Ashuelot River, 43.

Athenaeum, Portsmouth, 21.
Atkinson Academy, 210.
"Atkinson Waiter", 140.
Atwater, Mary Meigs, present-day weaver and author, 158, 159.
Ayer, Mrs. Frank P., quilt collector, 189.

Bachelder, O. L., potter, 99.
Badger, Stephen, itinerant artist, 218.
Bailey, Lawrence, bandboxmaker, 73.
Baker Memorial Library, Hanover, N. H., 109.
Baldwin, David, manufacturer, 35.
Baldwin, Elisha, 48.
Baldwin, Raymond, stonecutter, 113.
Baldwin Homestead, Stratford, N. H., 49.
Bandboxmaking, 73-75.
Bangor, Maine, 16.
Barnstead, N. H., 90, 151.
Barrett, Charles B., glassmaker, 125.
Barrington, N. H., 4, 64.
Bartlett, Levi, cabinetmaker, 46.
Basketmaking, 1-9, 251, 255, 257, 258.
Batchelder, John A., present-day cabinetmaker, 47.
Bath, Maine, 16, 19.
Bayeux Tapestries, 199.
Beal, Justus H., present-day cabinetmaker, 50.
Bedford, N. H., 43, 91, 152, 212.
Belknap County, N. H., 242.
Bellamy eagles, 17.
Bellamy, John Haley, wood sculptor, 16, 17-19.
Benjamin, Asher, architect, 34.
Benjamin Pierce House, Hillsborough, N. H., 216.
Bennington, Vermont, 167.
Berlin, N. H., 71, 77, 114.
"Berlin Work", 168.
Bethlehem, N. H., 49.
Biddeford, Maine, 192.
Bishop, Father Job, Shaker, 223.
Blackburn, Joseph, portrait painter, 206.
Blacksmithing, 134-135.
Blake, Mr. and Mrs. John W., present-day weavers, 158-159.
Blake, "Uncle Sammy", cabinetmaker, 48.
Blanchard, Porter, cabinetmaker, 46.
Blasdell, David, 55.
Blasdell, Isaac, clockmaker, 54-55.
Blasdell, Richard, 55.

274

Bleak House, Peterborough, N. H., 216.
Blinn, Elder Henry, Shaker editor, 233.
Block printing, 256.
Blodgett, Joe, cooper, 71.
Blodgett Yard, the, Hudson, N. H., 106, 109, 110.
Blood, Henry Ames, quoted, 119.
Boardman, Langley, cabinetmaker and architect, 33, 41.
Boar's Head Hotel, Hampton, N. H., 19.
Boatbuilding, 22-24, 76-77.
Bohonon, Ensign, 42.
Bohonon, Moses, cabinetmaker, 42.
"Bonnet Saloons", 11.
Boscawen, N. H., 3, 11, 26, 59, 94, 95, 101, 173, 180, 209, 241, 243.
Boscawen-Webster meetinghouse, 30.
Boston, Massachusetts, 3, 10, 15, 16, 18, 34, 43, 44, 55, 61, 65, 72, 81, 85, 100, 113, 118, 137, 138, 139, 142, 144, 146, 173, 193, 206, 213.
Boston Arts and Crafts Society, 6, 104.
Boston Directory of 1825, 120.
Boston Gazette, 139.
Boston Museum, 128.
Bouton, Reverend Nathaniel, author, 207.
Bow, N. H., 145, 186.
Boy Scouts, 258.
Boyden, Jabez, 10.
Boxmaking, 69.
Bradford, N. H., 213.
Bradford-Newbury Fair, 247.
Brentwood, N. H., 159, 200.
Brewster, Charles W., historian, quoted, 39, 214.
Brickburning, 92-93.
Brickmaking, 90-94.
Briggs, Eliphalet B. Jr., cabinetmaker, 42-43.
Bristol, N. H., 87, 98, 213.
Bristol Home Industries, 254.
British Museum, 145.
Broad Acres Farm, Randolph, N. H., 149.
Brookfield, N. H., 1.
Brookline, N. H., 73.
Brooks, Luke, 50.
Brown, Fred E., present-day woodenware maker, 75-76.
Brown, Hattie Gibbs, 189.
Brown, L. G., 189.
"Brownie Ware", 75-76.
Brussette, ship, 15.
Bulfinch, Charles, architect, 34.
Burbank, Barker, 172.
Burbank, William E., teacher of modeling, 255.

Burgum, Edwin Gannell, present-day ornamental painter, 214-215.
Burley, Nathaniel, carpenter, 30-31.
Burley, Sarah, 30-31.
Burns, John, 106.
Burns, Tom, 19.
Burpee, the family, potters, 94-95, 101.
Burpee, Jeremiah, brickmaker and potter, 94.
Burroughs, Paul, 43, quoted, 41-42.
Burt, Mrs. Edith, present-day weaver, 160.
Bussiel, "Widow", weaver, 155.

Craftsmen's Fairs, 254-255; Crawford Notch, Durham, Hancock, Laconia, Little Boar's Head, Plymouth, Whitefield; 248.
Cabinetmaking, 39-53, 76, 225, 227, 228, 240, 243, 251.
"Calico Party", 40.
Camisards, the, 222.
Campbell, James, weaver, 156.
Campbell, Ruth, 153.
Campton, N. H., 143.
Canaan, N. H., 135, 226.
Canaan Fair, 247.
Candia, N. H., 11, 64, 94, 209, 213, 218.
Candia Town Fair, 247.
Canterbury, N. H., 31, 70, 158, 220, 222, 225, 226, 228, 230, 232, 233, 234.
Cario, William, Boston Goldsmith, 139.
Cario, William II, Portsmouth Goldsmith, 139-140.
Carleton, Michael, cabinetmaker, 42.
Carlson, David, silversmith, 145, 146.
Carrick, Alice Van Leer, author, 210.
Carter, Eliza, quiltmaker, 185.
Cass, Mrs. W. Livesey, basketmaker, 255.
Castleton, Vermont, 203.
Caswell Carpet, the, 203, 204.
Caswell, John H., letterer, 214.
Cathedral of St. John the Divine, New York City, 84, 85.
Cato, ship, 15.
Centennial Exposition, Philadelphia, 1875, 111, 235.
Center Effingham, N. H., 5.
Center Sandwich, N. H., 250.
Central House, Stoddard, N. H., 217.
Chadwick, Joseph, clockmaker, 59.
Chamberlain, William, silhouettist, 210.
Chancy, Israel, Shaker missionary, 223.
Chandler, George A., present-day cabinetmaker, 200.

Chandler, Miss Helen, present-day jewelry maker, 256, 257.
Chandler, Timothy, clockmaker, 57-58, 60.
Charlestown, N. H., 106.
Charlestown Navy Yard, 18.
Chase, Moody, 62.
Chase, Mrs. Persis F., author, 203; quoted, 204.
Chase, Wells, traveling carpenter, 31.
"Checker Players, The", Rogers Group, 219.
Chelmsford Glass Company, 126, 127.
Cheney, Clinton, present-day wood carver, 82, 83.
Cheshire County, 239, 259.
Cheshire County Agricultural Society, 237.
Cheshire County Fair, 239.
Chester, N. H., 10, 31, 43, 54, 55, 105, 134, 150, 152.
Chester Congregational Church, 62.
Chester Town Fair, 247.
Chichester, N. H., 189.
Chickering, Jonas, pianomaker, 60, 61.
Childs, Amzie, basketmaker, 4.
Chipping Campden, England, 85.
Christophe, Elizabeth M., needleworker, 168.
"Circle-Head Man", 107.
City of Rome, ship, 20.
Claremont, N. H., 34, 47, 132.
Clark, Benjamin, potter, 96.
Clark, Daniel, Millville potter, 96.
Clark, Harry, present-day cabinetmaker, 52.
Clark, James, Loudon potter, 97.
Clark, John, Millville potter, 96.
Clark, Joseph, silversmith, 141.
Clark, John H., silversmith, 143.
Clark, Peter, Lyndeborough potter, 95, 96.
Clark, Peter II, Millville potter, 96.
Clark, Thomas, woodenware maker, 70.
Clark, William, Loudon potter, 97.
Clinesmith, John, glass blower, 123.
Clockmaking, 55-60.
Clothespin whittling, 69-70.
Clothmaking, 229, 230, 231, 238, 256.
Clotilde, ship, 20.
Clough, Albert L., 255.
Clovis, ship, 21.
Coffin, Charles Carleton, quoted, 95.
Coffin, Thomas, house raiser, 26.
"Coffin-Heart Man", 107.
Coffrin, Manley, present-day basketmaker, 5.
Colby, Betsy, basketmaker, 4.
Cole, James, clockmaker, 59.

Collins, Clarence, present-day clock collector, 60.
Collins, Mrs. Eliza Lane, basketmaker, 6.
Christianson, Thorwolde, jewelry maker, 256.
Collins, Miss Stella, 6.
Collins, Uncle Oscar, 230.
Colonial Dames of America, 179.
Colton, Robert P., glass blower, 128.
Colton, Walter Ewing, violinmaker, 65.
Columbia University, 80.
Columbian Centinel, 120.
Comolli, Frank, present-day stonecutter, 112.
Concord, 11, 16, 19, 26, 43, 46-48, 55, 57, 58, 61, 62, 65, 75, 76, 83, 85, 86, 94, 96, 113, 140, 143, 144, 145, 146, 162, 163, 182, 193, 198, 200, 204, 207, 208, 212, 214, 243, 255.
Concord Gazette, 173.
Concord Silversmiths, Inc., 144.
Conant, Doctor Mary, 37.
Connecticut River, 12, 34, 113, 203.
Connecticut Valley Fair, 247.
Collins, Susan Nason, present-day wood carver, 87.
Constitution, ship, 16.
Converse, Mrs. Carl R., 211.
Cooley, Ebenezer, Shaker missionary, 223.
Coolidge, Harold Jefferson, 215.
Coolidge, Mrs. J. Randolph, 196, 251.
Cooper, Mrs. Charlotte, present-day basketmaker, 5.
Cooperage, 72, 73.
Coös County, 27, 32, 114, 259.
Coös County Fair, 240.
Copley, John Singleton, painter, 16.
Corbett, Doctor Thomas, Shaker, 232.
Corliss, Arthur, basketmaker, 1-2.
Corliss, James, clockmaker, 55.
Cornish, N. H., 26, 99.
Corey, Mrs. Charles R., rugmaker, 199.
Couching, 166.
Countess of Rumford, 163, 182.
Country Fair, the, 236-249.
Cox, George J., author, quoted, 104.
Crafts, Mrs. Claude, present-day lacemaker, 169, 170.
Cragin, Francis, master builder, 118.
Cram, Ralph Adams, present-day architect, 35.
Cram brothers, ironworkers, 132.
Creole, ship, 17.
Crocheting, 257.
Culver House, Lyme, N. H., 217.
Currier Gallery of Art, Manchester, N. H., 128, 162, 166, 170, 198, 201, 206, 207, 255.

276

Currier, Mrs. Moody, 170.
Curtis, Mrs. Mary, present-day rugmaker, 202.
Cutter brothers, glass blowers, 126.
Cutter-Langdon House, Portsmouth, N. H., 33.
Cutwork, 170.
Chaucer, 176.
Clark, Deacon William, 62.
Crafts family, potters, 94, 101.
Croxford, Lydia, second wife of William Cario II, 139.
Craftworkers' Guild, 256.
Concord Coaches, 215.
"Crêche, the", wood carving, 87.

Daguerreotyping, 208, 242.
Dartmouth College, 150.
Dartmouth Gazette, 210.
Daughters of the American Revolution, 182.
Davenport, John, silversmith, 143.
Davis, George B., letterer, 214.
Davis, Hannah, bandboxmaker, 69, 74, 75.
Davis, Jacob, woodenware maker, 70.
Davis, Miss May, rugmaker, 195.
Davis, Moses, 110, 111.
Davis, Peggy, knitter, 172.
Davis, Peter, clockmaker, 74.
Davis Tennis Cup, 145.
Dearborn, Andrew P., musical instrument maker, 62.
Dearborn, David M., musical instrument maker, 62.
Dearborn, Shubeal, 45.
Decatur, Stephen, quoted, 41.
Dedham, Massachusetts, 10.
Deerfield, N. H., 79, 132.
Deerfield Fair, 247.
Dennis, Thomas, cabinetmaker, 44.
Derry, N. H., 95, 107, 200.
Derry Town Fair, 247.
Dickey, Matthew, 137.
Dodge, Mrs. Frank S., present-day craftswoman, quoted, 174.
Dodge, Jabez, potter, 95.
Dodge, Mrs. James, weaver, 160.
Dodge, Samuel, potter, 95.
Doherty, Joseph, figurehead carver, 16.
Dolls, 254.
Donahue, Jessie E., wood carver, 81.
Dorchester, Massachusetts, 106.
Dover, N. H., 12, 22, 31, 90, 254.
Dover Packet, river craft, 21.
Drage, Dorothy, author, 199.
Driscoll, Mrs. Josephine, present-day rugmaker, 197, 198.
Drown, Thomas Pickering, silversmith, 141.

Drowne, Benjamin, silversmith, 139.
Drowne, Daniel P., silversmith, 141, 142.
Drowne, Samuel, silversmith, 139, 140, 142.
Drowne, Shem, figurehead carver, 16.
Dublin, N. H., 92, 98, 216.
Dublin Lake, 215.
Dunbarton, N. H., 157.
Dunlap, Archibald, cabinetmaker, 43.
Dunlap, Major John, cabinetmaker, 43.
Dunlap, John Jr., cabinetmaker, 43.
Dunlap, Samuel, cabinetmaker, 43.
Dunlap, Samuel Jr., cabinetmaker, 43.
Dunlaps, cabinetmakers, 42, 43.
Dumas, Colonel Stebbins H., 19.
Dunklee, Mrs. Damaris, 106.
Durgin Company, 144, 145.
Durgin, Sister Dorothy, Shaker, 233.
Durgin, Mrs. Orpha, 178, 181.
Durgin, William, master builder, 29, 48.
Durgin, William B., silversmith, 143-144.
Durham, 22, 101, 163.
Durham Meetinghouse, 30.
Dutton, Daniel, clockmaker, 60.
Dyer, Elder Caleb, 229, 230.
Dyer, Jerub, 230.
Dyer, Orville, Shaker, 230.

Eaton, Allen H., quoted, 2.
Eaton, Dr., clothmaker, 239.
Eaton, John, woodworker, 68, 74.
Eaton, Moses, stenciler, 216.
Eaton, Moses, Jr., 216.
Eaton, Mrs. Roanna S., needleworker, 181.
Eagle Hotel, Keene, N. H., 213.
East Derry, N. H., 107.
East Jaffrey, N. H., 75.
East Northwood, N. H., 258.
East Rindge, N. H., 211.
Eastman, Cyrus, clockmaker, 58.
Eastman, Seth, silversmith, 144.
Edwards, Jonathan, 178.
Eliot, Maine, 14.
Ellis House, Keene, N. H., 197.
Embroidery, 162-169, 174, 211, 243, 257.
Emery, Jesse, clockmaker, 55.
Endicott, Governor John, 177.
Enfield, N. H., 60, 87, 220, 222, 223, 226, 234.
Eppes, Polly, needleworker, 178.
Epping, N. H., 94.
Epsom, N. H., 202.
Essex Institute, Salem, Mass., 219.
Evans, Mrs. Ezekial, quiltmaker, 184.
Everett, Richard Claire, 203.

Exeter, N. H., 12, 22, 35, 95, 139, 173.
Exeter Pottery Works, 95.
Exeter River, 22.
Exhibition of Rural Arts, Washington, 1938, 259.
Extension Service, University of New Hampshire, 258, 259.

Fanny M., gundalow, 22, 24.
Farmer and Mirror, 247.
Farwell, Ensign Joseph, 106.
Fawcett, John, pioneer builder, 32.
Fenderson, Franklin, present-day violin maker, 64.
Field, Darby, 116.
Figurehead carving, 14-19.
Fine Arts Department, Manchester Institute of Arts and Sciences, 255-257.
Fiske, Pliny, painter, 214.
Fitts, Deacon Frederick, tavern keeper, 213.
Fitz, William, clock trader, 56.
Fitzgerald, Sarah, needleworker, 181.
Fitzwilliam, N. H., 11, 32, 45.
Flax raising, 152-153.
Fletcher, Betsy, needleworker, 179.
Fletcher, Kimball, quoted, 25.
Fletcher, Rebecca, needleworker, 182.
Flint, William W., author, 96.
Flume, The, 84.
Flying Cloud, ship, 20.
Folsom, Josiah, cabinetmaker, 41.
Fosters, the, 106, 126.
Foster, Amos, 108.
Foster, Charles, glass manufacturer, 125.
Foster, Clara A., 189.
Foster, George W., glass manufacturer, 125.
Foster, James, 106.
Foster, Joseph, glass manufacturer, 123, 125.
Foster, Wallace, glass manufacturer, 125.
Forbes, Harriette M., author, 106.
Forest Hills Yard, East Derry, N. H., 107.
4-H Clubs, 258.
Francestown, N. H., 98, 112, 136, 155, 178.
Franconia, N. H., 50, 148, 158, 171, 197.
Franconia stoves, 133.
Franklin, Benjamin, 162.
Franklin and Tilton Driving Park, 247.
Freeport, Maine, 64.
French, Frank, quoted, 155.
French, Mrs. Nellie, present-day rugmaker, 199.

Fresco painting, 216-218.
Frost, Edward Sands, rug designer, 192, 193.
Fuller, Daniel, 112.

Gage, Elizabeth, needleworker, 179.
Gaines, George, cabinetmaker, 33, 36, 40.
Gaines, John, cabinetmaker, 33, 36, 39, 40.
Gale River, 133.
Gardner, the family, 141.
Gardner, Mrs. William T., present-day rugmaker, 198-199.
Gaverand, Christopher, English pianomaker, 61.
Gem cutting, 113-116.
Gem hunting, 114-115.
General Montgomery House, Haverhill, 61.
George's Mills, N. H., 60.
Geriche, Otto, silversmith, 146.
Germer, George E., silversmith, 146.
Gerrish, Andrew, silversmith and brass founder, 143.
Gerrish, Timothy, silversmith, 140, 143.
Gerrish, Woodbury, wood sculptor, 16-17.
Gesso, 256.
Gibbons, Ambrose, 131.
Gilford, N. H., 31, 98.
Gillet, John, maker of wooden dishes, 72, 73.
Gillette, Oliver, woodenware maker, 70.
Gillette, Timothy, woodenware maker, 70.
Gillingham, Elder John, clergyman, 213.
Gilmanton, N. H., 132.
Gilson, Fred A., manufacturer of glass bottles, 123.
Gilsum, N. H., 3, 156.
Girl Scouts, 258.
Glassmaking, 118.
Gleason, Mrs. M. E., basketry teacher, 255.
Glendale Bay, Lake Winnepesaukee, 16.
Glines, Mrs. Anabel, present-day craftswoman and collector, 4, 45, 46, 186, 187, 202.
Glover, Mrs., basketmaker, 4.
Goffe, Colonel John, ironmaster, 132.
Goffe, Mrs. Theodore A., silkmaker, 157.
Goldsmithing, 140-141.
Gonic, N. H., 94, 103.
Gooden, Benjamin and Diadamia, 206.

278

Gooden, Miss Kate, present-day leatherworker, 256.
Goodhue, Nathaniel, potter, 98.
Goodrum, Mrs. Alice, rugmaker, 196.
Goodwin, Fred, present-day gem cutter, 114, 115.
Gorham, N. H., 3, 114, 172.
Goss, Clifford, wood carver, 87, 88, 89.
Goss, Ephraim, 153.
Gould, John, Jr., cabinetmaker, 42.
Gould, Mary Ada, 111.
Gove, Moses, churnmaker, 73.
Gove, the family, woodworkers, 71.
Governor Gilman, ship, 15.
Gower, Anne, 176, 177.
Goyette, Major Erland A., 215.
Grafton, N. H., 114.
Grafton County Fair, 247.
Graham, Samuel, 62.
Grandee, ship, 15, 20.
Grange Fair Association, 247, 248.
Granite Glass Works, Stoddard, N. H., 125.
Grant, Major Samuel, 173.
Grasmere, N. H., 169.
Gravestonecutting, 105-112.
Gray, Robert, silversmith, 142.
Great Bay, 22.
Great Boar's Head, 19.
"Great Carbuncle", 116-117.
"Great Historical Clock of America", 60.
Green, Sister Myra, Shaker, 230.
Greene, Frederick W., silversmith, 145.
Greenland, N. H., 17, 91.
Greenleaf, Nancy, spinner, 203.
Greenwood, Washington, artist, 216.
Griffin, Earle R., present-day cabinetmaker, 52.
Griffin, Miss Kelsea, potter, 100.
Griffin, Wayne, present-day metalworker, 146.
Griffith, David, goldsmith, 139, 140.
Griffith, Nathaniel, goldsmith, 140.
Griffith, Samuel, goldsmith and jeweler, 140.
Guerin, E. R., glass collector, 129.

Hadley, Nellie H., woolworker, 211.
Haines, Mrs. Crosby Kimball, needleworker, 162.
Hall, Ivory, silversmith, 144.
Hall, Deacon Joseph, 55.
Hallberg, William, potter, 100, 104.
Hammond, Harry F., present-day cabinetmaker, 48.
Hampstead, N. H., 10, 185.
Hampton, N. H., 10, 12, 19, 45, 68, 95, 134, 138, 177.
Hampton Falls, N. H., 35, 199, 254.

Hancock, N. H., 30, 169, 183, 216.
Handicraft Guild, 85.
Handicrafts of the Southern Highlands, 2.
Handicraft Society of Peterborough, 168.
Hanover, N. H., 30, 60, 112, 114, 210.
Hanscom, Isaiah, 14.
Hanscom, Samuel, Jr., shipbuilder, 14.
Hanscom Shipyards, 14.
Hanscom, William, shipbuilder, 14.
Hanscom, William L., naval architect, 14.
Harding, Newell, silversmith, 144.
Hardy, Stephen, silversmith, 141, 142.
Hardy, the family, silversmiths, 142.
Harlow, Harry, present-day artist, 37.
Harriott, James, silversmith, 144.
Hart, Lydia, needleworker, 177.
Harvey, G. W. Jr., carver, 19.
Haselton, Ira, silversmith, 143.
Haskell, Moses, traveling carpenter, 31.
Hatmaking, 9-11, 234, 239.
Haverhill, N. H., 4, 42, 57, 61, 180, 186, 202, 203.
Haverhill and Franconia Iron Works Co., 133.
Hawthorne, Nathaniel, 16, 117.
Hayley, Rev. John, quoted, 149-150.
Hazelton, William, trader, 10.
Hazen, Moses, cabinetmaker, 42.
Head, the family, 91.
Heartz, Robert F., present-day weaver, 159, 200.
Hemphill, Agnes, spinner, 155.
Henderson, L. R., silversmith, 144.
Henniker, N. H., 26, 45, 62, 70, 153.
Herrick, John G., gem cutter, 115-116.
Hewes, Dr. Robert, glass maker, 118, 119, 120.
Hewings, P., portrait painter, 207.
Higgins, Wilson F., present-day metalworker, 256.
Hill, Mary E., 181.
Hills, Margaret, 155.
Hillsborough, N. H., 215.
Hillsborough Agricultural Society, 238, 245.
Hillsborough County, N. H., 242.
Hillsborough County Fair, 1819, 238.
Hilt, Nicholas, glass blower, 123, 124.
Hinsdale, N. H., 107.
Hirsch, Charles, glass blower, 123.
Historic American Merchant Marine Survey, 21.
History of Old Chester, 137.
Historical Records Survey, 207.
Historical Society, Portsmouth, N. H., 142.
Hoag, Albert B., present-day cabinetmaker, 51, 52.

279

Hoit, William B., portrait painter, 208.
Holderness, N. H., 52.
Hollis, N. H., 90, 109, 181.
Holton House, Lancaster, N. H., 32.
Home Demonstration Department, Extension Service, UNH, 258.
Home Industries for the Blind, 258.
Home Industries groups, 252.
Homer, John, stonecutter, 108.
Honeywell, Martha Ann, silhouettist, 210.
Hood, Wallace P., 128.
Hooksett, N. H., 91, 218, 219.
Hopkinton, N. H., 42, 157, 199, 207, 213.
Horne, Elba F., present-day woodworker, 76.
Horses, The, 84.
Hosmer, Josiah, cabinetmaker, 42.
Houston, Jemima, 109.
Houston, Ovid, 109.
Howells, John Mead, quoted, 13.
Howells, William Dean, 19.
Howison, Mrs. Arthur W., embroiderer, 188.
Hubbard, George, 219.
Hubbard, Guy, 219.
Hudson, N. H., 44, 106, 107.
Hudson, Mary, sampler maker, 181.
Hull, John, silversmith, 138.
Humphrey, Nicholas, silversmith, 144.
Hunt, Ephraim, mill owner, 68.
Hunt, Nathan, basketmaker, 3.
Hunts, the joiners, 31.
Hurlin, Mrs. William H., potter, 100, 103.
Hutchins, Abel, clockmaker, 58.
Hutchins, Levi, clockmaker, 58.
Hutchins, Martha, 59.

Index of American Design, 254.
Indians, 2, 7.
Indian Stream Republic, 25.
Ingalls, A. W., painter, 207.
Ingalls, Charles, sign painter, 213.
Ipswich, Massachusetts, 44, 45.
Iron Mountain, 133.
Iron Smelting, 131-133.
Ironworking, 131-137.
Iron Works Village, 132.
Isaac Newton, ship, 15.
International Exhibition, London, 13.
International Exposition, Paris, 1937, 159, 200.
International Rug Exhibition, Metropolitan Museum of Art, 200.
Intervale, N. H., 6.

Jackman, Samuel, joiner, 30.
Jackman, Samuel, blacksmith, 30.
Jackson, President Andrew, 123, 207.

Jackson, Clement, Jr., silversmith, 143.
Jackson House, Portsmouth, N. H., 32.
Jackson, Richard, builder, 32.
Jaffrey, N. H., 29, 56, 62, 68, 71, 74, 98.
James Brown, ship, 15.
Jamestown, Virginia, 118.
Jenks, Burton P., silver designer, 145.
Jennison, William, 173.
Jepperson, Mrs. Charles, lacemaker, 171.
Jesseman, Frank, present-day cabinetmaker, 49.
Jewelry making, 146, 256, 258, 259.
Jewett, James, Shaker, 223.
John Decatur, ship, 15.
John Hale, ship, 15.
John Paul Jones House, Portsmouth, N. H., 21.
John Taylor, ship, 15.
Johnson, Mrs. Carroll N., present-day potter, 100, 103.
Johnson, Edith Durgin, 180.
Johnson, Edward, present-day cabinetmaker, 76.
Johnson, J. Albert, present-day cabinetmaker, 47-48.
Johnson, Matthew, glass blower, 126, 129.
Johnson, Walter Leonard, model airplane maker, 48.
Jones, Abner, clockmaker, 55.
Jones, Elder Nathan, blacksmith, 135.
Joseph Judkins Communion Cup, 140.
Judkins, Joseph, silversmith, 140.
Judkins & Senter, cabinetmakers, 41.

Kassner, Myer, present-day gem expert, 114.
Kearsage, ship, 19.
Keen, Edgar, present-day wood carver, 85-86.
Keene, N. H., 42, 44, 56, 57, 68, 73, 108, 114, 115, 122, 123, 126, 134, 173, 185.
Keene glass, 122-126.
Keene Home Industries, 160.
Keene Window Glass Company, 122.
Kent, William Winthrop, author, quoted, 197.
Keyes, Charles, present-day cabinetmaker, 49.
Kidder Mountain, 118.
Kierstead, Mrs. Iona, present-day gem cutter, 116.
Kilkenny, N. H., 115.
Kimball, Mrs. Betsey, silk raiser and spinner, 157.
Kimball, Elipha S., woodenware maker, 70.
Kimball, Mrs. Ella, 211, 212.

Kimball, Joseph, spinningwheel maker, 70, 71.
Kimball, Richard, clothespin maker, 69.
Kimball, Samuel, wheelwright, 70.
Kimball, S. Warren, woodenware maker, 70.
Kimball-Union Academy, 116.
King, Seth, clothmaker, 238.
King, William, silhouettist, 209-210.
Kingston, N. H., 132.
Kirchmayer, John, wood carver, 84.
Kittery, Maine, 17, 18, 19, 138.
Knitting, 171-174, 234, 258.
Knowlton, Maud Briggs, present-day artist, 195, 255-256.
Koch, William, present-day cabinetmaker, 61.
Kraetzer, John F., knitter, 173.
Kuchler, Edith Wyckoff, present-day painter, 218.
Kunberger, Ernest, present-day woodworker, 76.

Lacemaking, 169-171.
Laconia, N. H., 114.
Laconia Company, 45.
Ladd, Daniel, ironworker, 132.
"Ladies Charitable Society", 173.
Ladies Manual of Fancy Work, 168.
Lady of the Lake, Steamboat, 16.
Lafayette, General, 163, 211, 212.
Lake Mascoma, 229.
Lake Sunapee, 60, 77.
Lake Winnepesaukee, 16, 155.
Lamb, Fred W., 212, 219.
Lambert, Julien, present-day wood carver, 87.
Lamont, D. G., portrait painter, 208.
Lamprey River, 22.
Lamprey River Iron Works, 131, 132.
Lamson, Asa D., potter, 95.
Lamson, F. H., potter, 95.
Lamson Pottery, 95.
Lamsons, the potters, 94, 95.
Lamsons, the stonecutters, 106.
Lancaster, ship, 17, 18.
Lancaster, N. H., 27, 59, 116, 203.
Landseer, artist, 201.
Lane, Mrs. Mary, glassmaker, 126.
Lang, Henry, glassblower, 123.
Lang, Louis, woodcarver, 84.
Langdon, Caroline, samplermaker, 182.
Langdon, John, 182.
Langdon, Woodbury, 182.
Langley Boardman—Marvin House, Portsmouth, N. H., 34.
Larcom, Lucy, 183.
Large, Harvey, cabinetmaker, 45.
Larken, James E., painter, 214.
Larkin-Rice House, Portsmouth, N. H., 34.

Lathrop, James, 167.
Lathrop, Polly, 167.
Lauder, George, present-day cabinetmaker, 48.
Laurent, Mrs. Joseph, present-day basketmaker, 6.
Lawrence, Mrs. Betsey, 239.
League Governing Council, 253.
League of New Hampshire Arts and Crafts, 51, 52, 75, 85, 98, 100, 113, 116, 146, 158, 159, 160, 168, 169, 196, 198, 248, 249, 250, 255, 257.
Lear, Captain Tobias, 40, 108.
Leathhead, Robert, pewterer, 137.
Leathers, the family, basketmakers, 4.
Leathers' City, 4.
Leavitt, Frank A., present-day silversmith, 144.
Leavitt, Samuel, potter, 95.
Lebanon, N. H., 44.
Lee, Mother Ann, founder of Shakerism, 222, 224.
Leeman, Samuel, 109, 110.
Leggett, Percy, present-day gem cutter, 114, 115.
Lempster, N. H., 210.
Lewis, "Uncle Jimmy", cabinetmaker, 48.
Lexington, Massachusetts, 42.
Libbee, Nathaniel, potter, 94.
Library of Congress, 112.
"Lilacs", 183.
Linchey, Bernard, present-day maker of ships' models, 19.
Lind, Albert, Boston violinmaker, 65.
Lind, Jenny, 14.
Linen manufacture, 152, 230.
Lisbon, N. H., 133.
Litchfield, Lewis L., present-day violinmaker, 64.
Little, Amos, silkmaker, 157.
Little Boar's Head, 248.
Little, Sarah K., samplermaker, 178.
Littleton, N. H., 42, 49, 50.
Locke, Cynthia, samplemaker, 182.
Locke, Polly, weaver, 154.
Londonderry, N. H., 62, 107, 236, 259.
Londonderry Grange Fair, 1910, 248.
Loudon, N. H., 97.
Lougee, John, knitter, 173.
Lovejoy, Captain Henry, 132.
Lowell, Amy, poet, 183.
Lowell, James Russell, quoted, 180.
Lowell, Massachusetts, 75, 126.
Lull, Colonel Oliver W., 188.
Lundberg, Mrs. Henry, lacemaker, 171.
Lyme, N. H., 37, 218.
Lyndeborough, N. H., 94, 96, 105, 106, 128, 132.
Lyndeborough Glass Company, 128.

MacDowell Colony, 215.
MacGregor, Rev. James, 62, 259.
MacLean, Mrs. Marion M., present-day rugmaker, 199.
MacMillan, Donald, explorer, 64.
MacPhaedris, Archibald, maritime merchant, 131.
Madeira Islands, 17.
Madison, N. H., 194.
Magraw, Charles H., 37.
Malm, Leo, present-day wood carver, 83-84, 257.
Manchester, N. H., 6, 11, 43, 65, 75, 80, 81, 82, 87, 91, 93, 113, 128, 160, 162, 163, 164, 167, 170, 178, 181, 198, 199, 201, 206, 218, 219.
Manchester Art Association, 246, 255.
Manchester Electric Club, 255.
Manchester Historic Association, 113, 179, 206, 212.
Manchester Institute of Arts and Sciences, 6, 80, 81, 100, 146, 158, 159, 160, 165, 168, 171, 195, 225, 256.
Mangano, Mrs. Rose, present-day needleworker, 164.
Manifesto, The, 233.
March farm, Greenland, N. H., 17.
March, Hopestill, master carpenter, 31.
March, John Howard, wine merchant, 17.
Marcoux, Omer, present-day wood carver, 86.
Marine Room, John Paul Jones House, Portsmouth, N. H., 21.
Marine Room, Museum of Fine Arts, Boston, 17.
Mariners' Museum, Newport News, Va., 14, 17.
Marlborough, N. H., 98.
Marquetry, 47, 50, 87-89.
Marsland, Elizabeth, E., present-day weaver, 161.
Marsland, Mrs. Hilda, weaver, 161.
Martin, James, ironworker, 132.
Martin, Mrs. Louise C., present-day weaving, weaver, 160, 256.
Martin, Governor Noah, 162.
Marvle, Mark, woodworker, 71.
Mascoma River, 229.
Mascoma Valley Fair, 247.
Mason, N. H., 146.
Mason, Captain John, 131.
Mason, Madam, weaver, 155.
Mason, Colonel Stephen, 155.
Massachusetts Bay Colony, 45, 148.
Massachusetts Institute of Technology, 103.
Mather, Frank J., quoted, 14.
McIntire, Samuel, wood carver, 60.

Meacham, Elder Joseph, Shaker, 222, 223, 224.
Mead, Israel, brickmaker, 90.
Mechanics Reading Room, Portsmouth, N. H., 39.
Meindl, Peter, present-day wood carver, 84.
Meredith Home Industries, 254.
Meredith, N. H., 253, 254.
Merrill, Deacon John, cabinetmaker, 49.
Merrimack County Agricultural Society, 157, 241, 245.
Merrimack County Fair, 241-242, 246.
Merrimack River, 43, 55, 91, 127, 132, 134.
Messer, Stephen, basketmaker, 3.
Metalwork, 131-147, 254, 256.
Metcalf, Jonathan, 108.
Metcalf, Sarah, 108.
Metropolitan Museum of Art, New York, 82, 126, 198, 200.
Middlesex Canal, 43.
Milford Historical Society, 188.
Milford, N. H., 46, 112.
Miller, Alec, sculptor, 85.
Millville Pottery, 96-97.
Mitchell, Charles, 64.
Mittens, 254.
Modeling, 255.
Moffatt, Mrs. Catherine, 181.
Moll, Richard, present-day potter, 99, 100, 256.
Monroe, President James, 223.
Mont Vernon, N. H., 26, 60.
Montgomery, General John, 21, 61.
Montgomery, ship, 21.
Moore, J. Baily, author, quoted, 209.
Morin, J. Phillip, present-day gem cutter, 114.
Morgan, John, maker of woodenware, 72, 73.
Morrill, Benjamin, clockmaker, 59, 241.
Morrill, Moses, ironworker, 132.
Morris, William, wood carver, 79-80.
Morrison, Arthur J., present-day clock collector, 60.
Morrison, Miss Mary, craftswoman, 257.
Morse, Deacon Jesse, brickmaker, 92-93.
Morse, Samuel F. B., inventor, 208.
Morse, Stephen, silversmith, 31, 143.
Moulton, Edward, clockmaker, 59.
Mt. Monadnock, 215.
Mt. Washington, 12, 48.
Mountain View House, Whitefield, N. H., 174.
Munroe, Miss Helen, potter, 100.
Munsonville, N. H., 125.

Murdock, Ephraim, mill owner, 69.
Murphy, John D., silversmith, 144.
Museum of Fine Arts, Boston, 16.
Museum of Society of the Daughters of the American Revolution, Washington, D. C., 167.
"Musicians, The", bas-relief plaque, 84.

Nailmaking, 135.
Nansen Ski Club, 77.
Nashua and Nashville Directory for 1843, 110.
Nashua Manufacturing Company, 34.
Nashua, N. H., 34, 43, 44, 84, 91, 94, 101, 106, 109, 110, 111, 179, 185, 198, 254.
Nathan Fay House, East Alstead, N. H., 217.
National Youth Administration, 196, 257, 258.
Needlework, 162-175, 243, 254.
Nelson, Mrs. Elwyn, 50.
Nelson, John, silversmith, 143.
Nelson, Mark, silversmith, 143.
Netting, 253.
Newbury, Massachusetts, 31.
Newburyport, Massachusetts, 26, 55.
Newfields, N. H., 42, 140.
Newing, Charlotte M., 258.
Newington, N. H., 138.
Newington, Church, 138.
Newmarket, N. H., 22.
Newport, N. H., 44.
New Castle, N. H., 19, 21, 236.
New England, 1, 2, 8, 10, 15, 16, 21, 33, 34, 45, 64, 165.
New Hampshire State Agricultural Society Fair, 218, 242.
New Hampshire, ship, 145.
New Hampshire Art Project, 84.
New Hampshire Business Directory, 125.
New Hampshire Crippled Children's Society, 258.
New Hampshire Exhibit, World's Fair, 159.
New Hampshire Federation of Women's Clubs, 183, 257.
New Hampshire Gazette, 138, 139, 141, 210.
New Hampshire Glass Factory, 122.
New Hampshire Historical Society, 16, 113, 128, 140, 145, 162, 163, 177, 182, 185, 186, 193, 198.
New Hampshire Historical Society Exhibit of 1939, 189.
New Hampshire Iron Factory Company, 133.
New Hampshire Mirror and Farmer, 247.

New Hampshire Patriot, 46, 238.
New Hampshire Patriot and State Gazette, 127, 212.
New Hampshire Silex Company, 128.
New Hampshire State Agricultural Society, 242.
New Hampton Literary Institution, 18.
New Ipswich, N. H., 42, 44, 60, 61, 118, 154.
New London, N. H., 210.
New York City, 11, 18, 81, 139, 146, 198, 200.
New York Historical Society, 219.
New York State College of Ceramics, 100.
New York World's Fair, 52, 86, 215.
Nicoll, Andrew, silversmith, 145-146.
Nichols, Moses, 110.
Nicolosi, J., sculptor, 112.
Nightingale, ship, 13-14, 20.
Noah's Ark Tavern, Portsmouth, 143.
Northfield, N. H., 45, 98.
Northwood Meetinghouse, 29.
Norton, Prof. F. H., 95, 103.
Noyes, Cutting, blacksmith, 134.

Odiorne's Point, 15.
Old Burying Ground, Nashua, N. H., 106, 109.
Old Dover Pottery, 101.
Old Man of the Mountain, 215.
Old North Meetinghouse, Concord, N. H., 55.
"Old Settler's House", Orfordville, N. H., 136.
Oleson, Olaf, present-day ski maker, 77.
Orchard Pottery, Cornish, N. H., 99.
Ordway, Colonel George L., 248.
Ordway, John, trader, 10.
Orford, N. H., 34, 113, 136.
Orfordville, N. H., 136.
Ornamental Painting, 211-215.
Osborne, Elijah, potter, 97.
Osborne, James, potter, 97.
Osborne, John, potter, 97.
Osborne, Oliver, potter, 95.
Osborne Pottery, 97, 103.
Osborn, Jonathan, buttonmaker, 72.
Osborn, Samuel, buttonmaker, 72.
Osborne, S. D., cabinetmaker, 244.
Osborne, the family, 94.
Osgood, John, clockmaker, 57.
Ossipee Lake, 132.
Ossipee Mountains, 12, 50.
Otterson, Mrs. M. J., rugmaker, 204.
Oyster River, 22.

Page, David, blacksmith, 134.
Painting, 210.
Palladino, Andrea, Italian architect, 35.

Paris Exhibition, 1937, 256.
Park, John, stonecutter, 109-110.
Park, William, stonecutter, 109-110.
Parker, David, Shaker, 232, 235.
Parker, Robert, cabinetmaker, 43, 212.
Parker, William, agent for Chelmsford Glass Co., 127.
Parker, the family, 91, 220.
Parry, Captain Martin, silversmith, 139, 141.
Parsons, Mrs. Ralph, rugmaker, 201.
Patenaude, Charles, cabinetmaker, 50.
Patrick, Joel O., steeplebuilder, 29.
Paul Revere Potteries, Boston, Massachusetts, 100.
Peabody, Mrs. R. P., author, 184.
Pearson, Hannah, samplermaker, 180.
Peavey House, Bennington, N. H., 217.
Peckett, Robert P., rug collector, 196, 197, 215.
Peirce Mansion, Portsmouth, N. H., 34.
Pembroke, N. H., 41, 49, 128.
Pembroke Glass, 127-128.
Pennacook, N. H., 55, 134.
Pennsylvania, ship, 19.
Pepperrell, Sir William, 138.
Pewter, 146, 253.
Perkins, Robinson, clockmaker and blacksmith, 56.
Perley, Squire Stephen, 29.
Perreault, Charles, present-day violinmaker, 63.
Perry, Justus, glass manufacturer, 122.
Perry and Wheeler, glass manufacturers, 122.
Perry and Wood, glass manufacturers, 122.
Peter Farnum House, Francestown, N. H., 216.
Peterborough, N. H., 4, 152, 215, 254.
Peters, John, cabinetmaker, 42.
Phelps, Miss Helen B., potter, 100.
Phenix Hotel, Concord, 19, 59.
Philadelphia Art Alliance, 256.
Philbrick, William, potter, 95.
Phillips Church, Exeter, N. H., 35.
Photography, 242.
Pierce, Governor Benjamin, 58, 217.
Pierce, Edward, painter, 214.
Pierce, President Franklin, 58, 215.
Pierce, Mary H., collector, 19.
Pike, N. H., 4.
Pinkham, Enoch, brickmaker, 91.
Pinkham, Frank C., present-day designer of ships' models, 19.
Piscataqua, 131, 137, 148.
Piscataqua craftsmen, 20.
Piscataqua River, 12, 14, 21, 22, 39, 132.
Pitt, William, glass collector, 129.

Pittsburg, N. H., 25.
Pittsfield, N. H., 62.
Pittsfield Cattle Show, 239.
Pittsfield Fair, 247.
Place, Samuel, silversmith, 143.
Plaistow, N. H., 91.
Ploof, Mrs. Anna L., present-day spinner and weaver, 149.
Plymouth, N. H., 3, 158, 248.
Point of Graves Cemetery, Portsmouth, N. H., 108.
Poletti, Cesare, stonecutter, 112.
Polk, Patty, samplermaker, 180.
Polleti, Marco, stonecutter, 112.
Ponds, the, silversmiths, 143.
Portrait painting, 206-208, 212.
Portsmouth, N. H., 3, 12, 13, 15, 16-19, 29, 31-37, 39, 40, 42, 44, 45, 54, 55, 72, 95, 106, 108, 131, 137, 138, 139, 142, 164, 181, 182, 202, 206, 209, 213.
Portsmouth Gazette, 41.
Portsmouth Historical Society, 21.
Portsmouth Navy Yard, 17, 20.
Portsmouth Yacht Club, 17, 21.
Potter, Ephraim, builder and clockmaker, 29, 55.
Potter, Jacob A., artist and inventor, 209.
Pottery, 2, 94-104.
Prescott, Abraham, musical-instrument maker, 61, 62, 63.
Prescott, Mrs. Elvin J., present-day rugmaker, 199.
Prescott, John, woodenware maker, 69.
Prescott Tavern, East Jaffrey, N. H., 217.
Pridham, John R., figurehead carver, 19.
Prince, Calvin, clothmaker, 245.

Quakers, the, 222.
"Queens'-ware," 94.
Quilting bees, 184-185.
Quiltmaking, 183-191, 242.
Quint, Edgar, present-day violinmaker, 65.

Rambles about Portsmouth, quoted, 39.
Ramsay, John, quoted, 94.
Rand, John, portrait painter, 212.
Rand and Abbott, cabinetmakers, 44.
Randolph, N. H., 149.
Ranney, Frank G., present-day cabinetmaker, 44.
Raynes, George, shipbuilder, 13.
Recollections, quoted, 208.
Reticella, 170, 257.
Revere, Paul, Massachusetts silversmith, 141, 142.

Rhode Island School of Design, 145.
Rhodes, Rowland, silversmith, 145.
Ribberhold, James T., 258.
Rice, Ebenezer, master carpenter, 34.
Rice, Ebenezer A., manufacturer of glass bottles, 124.
Rice, Emery, stenciler, 216.
Rice, Captain William, privateersman, 40.
Rich, Mrs. Inez, present-day craftswoman, 258.
Richardson, Charles, 218.
Rindge, N. H., 11, 69, 211.
Rinta, Sylvester, present-day ironworker, 137.
Risley, Asa (also Wrisley), stonecutter, 108.
Risley, Asa, Jr., (also Wrisley), stonecutter, 109.
Risley, the family, stonecutters, 112.
Roberts, Fred R., silversmith and designer, 145.
Rochester, N. H., 59, 93, 95.
Rochester State Fair, 164, 165, 187, 247, 248.
Rockingham Agricultural Society, 237.
Rogers, George W., cabinetmaker, 46.
Rogers' Groups, 219.
Rogers, John, sculptor, 218-219.
Rolfe, Benjamin S., sign painter, 214.
Rowan, William, silversmith, 145.
Rowell, Mrs. Moses, weaver, 154.
Royal Academy of Arts, London, 208.
Rugmaking, 158, 192-205, 231, 251, 254, 257, 258, 259.
Runnells, Mrs. Nellie, present-day rugmaker, 199.
Rural Arts Exhibition, Washington, 86.
Rydingsvard von, Karl, present-day wood carver, 80-82.
Rydholm, Alfred, present-day cabinetmaker, 47.
Rye, N. H., 5, 15, 19.

Saco River, 6.
Saddleback Mountain, 132.
Saffron and Indigo Society, 254, 257.
St. Francis d'Assisi, 87.
St.-Gaudens, Annetta J., present-day sculptor, 98-99.
St.-Gaudens family, potters, 98.
St.-Gaudens, Louis, 99.
St.-Gaudens, Paul, present-day potter, 98-99.
St. Jean-Baptiste Church, Manchester, N. H., 87.
St. John's Church, Portsmouth, N. H., 138.
St. Johnsbury Granite Company, 111.
St. Paul's School, Concord, N. H., 86.
Salem, Massachusetts, 16, 60, 118, 142.

Salem, N. H., 10, 11, 107, 210.
Salisbury, N. H., 42, 43.
Salmon Wood House, Hancock, N. H., 216.
"Sam-cloths," 177.
Samplers, 176-183.
Sampson, James, figurehead carver, 16.
Samuel Fitts Houses, Candia, N. H., 218.
Sanborn, Daniel Hall, basketmaker, 1.
Sanbornton, N. H., 30, 48.
Sanbornton Meetinghouse, 29.
Sanders, James H., painter, 214.
Sanderson, Lydia, 138.
Sanderson, Mary, 138.
Sanderson, Robert, silversmith, 138.
Sandown Meetinghouse, 26.
Sandwich, N. H., 50, 51, 52, 86, 94, 116, 135, 250, 251, 253, 255.
Sandwich Historical Society, 250.
Sandwich Home Industries, 116, 158, 196, 253.
Sandwich Mountains, 50.
Sandwich Town Fair, 247.
Sargent, Mrs. Eaton, 179.
Scabbard Mill Brook, 73.
Schiller, Rudolph, 65.
Schoepf, Martin, present-day violin maker, 65.
School of Ceramics, Alfred, New York, 99.
Schoolcraft, Henry Rowe, glass manufacturer, 122.
Schoolcraft, Colonel Lawrence, 122.
Schoolcraft and Twitchell, glass manufacturers, 122.
Scotch-Irish, 152.
Scott, William W., 20.
Sculpturing, 218-219.
Seabrook, N. H., 5.
Sea Serpent, ship, 13, 15.
Searle, William, 45.
Seavey, Mrs. Burton, present-day weaver, 160.
Seavey, W. L., figurehead carver, 16.
Second Burying Ground, Keene, N. H., 108.
See, Mildred P., present-day weaver, 160.
Shades of Our Ancestors, 210.
Shakers, 158, 220-235.
Shaker Bridge, Enfield, N. H., 229-230.
Shaker Crafts, 220-235.
Shaker Hill, 223.
Sharon, N. H., 118.
Sheepshearing, 149-150.
Shelburne, N. H., 172, 184.
Shepheard, Mary, 220, 223.
Shepard, Samuel, architect, 34.

285

Sherburn, Mrs. Joseph, present-day spinner, 148-149.
Sherwin, Captain David, mill owner, 69.
Shipbuilding, 12-14, 237.
Ship model making, 19-22.
Silhouette, Etienne de, 208.
Silhouette making, 208-210.
Silhouettes, 208-209.
Silk raising, 241, 157.
Silk spinning, 157-158.
Silversmithing, 47, 137-147.
Simes, William, silversmith, 141.
Simms, Charles F., silversmith, 145.
Skillings, John, wood carver, 16.
Skillings, Simeon, figurehead carver, 16.
Skimaking, 77.
Slason, Mary, basketmaker, 6-7.
Smart, Lucetta, rugmaker, 204.
Smith, Augustus, glass blower, 123.
Smith, Horatio, glass blower, 126.
Smith-Hughes Act, 252.
Smith, Jim, 126.
Smith, Luther, clockmaker, 56.
Smith, Mary Jones, weaver, 156.
Smithsonian Institution, 21, 22.
Snow, Penelope W., 256.
Soapstone carving, 112-113.
Society of Colonial Dames of Massachusetts, 176.
Society for the Preservation of New England Antiquities, 32, 96.
Somers, A. N., Reverend, quoted, 28.
Somersworth, N. H., 26, 99, 165, 187.
Somerville Lake Yacht Club, 77.
Soule, Ebenezer, stonecutter, 107, 108.
South Acworth, N. H., 254.
South Baldface Mountain, 114.
South Keene, N. H., 217.
South Lyndeborough, N. H., 128.
South Tamworth, N. H., 1.
Spencer, Elmer, blacksmith, 136.
Spicer, W. T., figurehead carver, 17.
Spinning, 68, 149, 231, 251; wool, 150-151; flax, 151, 153-154; silk, 157.
Sprague, Charles A., present-day basketmaker, 5.
Sprague, John, master carpenter, 30.
Sprague, Nathaniel, glass manufacturer, 122.
Squam Lake, 77.
Squantum Mills, 68-69.
Stark, N. H., 111.
Stark, Mrs. C. F. M., 58.
Stark, Charles, potter, 98.
Stark, Major General John, 42, 182.
Stark Mills, Manchester, N. H., 146.
Stark, Molly, 167-168, 260.
State Board of Education, 252.

State Fairs of 1850, 1854, 1874, 1885, 243, 244, 246, 247.
State Federation of Women's Clubs, 183.
State Gazette, 212.
State Rug Group, 254.
Stearns, Mrs. Foster, craftswoman and editor, 169, 183, quoted, 52-53.
Stenciling, 256.
Stevens, Lydia, blacksmith, 135.
Stiegel, Baron, glass manufacturer, 118.
Stockwell, Eunice, weaver, 203.
Stoddard, N. H., 123, 126.
Stoddard Glass, 123-126.
Stoddard Glass Company, 123.
Stonecutting, 105-116.
Storer, Mary Lear, samplermaker, 182.
Stradivarius, 64.
Strafford County Fair, 240.
Stratford, N. H., 48.
Stratton, the family, 73.
Stry, Augustrofus van, wood carver, 84.
Sugar River, 44.
Sugar Hill, N. H., 215.
Sullivan, N. H., 3, 182.
Sullivan, General John, 163.
Suncook Glass, 127, 128.
Suncook River, 127.
Suncook Village, N. H., 127, 166.
Sutton, N. H., 70, 128.
Swanzey, N. H., 73.
Swiftwater, N. H., 3.
"Swiss Family Robinson", 155.
Sylvester, S. G., glass painter, 212.
Symonds, John, 125.

Tabor, Parker, 25.
Talbot, Mrs. Loren, 211.
Tappan, Abraham, 50.
Tappan, Daniel, chairmaker, 50.
Tappan, Walter S., chairmaker, 50.
Tamworth, N. H., 116, 155.
Taylor, John, poet, 177.
Taylor, Mr. and Mrs. Joseph, present-day basketmakers, 8-9.
Temple, N. H., 118, 120, 132.
Temple Glass, 118-120.
Temple Mountain, 118.
Tenny, Mrs. Sally, weaver, 155.
Terry, Eli, Connecticut clockmaker, 60.
Thompson, Benjamin, Count Rumford, 163.
Thompson, John, Sr., master builder, 30.
Thompson, Mrs. Mary, 178.
Thornton, N. H., 26.
Timber Salvage Administration, 84.
Titanic, ship, 20.
Tobias Lear House, Portsmouth, N. H., 182.

Toledo Art Museum, Toledo, Ohio, 126.
Towle, Isaac, figurehead carver, 16.
Town Fairs, 246-247.
Treadway, Mr. and Mrs. Charles, 33.
Treadway, Jacob, 33.
Treat, John I, stonecutter, 110.
Treat, Samuel, stonecutter, 110.
Treat, the family, stonecutters 110.
Troy, N. H., 70, 98, 178, 211, 212.
True, Joseph, figurehead carver, 16.
Trufant, Converse P., blacksmith, 136.
Tucker, Micaijah, Shaker carpenter, 226.
Tuckerman Ravine, 114.
Tuftonboro, N. H., 149.
Turkey River, 132.
Twain, Mark, 19.
Twitchell, Doctor Amos, 185.
Tyler, Benjamin, ironworker, 132.

Underhill, Lieutenant Josiah, smith and toolmaker, 134.
Union Grange Fair Association, 248.
Unity, N. H., 26.
United Society of Believers in Christ's Second Coming, 220.
University of New Hampshire, 98, 100, 104, 137, 248.

Varick, Mrs. Melusina, wood carver, 80, 255.
Verge, Starr K., Sr., rugmaker, 200.
Virgin, Ebenezer, cabinetmaker, 46.
Virgin, Lloyd R., present-day boatbuilder, 76, 77.
Virgin, William E., boatbuilder, 76, 77.

Wakefield, N. H., 1.
Walker, Rev. Timothy, 55.
Wallace, Woodman L., 49.
Walpole, N. H., 31, 173, 239.
Ward, Mrs. Josiah, 45.
Warner, N. H., 85.
Warner-MacPhaedris House, Portsmouth, N. H., 132.
Washington, General George, 40, 162, 182.
Washington, Martha, 182.
Watercraft Collection, Smithsonian Institution, 22.
"Watch on the Santa Maria, The", Rogers Group, 219.
Watson, Mrs. Martha S., present-day needleworker and rugmaker, 165, 196, 256, 257.
Watson & Twitchell, glass manufacturers, 122.
Weare, N. H., 4, 42, 55, 72, 135.
Weaving, 43, 154-161, 230, 238, 245, 251, 254, 258, 259.

Weaver, Constant, **pottery manufacturer**, 98.
Weaving Guild, 254.
Webster, Daniel, 182, 209, 243.
Webster, Mrs. Ellen Emeline, quilt pattern collector, 189, 190, 191.
Webster, Ezekiel, 209.
Webster, Isaac, 113.
Webster, Joseph, cooper, 72.
Webster Lake, 77.
Webster, Susannah, 42.
Weeks House, Greenland, N. H., 91.
Weeks, Luman, bottle manufacturer, 124.
Weeks and Gilson, glass manufacturers, 125.
Welch, David, basketmaker, 3.
Wellington, Mary Jane, 182.
Wells-Fargo Co., stagecoach line, 214.
Wentworth, N. H., 26, 32, 71.
Wentworth, Governor Benning, 132.
Wentworth-Gardner House, Portsmouth, N. H., 36.
Wentworth, Governor John, 34.
Wentworth, Thomas, 36.
West Concord, N. H., 26.
West Henniker, N. H., 42.
West Indies, 33, 73.
West Manchester, N. H., 63.
Westmoreland, N. H., 115.
West Rindge, N. H., 8.
Weston, Mary Pillsbury, artist, 213.
West Rumney, N. H., 204.
Weygandt, Cornelius, author, 135.
Wheat House, Candia, N. H., 218.
Wheeler House, Orford, N. H., 34.
Wheelock, Eleazar, founder of Dartmouth College, 30.
Wheelock, James, 210.
White, Rev. and Mrs. Broughton, 207.
White, Lucy, spinner, 203.
White, Mrs. Miles, Maryland silver collector, 147.
White, Philips, 32.
Whitcher, Benjamin, Shaker, 220, 223.
Whitcher, Reuben, builder, 32.
Whitefield, N. H., 174.
Whitefield, Benich, basketmaker, 1.
Whitefield, Craftsmen's Fair, 1938, 248.
Whitehouse, Mrs. C. R., present-day needleworker, 163-164, 168.
Whitney, Irmi, music teacher, 65.
Whittemore, William, silversmith, 138-139.
Whittier, Mary J., present-day wood carver, 86.
Wiggin, Henry, Jr., cabinetmaker, 42.
Wight, John, stonecutter, 107.
Wilder, Major Jonas, 32.
Wilder, Peter, chairmaker, **44.**

Willard, Cecelia C., weaver, 159.
Willard, Simon, clockmaker, 58, 60.
William Long Memorial Building, 207, 213.
William Pitt Tavern, Portsmouth, N. H., 213, 214.
Williams, John, figurehead carver, 19.
Williamson, Daisy Deane, 258.
Wilman, Mrs. Fred, present-day craftswoman, 183, 257.
Wilmot, N. H., 114.
Wilson, George, 19.
Wilson, Jehiel, pailmaker, 73.
Wilson, M. L., U. S. Dept. Agriculture, quoted, 259.
Wilson Tavern, Peterborough, N. H., 216.
Winant, Governor John G., 251.
Winchester, N. H., 133, 254.
Windham, N. H., 155.
Wingate, Mary, samplermaker, 177.
Winnepesaukee River, 98.
Wistar, Caspar, glass manufacturer, 118.
Witham, Miss Minnie F., crafts instructor, 258.
Wolfeboro, N. H., 34, 254, 257.
Wood Carving, 47, 240, 254.

Wood family, sheep raisers, 149.
Wood, Dr. Samuel, 150, 241.
Woodcock, Virgil, inventor, 245.
Woodenware making, 52, 67, 69, 70-73, 75-77.
Woodman, Caleb, joiner, 31.
Woods, Almon, glass manufacturer, 124.
Woodworking, 47, 48, 51, 52, 67-78.
Wool carding and combing, 150.
Woolson, Thomas Jr., clockmaker, 57.
Work Projects Administration, 84, 207.
WPA Art Program, 254.
Wren, Sir Christopher, English architect, 29.
Wright, Samuel, clockmaker, 59.
Wrought-iron utensils, 251.
Wyman, Linnie Varney, quoted, 93.

Yates, Thomas, ornamental painter, 214.
Young, Miss Laura E., present-day gem cutter, 116.
Young, David, cabinetmaker, 42.
Young, Mrs. Jennie C., craftswoman, 255.